Raven Mother

Jane Messer is the accomplished writer of novels, short stories and essays, is a regular contributor to *The Conversation*, and is a former Associate Professor of Creative Writing at Macquarie University. She is the founder and director of StorySALOON, a live show and podcast dedicated to Australian short stories.

As the daughter of a refugee, she finds herself compelled to write about fractured lives, marginal people and migration.

'In seeking the truth about her grandmother, Messer uncovers far more than a family history. Her thorough journey reveals profound questions of identity, loss, and displacement, while exposing the deep-rooted racism and injustice woven through the world she explores.'

Majeda Awawdeh

'With evenhandedness and generosity of spirit, Jane Messer's minutely researched history of dispossession and genocide embraces both her Jewish roots stretching back to Berlin before the Holocaust and, with unflinching clear-sightedness, the story of Palestine. It is a plain-speaking, remarkable and deeply affecting book.'

Robert Dessaix

'*Raven Mother* takes us on a deeply moving journey of discovery. While we have begun to understand how tenaciously the traumas of our parents live on within us, it takes a writer of Messer's calibre to apprehend this phenomenon with such verve, candour and insight. As her travels into her father's past demonstrate so palpably, what we draw from our parents' complex histories can change over time if we are brave enough to face them.'

Sara Dowse

'A beautifully etched excursion through muddied layers of history and memories of place, *Raven Mother* is an unexpected homage to the fault lines of family.'

Andrea Durbach

'An important work of enquiry into one of the most contested pieces of land on this earth through one family's story. A fine book illustrating the sorrows and resilience of life and why we must not look away from the suffering of others.'

Susan Johnson

'Wise, poignant and beautiful, *Raven Mother* builds an arch over the here-and-now to connect an individual life with a family and communal past. This is a book that matters. It can only enrich our understanding of the present.'

Malcolm Knox

'Messer's search for her grandmother is gripping and forensic, asking difficult questions about history and memory. It is both epic and personal. A moving and beautifully written memoir.'

Catharine Lumby

'... poetically beautiful, fascinating, special ... so rare in the landscape of writing about Israel–Palestine and Jewish–Arab relations.'

Yonatan Mendel

Also by Jane Messer

Fiction

Night by Night

Hopscotch

Provenance

As editor

Bedlam: An anthology of sleepless nights

Certifiable Truths: Stories of love and madness

Raven Mother

War, family and inheritance: a memoir

Jane Messer

NEWSOUTH

UNSW Press acknowledges the Bidjigal people, the Traditional Owners of the unceded territory on which the Randwick and Kensington campuses of UNSW are situated, and recognises the continuing connection to Country and culture. We pay our respects to Bidjigal Elders past and present.

A NewSouth book

Published by
NewSouth Publishing
University of New South Wales Press Ltd
University of New South Wales
Sydney NSW 2052
AUSTRALIA
https://unsw.press/

The writing of this project has been assisted by the Australian Government through Creative Australia, its principal arts investment and advisory body.

The writing of this project has been assisted by a grant from Create NSW.

A catalogue record for this book is available from the National Library of Australia

ISBN: 9781761170638 (paperback)
9781761179396 (ebook)
9781761178658 (ePDF)

Cover design Mika Tabata
Cover images Bella on yacht, c.1930s; textured background and feather / shutterstock
Internal design Josephine Pajor-Markus
Inside cover images Bella holding Michael at seaside beach, c.1929 (*inside front*) and Bella's 'J' (Jew) passport *(inside back).*

For my father, Michael.

For my mother, Judy. I wish you were here to read this with us.

And for Martin, Lottie and Louis.

Contents

Raven's cry xi

Part One

'A History of My Family' 3
Walking in Berlin 14
A bit of a Jew 22
Family traits 30
Pestalozzi-Fröbel Haus 40
The Spirit of 1914 44
Fighting for Germany 55
Spring arrival in Berlin 62
The monkey out of her cage 66
The slap 72
The children's war 79
The price of escape 86
A bad time to be in Berlin 93
Rubble women 100
Finding Goethe 103
The worst of mothers 107
Translations 112
Berlin Porn Film Festival 116

My Germany 122
Reading Goethe 130
Rolf and the 5767 136
The torn page 143
From Bunce Court to Melbourne 150

Part Two

The Land of Promise 159
The land called Palestine 162
Aliyah 168
al-Thawra al-Kubra 175
Arrivals, departures and the Palestinian No 181
World War II 189
The fortunes of war 198
Now: Jerusalem and the archives 204
My Jaffa apartment 211
'A Palestinian Day Out' 218
What is lost was needed 225
Walter Strauss 235
Grave relations 242
Return from Israel 248
The found letter 252
And now 255

Afterword 258
References 260
Acknowledgements 275

Raven's cry

'My mother was *Die Rabenmutter*, a "raven mother",' my father said, using the old German expression for a mother who is harsh and abandons her children – an expression that I discovered and he then grasped hold of. She'd left him twice: in 1935 and in 1949.

'She never loved me,' he said. 'Bella never once said the words, "I love you".'

Never is such a strong word. Was this true? I hadn't seen my father with my grandmother, that was certain. She died long before I was born. I was a witness to nothing between them.

So began the search for the answer to the absence of loving words, which might have been flaws in his recollection – or flaws in her.

In place of recollection, I've spent years researching her by talking with him, finding lost letters, travelling to sites, archives, speaking to people, reading histories, and much more. I've gone back in time to where she began in Berlin, to the last years of Jewish Berlin, through to the mid-twentieth century and its eventful years, to our here and now.

The result is this book, that's portmanteau memoir, social history, biography, the story of three people – me, my father, Michael, and his mother, Bella – and of four countries: Germany, Palestine, Israel and Australia.

In an afterlife, if Bella and I were to pass each other on the street, she would walk on by without knowing me in any way. And for most of my life, it would have been the same for me; I wouldn't have recognised her. The work of this book has changed that. I'm bringing us together, here in these pages. I'm looking her in the face, checking her pockets, looking under her skirts, reading her letters, searching out her confidences. Honouring the welfare work she did with children who suffered in World War I, with the poor of postwar Berlin, with the child refugees who fled to Palestine, and recognising that she brought her own children to safety out of Nazi Germany.

Bella's life came to span the two world wars, the collapse of Germany and the annihilation of herself as a German. As millions of others did, she lost colleagues, friends and family during World War II and the Holocaust. After fleeing Germany in 1937, she lived for ten years in what was then the nascent, polyglot city of Tel Aviv, amid a scattering of old Palestinian villages, among dispute and collaboration, amid new and old friends – without her husband or children. As a corporal in the Palestinian Auxiliary Territorial Service (ATS) stationed in Egypt during the war, she worked to protect Palestine. In her few remaining letters that we have, she writes about the present and the future, matters to do with her new life in Palestine, and later Melbourne. Her two children grew up without her. In many ways they stopped caring about her over the many years they lived apart from her. She had a long affair with a man who was also married, but that relationship ended in grief and bitterness and my grandfather never forgave her for it. She left Palestine for Australia in 1947, arriving a few months before the nation state of Israel was declared.

There seems to be a pattern to her, of making a life that is full and rich despite everything, year upon year, until Melbourne. She had survived the war and the Holocaust, but didn't survive the surviving.

Mine is also a father-daughter story. I'm the daughter who asks questions of my father, studies his pauses, pokes away at the archives, and writes about death and love, sex and grief, silence and action. Each of these words is loaded with heartache. I wanted to give him a different past, one in which he'd been loved, even if not well enough. If I'd not had the dozens of conversations with him for this book, I'd barely know my father, or I'd know a different man.

Now that the book is done, I want very much to leave the deep past. And yet, here we are, here am I, Bella's grandchild, jostling and fractious, still talking to the un-still, unsettled past, and its worsening present.

Part One

'A History of My Family'

The details of my father Michael's family are documented in his rather promisingly titled 'A History of My Family', a ten-page account of the Messer and Riess families. It arrived out of the blue one day in 2010, via email, with one of his usual brief missives: *You probably have no interest in this, but in case you do, here is the story of your German family. xx love Dad.* He'd sent it to me and my younger brothers, David and Jacob. We lived then, and still do, a few kilometres from each other in Sydney, along with our children, Dad's grandchildren, the six cousins.

My father, Michael, now close to a hundred years of age, is a great reader of fiction, histories and serious science, and a film-goer. He has seen films as varied as Greta Gerwig's exuberant *Barbie*, and Hlynur Pálmason's cold-drenched *Godland*. He's interested in people's life stories and cultural origins, and has friends, even at his great age, when so many of his earliest friends are long dead. He's cheerful in his own way, and willing to like people, but often suspects others' motives and capacity for genuine and generous feeling. Paranoid is too strong a word; untrusting is about right. His emailed missive saying that we, his children, probably had no interest in his family history, surprised none of us.

The History was short, but dense with names, addresses and dates, the kind of data that I needed to know more about. Without it I'd have had to engage a bevy of genealogists and historians from the very first. It was the beginning of my forays into this vast past of foreign places and times, in which each birth, street and incident had its own complex resonances. The History explained, in the briefest way, how it was that he, his mother, Bella, his father, Willy, and his older sister, Ruth, came to be separated across three continents for ten crucial years of his growing up, from before the war began to Bella's death in 1949. At the outbreak of World War II, my father was living in a German Jewish school in England, Bella was in Tel Aviv, and my grandfather Willy and aunt Ruth were in Melbourne.

World history courses through every line: ancestors flee pogroms and poverty, enlist to fight in World War I, live as naturalised Germans, then as stateless people. A great-uncle is picked off the street for the 'race-defilement' crime of *Rassenschande*, being a German Jew married to a German; others are deported and die in the camps, or vanish, their whereabouts unknown. There were rumours, writes Dad, that his uncle Martin, 'converted to the Christian faith and was a secret agent for the British' during the war.

For every tiny question I had, there'd be so much more to learn. Dad mentioned that Willy's parents, Adolf and Emma, had immigrated to Berlin from towns in what is now Poland. Following that trail, I read about the movement of tens of thousands of Jews from Russia, Poland, Romania and elsewhere, leaving towns and cities because of pogroms (a word that specifically designates violence against Jews) or changes in laws or economic circumstances that made life impossible.

Bella's parents, Doris and Max Riess, both came to Berlin from Pomerania, which had been annexed into Prussia in the late 1700s. Like many others leaving the province, theirs was part of an economic emigration that had begun in the 1850s. People left their villages and their tenant farms for the city's new factories and commercial centres to seek a better life, economically and socially, though many of these new Berliners ended up criminally poor.

Doris, Julius, Minnie and Bella, 'Mai 1916'.

A joke Berliners shared back then was that every Berliner was from somewhere else.

The Riess family thrived: Doris had left Wangerin (now Węgorzyno) where her father owned two mills, after her marriage to Max Riess, who was from a town in Posen (now Poznań). Max established a business manufacturing men's shirts in Berlin. The business grew, and the family became reasonably affluent. Bella Rosa Riess was the last of the five children, born in May 1893, when her mother Doris was aged thirty-five.

Bella was fourteen and still in high school when Max Riess died in 1907. The siblings she was closest to were the beautiful Minnie, who was three years older (b. Minna, 1890), and Julius, five years her senior (b. 1888). Her other two sisters were Lotte (b. Charlotte, 1889) and Hedwig (b. 1884). (According to my aunt Ruth, Hedwig was her and Michael's favourite aunt.)

Bit by bit I added to what Dad had written down in his History, asking him questions, talking about his memories, cross-examining him, even challenging what he recalled. I drew on my aunt Ruth's life story, twenty-five pages that she composed when she was taking courses with the University of the Third Age in the late 1990s. She had given me a copy in 2001, when she was dying. As with many of the letters and other documents I have at home, I read Ruth's pages quite a few times over the years, and as with all this 'data', I'd remember some of it and forget other parts. I was constantly learning and then forgetting certain elements because writing the book took so long. There was so much else going on in my life: work, births, deaths, divorce, caring for parents, for my children, time with my friends, marriage, travels. Other words being written.

There was also my close reading of the photographs and school certificates from the boxes of memorabilia Bella had carried with her across continents, from Germany to Palestine and then Australia. I learned that she had an unremarkable liberal Jewish upbringing amid a family that was acculturated, as were many middle-class German Jews. According to Bella's niece Susanne Arendt, who'd lived in the USA since the late 1920s and was quoted in the History, Doris and Max had raised their children in the Reform Jewish movement (the more liberal, more secular Judaism that predominated after 1900 among urban German Jews). This was, she said, 'even for Berlin, a very advanced education'.

The family saw themselves as German. They referred to Christian calendar dates and read German writers popular with other Jews, such as Goethe and Schiller. As teenagers, Bella and Minnie dressed up in the Tyrolean dirndl costume (the Bavarian version now associated with beer and Oktoberfests) consisting of a colourful, heavily embroidered neckerchief, fitted bodice and gathered skirts with a plain apron. In all these photographs, there's about three or four of them, the sisters are smiling broadly, and

Minnie and Bella wearing matching dirndl dresses.

Bella, standing top left, back row, with girls from her high school.

you can tell that they feel very chic and pretty. They seemed to wear these outfits when holidaying in the countryside and were also photographed together in studio portraits with snow-peaked alpine backdrops.

Like her older sisters, Bella attended a girls' high school, a *Höhere-töchterschule*. In 1909 or 1910 she began post-secondary studies in the revolutionary new field of early childhood education at the internationally renowned Pestalozzi-Fröbel Haus. She was still a fresh-faced twenty-one year old when Germany declared war on Russia in 1914 and she signed up to train as a volunteer nurse's aide.

*

My father wrote 'A History of My Family' as a Word document on his iMac in his study-slash-dressing room. Dad had got Mum's old iMacs (she churned through them; they were essential to her environmental and academic work) and he took up emailing, reading journal articles online, even shopping online. He'd visited his long-lost Jewish relatives on trips to the USA in the 1980s; now he emails back and forth with them.

His study is quite untidy. He retired around 1990 from his job at the University of Sydney where he'd been a professor of biochemistry, but maintains a keen interest in science, and well into his eighties he collaborated with a few colleagues on their projects. There's often a discarded shirt and some socks lying near his computer desk. Papers and pens litter the desk, and his electric shaver seems to live beside the keyboard. He still shaves while checking his emails. On the shelf above his computer he keeps the funeral programs of his dearest friends, each with its photo portrait: Max, Frank, Emil, Peter, Peggy. Framed photographs of my mother sit on his bookshelves. She keeps loyal watch over him.

There is no preamble to the History. It begins straight-up with his paternal great-grandparents Isaac Messer and Rosa Deckman's family tree. There is a short narrative about the paternal and then the maternal ancestors, illustrated with family trees that begin in the 1820s. These are laid out a little erratically. Birth and death dates don't always visually align beneath the names, and some dates are missing. But without this modest document my brothers and I would know little about his family, who our great-great-grandparents were, their children, what they did for a living, nor who had lived and then died during the Holocaust. The closer he gets to his own generation, the more detail there is.

Of Bella, he writes that:

> According to her passport (dated 1936) her eyes were blue, though I remember them as more blue-grey. Her hair was

> stated to be brown, but this was not necessarily its natural colour, as it became grey at a young age.

There are so many more questions that arise, amid the titbits such as that his aunt Lotte's daughter, Ilse, married a Jack May who owned a pharmacy on 48th Street, Manhattan, where the young writer and cartoonist Stan Lee worked before becoming the creative lead at Marvel Comics.

The little that Dad knows about his parents' marriage is distilled in a few telling lines:

> She once told me, in Melbourne, that she had got married mainly to get away from her unpleasant mother (Doris), but it seems that another reason was that she got pregnant (with Ruth, b. 1922).

Nevertheless, judging from photographs, for quite some time the marriage appears to have been a very happy one.

I return to the brief History regularly. I add corrections based on my own research. For instance, the History states that his aunt Minnie and her husband Kurt Fuchs immigrated to South Africa to escape the Nazis. They didn't. We have no idea where the idea of her having immigrated to South Africa came from.

Dad isn't signed up with any genealogy sites, has not used the Holocaust victim and survivor databases, or any of the major Holocaust photographic and text-based archives. Nothing in the family history document comes from online archives or databases. It is either in his head or was already written down on paper. I asked him how he knew all these dates and facts in the first place. He couldn't remember. 'Maybe it's in *das familienbuch*?' he said. Even now many Germans keep a *familienbuch*, a 'family book', in which they record births, deaths, marriages and places of domicile. Where is the Messer *familienbuch* then? At the start of this century, my parents left the small harbourside suburb of Greenwich where they'd lived for the past thirty years and moved across the Sydney Harbour Bridge to Balmain. They brought everything with them, threw nothing away. The four-drawer filing cabinet in Dad's study seemed infinitely deep. I'd plough through the shelves in the living and dining rooms and abscond with boxes and photograph albums. But I didn't find the *familienbuch*.

When I asked my father, via email, could he expand on the History seeing as it was brief, he emailed back, 'How is it brief?'

There *is* more to say, though. It doesn't include details of his marriage to my mother, Judy, and the children they had, me and my two brothers, our marriages and children, nor details of Ruth's son Leigh's marriages and his three children, or Dad's surviving cousins Edith, Alice and Helga and their children and grandchildren, nor the deaths of Willy, Erica (Willy's second wife) and Ruth. The focus of the History is on what is lost: that is the meaning and heart of 'history'; it's what's gone, what was savaged and ruined and murdered, it's what somehow survived against the odds, and those who did not survive. This isn't a living family history. The document doesn't mention that he is once again a naturalised German, regaining the citizenship that he and his family had taken from them, nor the debates he had with himself about the decision to take up the opportunity that Article 116 par. 2 of the Basic Law (*Grundgesetz*) offered. The law applies to victims of persecution by the Nazi regime who were deprived of their German nationality on political, racial or religious grounds between 30 January 1933 and 8 May 1945. It returns to them the citizenship that was taken from them. It is a sad good fortune that I, my brothers and Dad's six grandchildren all now have two passports: German and Australian. Sad because my good fortune has come out of so much suffering, and when others have no citizenship at all.

Dad keeps himself at arm's length when he writes:

Bella playfully holding Michael, 1933.

> Evidently she [Bella] had intended to collect me from England and take me to Australia, but the war, which broke out in September that year, prevented that, the result being that she remained [in Tel Aviv] on her own.

Thus, for the duration of the war the family lived across three continents. Dad was a boy in England, Bella was in Palestine, while his sister, Ruth, and father, Willy, were in Melbourne.

He holds himself apart. He cannot speak for himself within the document, as if he's just a conduit for the history, an incidental character, barely inflecting it with his own meanings.

At the end of 1949 Bella died, and Dad blamed himself, as children do, and none of the three survivors, my father, Willy or Ruth, talked about it.

*

In my attempts to make sense of the lives of Bella and Michael and Willy and Ruth, I've turned often to German, Jewish and Palestinian writers who lived through those days or who grew up with stories from their diaspora parents. Amos Oz's memoir *A Tale of Love and Darkness* is mostly set in Jerusalem, not Tel Aviv where Bella lived for ten years, and Amos was a boy in the years when she was a woman. But his mother, Fania, died by suicide, in 1952, when he was twelve, so he'd had that to contend with. He asked questions that resonated with me: about his parents and their friends who were Jewish, Palestinian, some poor, others influential and wealthy. Oz wrote about the repressions that afflicted many postwar European Jews and shaped his father, Arie, observing that there'd been

> ... generation upon generation of repression and negation. A double negation in fact, two sets of brakes, as bourgeois European manners reinforced the constraints of the religious Jewish community.

I found his words peculiarly reassuring, providing an unexpected context for me to understand my grandparents and perhaps my father, too.

Bella's cremation brings 'A History of My Family' to its last line. It took me a hundred re-reads before I noticed. 'Her ashes are interred in the cemetery and crematorium at Springvale, Princes Highway, Victoria in the Tristania Garden G3, Bed No 6, Tree No 23.' The tree is a small, heavily pruned rose bush that her son has never seen.

Walking in Berlin

I had imagined from afar, from my other nation and my generations later in Sydney, Australia, that the Weimar Republic had been all boisterous risqué *kabarett*, and late-night drinking of beer and vodka, then tart black coffees, and splashing about in chilly lakes while a friend lay back on the rug beside a picnic of fresh breads and Bavarian cheeses, laughing back shots of pear schnapps.

I had imagined that the crowds were utopian, hyper-inflated, political, defeated and exultant. They knew that life could be ended in an instant – heard the ghosts of the wailing men and screaming horses killed at the front.

How to live after that first world war? I imagined signs of disruption, dissidents waving flags, bearing witness, singing manifestos. Anita Berber danced. Alienation and melancholy, a dangerous, slow burning smell coming from, somewhere. Fritz Lang filmed. Käthe Kollwitz's paintings cried out, 'It is my duty to voice the suffering of men, the never-ending sufferings heaped mountain-high.' *The Threepenny Opera* declared, 'My business is too difficult. You see, my business is trying to arouse human pity.' Liza Minnelli wasn't there, actually. Lotte Lenya was asked, 'Fräulein Lenya, is it only on stage that you notice a blind beggar?' Rosa Luxemburg prophesied totalitarianism.

Somewhere in the background, there were huddled refugees, potato eaters, solid women in headscarves, grim men in tired caps, children with sodden coughs hanging on for dear life. Food queues, and immigrants sleeping out in the Tiergarten. Someone cringing beneath the words hurled at them – people I knew little about.

The social democrats, the communists and the Nazis clashed, the noise was louder and louder, the dancers scattered, knives were thrown, the streets became bloodier, Jews were the bullseye. And then the red velvet curtain tumbled down, the music stopped, the police arrived and bundled the republic into trucks and camps, using batons, churlish words, ropes, interrogations, guns. Then up, up, up went the curtain to a roar of applause, and Hitler was shouting on the podium at Nuremberg and planning grandiose horse statues.

This history, this ferment of violence and beauty and lives crushed and others achieved – I am one of its many, many offspring.

*

So here I was at last. Berlin. It was the European spring of 2014, and I was going to be a Berliner for just a few months, living in the city that my father and grandparents had been forced to leave decades ago. Both Willy's and Bella's families had found succour here for only a generation or two before they had to leave again.

Despite Imperial Germany's restrictive immigration policies, there was migration to Germany from eastern Europe in the mid-1800s onwards. Jews from Central and Eastern Europe and particularly from Russia's designated area for Jews, the 'Pale of Settlement', were on the move, some transiting through the port cities of Antwerp, Bremerhaven, Hamburg and Rotterdam en route to America; others staying in Germany.

Many settled in Berlin's Scheunenviertel, literally the 'barn quarter'. The area was known as *das Elendsquartiere*, the 'quarter of misery'. But for the Eastern European Jewish immigrants, the low rents, the proximity to the Old and New Synagogues and the polyglot Jewish community made it a place of relative safety.

Exterior, Number 22 Hufelandstrasse
and Hufelandstrasse street view.

Scheunenviertel's name had its origins in the twenty-seven grain barns that serviced the Alexanderplatz cattle markets from mediaeval times to the mid-1800s. When they were razed, the barns were replaced with three- and four-storey apartments built on small plots. There were food and beer halls, community centres, stores and shopfronts. Everyone was poor but hoping for a better life.

According to Dad's History, my great-grandparents, Adolf Messer and Emma Wolke, began their German lives in Scheunenviertel. An orphan raised by one of his brothers, Adolf had left Krakow in 1875 as a young man. Emma came from Murowana

Goślina, an ancient Polish town. They married in Scheunenviertel in 1885. My grandfather Willy was the third of their four children, born in June 1891 at Linienstrasse 47, an apartment block that's still intact. I've found photographs of it on history-of-Berlin sites: blank-walled, without balconies or ornament. The family grew a little better off, and moved to a better building in Prenzlauer Allee, and then as Adolf's menswear manufacturing business grew, they moved again, to Hufelandstrasse, in Prenzlauer Berg. This was another working-class and sometimes impoverished Jewish neighbourhood. The apartment at Hufelandstrasse was a short walk from where Adolf established a larger factory and business.

*

Berlin. It must have been a city Bella loved, that she felt a powerful affinity with for its thriving, wakeful, eclectic character; it was a city Berliners were proud of. It was the home she lost to the Third Reich. Berlin had been wilfully, avidly cosmopolitan before the Third Reich, from the wealth of the western boroughs to the working-class manufacturing hub in the east. There were the suburbs of the very rich bourgeoisie to the west, and there were the slums to the south and east, the river Spree wending its languid way westwards, busy with tugs and barges docking at the many commercial ports. The city's population had always been mongrel: gentile and Jewish, communist, socialist, nationalistic and antisemitic, 'slum-dwelling', Sinti and bourgeois. Working Berliners spoke a brash *Berlinerisch*, an idiom distinctive for its tendency towards occasional crudity and Yiddish flippancy. Its *rotwelsch* language of thieves and French Huguenot élan was knitted together with intentionally bad grammar. Berliners talked a lot. They also read the most newspapers in all of Europe. Of all the cities in Germany, its politically and socially diverse residents were among the most resistant to the Nazis, to begin with.

Bella had danced, partied, fallen in love (at least twice), and given birth to her children in Berlin. She and my grandfather Willy knew the popular songs of the time. They sang songs from Kurt Weill and Bertolt Brecht's *The Threepenny Opera,* which had opened at the riverside Theater am Schiffbauerdamm in Mitte in 1928 and become crazily popular. Six months later, in March 1929, my father's second birthday was celebrated with family and friends. He recalls the grown-ups singing 'Die Moritat von Mackie Messer' – 'The Ballad of Mack the Knife' – at the party. The lyrics about the killer Mackheath are macabre, but also a bit sexy, a bit jaunty. Mackheath is the shark, his knife its teeth, hunting the streets at night. I grew up with two versions of the song, the one Dad sang in German, and Louis Armstrong's version where he sings in his rich gravelly voice along with the horn, the famous Grammy Award–winning recording that we'd listen to on Dad's 45-inch single. My father could even whistle Armstrong's horn opening. The song invites you to like the murder mystery, to enjoy its thrills. It's so very Berlinesque – here, come enjoy the risk and wickedness of the dangers of the streets and bodies 'oozin life'.

My father left Berlin in 1935, aged eight. Before that, he remembers a nanny and a cook working in the family's apartment and a holiday on ski slopes in Czechoslovakia with his parents and sister. Photographs show my grandparents out in the evening with friends, at fancy-dress parties, nightclubs and restaurant dinners. The recollections swing from one extreme to another. In 1933 when the family moved from Prenzlauer Berg to a larger apartment in Charlottenburg, the move was short-lived, coinciding with a weekend of pogroms and window-smashing. Until then Bella's experience of Berlin would have been heterogeneous, liberal, secular.

My grandparents' city came to fascinate me. I imagine Bella crossing paths with locals such as the writer Franz Hessel. After all, Berlin's Jewish community wasn't that large, less than 160 000 – less than 4 per cent of Berlin's population. In the 1920s Hessel embarked on his book *Walking in Berlin*. Beginning at Potsdamer Platz, Hessel crisscrossed the city. Reading the book, following Hessel's walks, brought me closer to my grandmother's city. He walked on his own or with locals or friends, such as the Jewish writer Walter Benjamin. He'd gently connive invitations into homes and workplaces, taking note of overheard conversations, delving into courtyards, dingy basements, shops and stores of all kinds. He'd find women willing to take him into their haberdasheries and washhouses, to the stocking repair shop with the sign 'Fallen stitches taken up'. When women accompanied him, he'd get entry to interiors not usually open to men. Hessel looked 'closely at all of it and gleaned a piece of the city's and the world's history from it'. Bella could have shown him a thing or two; in the 1920s, before she married, she worked as a district welfare officer supporting people living in the tenements and slums.

Berlin's modernisation continued apace through the 1920s. It isn't easy, wrote Hessel, 'neither the viewing nor the dwelling in a city that is incessantly on the go' and 'always in the middle of becoming something different and never at rest in yesterday's form'. Hessel loved it. The pneumatic drill, invented a few decades earlier, had revolutionised building techniques, and new materials were being introduced into construction, including ultra-modern glass and concrete. Streets were being rebuilt and surveys undertaken for new roads. Factories, offices and apartment buildings were proliferating. There was coal smoke and clouds of grit and the noise of drill presses and hammering. But inflation was soaring from the impact of the post–World War I reparation payments and the chaotic, multi-party Reichstag coalition. Many Germans were unemployed or struggling with housing. International trade was constrained by worldwide protectionism. Even so, scientists, educationalists and even sex therapists gave lectures in packed halls. The river ports along the Spree burgeoned. Alexanderplatz was being rebuilt with omnibuses, horse-drawn trams and city and regional trains making it the city's transport hub and central to the country's rail network.

Berlin's first department store – a concept entirely novel to most Berliners, who'd never been to Bon Marché or Printemps in Paris – had been opened by the Jewish entrepreneur Georg Wertheim on Leipziger Platz in the 1890s. Designed by the architect Alfred Messel, the store was the largest in Europe. Over a period of twenty-five years, Wertheim opened five more. Bella and her glamorous sister Minnie would have shopped or had coffee and cake at the Leipziger Platz store, nearest to the family's Schöneberg apartment. Perhaps they bought their corsets from Wertheim's, while they were still wearing them, before bobbing their hair and throwing off their Victorian dresses in the late 1920s. Wertheim's introduced both everyday convenience and extravagance: sculptures, ornate stairways, carved reliefs, two glass-roofed atriums, and more than eighty elevators servicing movement around the building's 26 000 square metres. At Christmas, the store was transformed into a fairytale kingdom, and families travelled from far away to view the nativity displays. The Riess family were Jewish, but they too used the Christian calendar to set the rhythm of their days. Perhaps, like Walter Benjamin's family, they even decorated a Christmas tree.

The store's history also encapsulates what was brewing. Some smaller shopkeepers didn't like the popularity of the new department stores, the modernisation and acceleration of crowds. The Wertheim stores seduced their customers. Antisemites didn't like who'd built it. It was described in the antisemitic press as a 'socialist Jewish bazaar'. Antisemitic and anti-communist propaganda proliferated after the Russian revolution of 1917.

By 1939, Georg Wertheim, like many thousands of other Jewish business owners, including my grandfather, was forced to sell all his stores to 'Aryan' buyers at reduced prices. In the last days of World War II, the original Wertheim's was destroyed in an Allied bombing raid. Most of central Berlin was razed to the ground in the bombing and street fighting. So it was extraordinarily good luck that the Hufelandstrasse apartment in Prenzlauer Berg, in which my father had been born, survived the war unharmed. And in the spring of 2014, when I arrived in Berlin for the first time, I found myself living in Hufelandstrasse. The street was much the same as it had been when my father and grandparents left in the 1930s. Only the people had changed.

A bit of a Jew

Who was I to have taken on this search into my grandmother's life? I began knowing so very little, but needing to know more, to see if what my father said about her really was true. I guess I was trying to find my own place in the history, too, both as my father's daughter and as a Jew, to have a stronger sense of our family history as Jews. Isn't that the burden and the great opportunity for the children of refugees, to look back across the oceans to whence our parents came?

My parents had met and married in Melbourne in 1957, where I was born in 1960. We lived in North Carlton when the neighbourhood was populated by Italian and Greek postwar migrants and a smattering of students. When I was three, Dad was awarded a research contract in Copenhagen and we left for Denmark. After returning to Melbourne, we left again, this time for Stanford University in California. Aged five I boarded the vast SS *Oriana*, a P&O passenger ship. In San Francisco, I remember Haight-Ashbury musicians sitting around with their guitars and tambourines in the parks, folk smoking hookahs, a man with a long ponytail loping along the sidewalk wearing checked pyjamas. Joan Baez and the Grateful Dead hung out there. Palo Alto was a mix of conservatives, academics, students; it would later produce Silicon Valley. In one of my school-year photos I sit next to an Indian girl who wears a sumptuous crimson velvet pinafore – she may have been a local or the child of an international professional like my dad. I'm dressed in a winsome gingham dress that my mother had expertly sewed.

When we returned to Australia in 1968, we moved to a small peninsular suburb on Sydney's lower north shore. Greenwich was nothing like Palo Alto or North Carlton. Weekends had their own sounds, of church bells and lawnmowers, the pinging bells of Dragster bikes, and Mrs C up the street yelling at her husband the butcher from her seat on the outside dunny. There was the thump of trampolines, the urgency of transistors broadcasting the races, the drone of cicadas from the bush that ringed the bay, and the thwack of tennis balls on the local courts.

With the move back to Australia, I discovered I was different. Kids, teachers and parents showed me I was. The markings had been invisible to me until now. I found that I didn't look like anyone else. My hair was almost black, my skin olive and my eyes 'almond' shaped. I'd be asked at school, on the street, in shops, 'Are you Jewish?' Sometimes I was told, 'You look Jewish.' Did I? There was no getting away from explaining myself. I sensed a silent, shared disapprobation from other parents and teachers that I hadn't felt before, of being different in ways that always led back to being of Jewish origin.

My responses sometimes led to a new statement, 'So your mother's not? Oh, you're not Jewish then.' Within minutes I could be spotted as a Jew, then confidently un-Jewed. The experience was often hurtful and confusing. We didn't attend synagogue, and I knew almost no religious lore or stories. Every few years Grandfather William, as we called Willy, would visit from Melbourne with Erica, his second wife. They'd stay at a motel in nearby St Leonards and come for meals. Both were secular, godless after the catastrophe, unwilling to live in the dark past. They were sweet and old, both unused to children.

Dad gave us matzos during Passover and told stories of Jewish life and his family history. He talked sometimes about religion and

Jewish tradition but could recall very little of his family's religious observance before leaving Germany. And yet here we were, in Australia, me and my brothers, Jacob and David, the children of a Jewish refugee.

The first Greenwich house we moved to was in the same small street as the local Anglican church. The suburb had more churches than any other in Sydney. I was eight when I first saw the Carter family, who lived opposite us, filing out on Sunday mornings in their good clothes, past the beds of low-growing plants and their neatly edged lawn. My family went bushwalking and swimming on the weekends, and our garden was wilder, with sandstone rock saddles a metre wide, and an old lemon tree. We had a rope to swing on. Weekends, I'd lounge around in my cotton shorts, maybe watch a bit of television, play LEGO with my younger brothers, or head down into the bush for some tadpole hunting along Berrys Creek in the bushland reserve below the cul-de-sac. Our parents were atheists and environmentalists. We didn't have family nearby. On a day-to-day basis, we didn't have aunties or cousins or grandparents, and this was another point of difference between our neighbours and us.

Dad was not troubled by his Jewishness. He knew who he was and what he'd been through. He thought he was leaving the past behind. Everything Jewish, the little I knew beyond my father's terrible stories, was tainted with a tricky combination of sorrow, knowingness, silences and pride when another Jewish person made good, invariably as an intellectual or scientist. These other Jewish people lived elsewhere, in other times or other nations. Occasionally one of them visited the house.

For me, whatever it meant to be Jewish, or a bit of a Jew, got muddled up with other stuff. I was playing elastics at school when a girl told me that I was going to Hell because I wasn't baptised. Her curse is now forever imprinted in my memory, along with her long slim legs scissoring the parallel bands of white elastic as her light brown hair bounced. The incident confirmed that my thick black curls – brushed by my mother every day till each hair was separated and the whole of it was in a major frizz – had doomed me. I began to plan for emergencies and imagined that if I had only one room to live in like Anne Frank, the bathroom would be best. It had running water and a toilet, and I could sleep in the bath.

My parents were way out in their own orbit, evidenced by the foreign novels on the 1970s pinewood shelves, the European foods we ate, the countries we'd lived in, the friends who visited: well-travelled scientists, policy writers, social workers, paediatricians. We moved to a larger house in Greenwich, that looked out over bush, well away from the churches, but alongside the Shell Oil terminal and storage facility. Each Saturday, Dad returned from the delicatessen in Crows Nest with his week's supply of Estonian dark rye and ripe cheeses. We went to Paddington art galleries, didn't observe Shabbat, didn't attend a synagogue or play football, cricket or tennis. My mother was no libertine, but had danced to Jefferson Airplane and Janis Joplin, and seen Woody Allen do stand-up in San Francisco. She was bored by netball and Girl Guides. She took me to small community halls for critiques of environmental degradation. We sat on hard chairs to watch the documentary *Red River*, about slaughterhouse waste emptying into the Missouri River, the gushing water heavy with blood. In sum, we did little that was Jewish or popularly Australian in character.

The years hurtled along. I heard that the personal was political and never forgot it. Thousands marched for nuclear disarmament year after year. The Berlin Wall came down and the Soviet Union imploded, and the Cold War was declared over. I finished high school and moved across the harbour to the multicultural south side of the city, shifting between various share houses, unable to settle. I lived in old cottages next door to old workers who still used wood-fired coppers to heat water. Fridges frequently rattled all night, and I had not yet met anyone who had an ensuite bathroom.

When Israel's Prime Minister Yitzhak Rabin was assassinated

in 1995 after speaking at a rally in support of a peace agreement with Palestinians – 'Yes to Peace, No to Violence' – I was barely aware of it. I had just given birth. I'd stopped moving around, finished my arts degree, done postgraduate study in the USA, married, and was living with my husband and baby. I was a mother now. I began to see Bella's situation differently, the little I knew of her.

*

The only image of Bella that I can recall seeing for all the years that I was a child was a framed photo of her standing outside somewhere in Berlin, wearing a coat and skirt, thick-waisted, pensive. She's perhaps in her mid-thirties. This was the woman I knew as my father's mother, the woman Dad talked about at the dinner table. The photograph was kept in a drawer somewhere. And so, when I took an active interest in her, I was surprised to find images of a very different Bella in her German photograph albums and old sewing boxes. Where had these albums been all these years? They didn't appear until after my parents moved house in 2001. This woman seemed warm and tactile: cuddling my father, Michael, as a little boy, hoisting him up playfully, sitting on the grass or the sand with him, or with both her children, Michael and Ruth. She's plain-faced, or perhaps handsome, with plump cheeks and wide brows and forehead. Her eyes are also wide and slant downwards, and her hair is dark and wavy. Her expression is sometimes reflective, often mischievous. In photos with others she's among the tallest, and she's a little taller than Willy, so maybe 170 centimetres. In the albums she created, many of the photographs have a precise description written with a fountain pen in white ink on the black page. Her names for the children are *Micha* and *Ruthen*.

A loving mother places her child in the safest place she can during a war, which might be with her, or somewhere else. We know this from the thousands upon thousands of mothers and fathers who have sent their children away on perilous journeys to safer countries, to Australia, Germany, Britain, Palestine, the USA. Most famously, 10 000 German, Austrian, Czechoslovak and Polish children were put on the Kindertransport boats in the 1930s. There are many others down the years, stories of children sent to what their parents hope will be a safer country than Kampuchea (now Cambodia), Vietnam, Syria, Sudan, Afghanistan, Iraq, Ukraine. There are no estimates for unaccompanied children leaving Gaza, because so few have been able to leave.

My thinking about Bella shifted during the early 2000s, especially after Australia's minister for immigration controversially accused asylum seekers of throwing their children overboard in a bid to be rescued. I began to think of Bella as part of a history of parents forced by war, starvation, persecution, to send their children to safety elsewhere to ensure their survival.

I re-read the Vietnamese-Australian writer Nam Le's short story 'The Boat' and set it as a study in technique and voice at the university where I was teaching creative writing. I was hoping the conversation would spill over into what the story was about. And it did. Many students said they had no idea what it meant to be a 'boat person', or how child refugees came to be in the boats or what being on a fragile boat in a vast sea was like. In common with many Australians, they hadn't met a refugee, or not knowingly. They'd not had conversations such as those I'd had with my father.

In 'The Boat', Mai's mother arranges for sixteen-year-old Mai to be smuggled with dozens of others from Vietnam to Australia. When they part, Mai recalls her father's return from a re-education camp, broken and blind. She understands why her mother is sending her away, and that their separation is very likely final. Now I and my students learned through visceral detail about the fear, the deaths on board from illness, overcrowding and dehydration, and the deep hope of staying alive wedged inside the trauma of flight.

Nam's stories are drawn from those of his family, who arrived as refugees from Vietnam in the 1970s.

But my educated, historical perspective isn't my father's. He was a child of eight when he left Germany. What he felt and knew was that his mother abandoned him at a strange school in a strange land. She'd said goodbye at the school in Kent as if she'd be back soon, knowing that she wouldn't be. There is no 'going back' on those feelings that are long embedded in my father. But could her leaving be understood differently by us both, in this broader context of war and persecution?

That's when my interviews with my father began. My earliest recording is dated 2007. We would agree on a time, or I'd drop by and we would start talking. To begin with I used a digital recorder, then as the technology improved, I used my phone. Often my mother would be there, and so we'd have a three-way conversation and she'd ask him questions too.

It wasn't enough, though, to talk to my father and go through the photographs, letters, Holocaust databases, history books. In 2014, I went to Germany, and the next year, Israel. From what Ruth said, and a few letters that have survived, and what I learned about Bella's work during World War II, she had thrived first in Germany and then in Palestine. I had to go to Israel, too, even though I viewed Germany and Israel with much ambivalence. Both have waged acts of persecution, assassination, dispossession, and now genocide. (I write the word 'genocide' fully aware of how controversial it is for some Israeli and Jewish people to hear Israel accused of it.)

After spending years reading, listening and thinking about the lives, persecution and survival of Jews in the twentieth century, I am compelled to understand the Palestinian experience. I cannot turn away from it. This is the burden, and the gift of history: you're born into it whether you choose to recognise it or not. I needed to see for myself the consequences of the Jewish migrations that brought Bella and hundreds of thousands of other Jews to safety, but led to an exodus of 700 000 Palestinians and, for those who remained, a precarious and insecure life.

In searching for knowledge and some sense of what life had been like for Bella in the ten years she lived in Palestine, I confronted the violence that her migration, and those of the many hundreds of thousands who followed her, has brought upon Palestinians.

Family traits

I was in my early twenties in Sydney, and I was restless. I'd been on the move since I was seventeen, searching for the right fit of house and housemates. On this day, I arrived at my parents' place in Greenwich looking for a home-cooked meal. Why else would I have been there? I lived in a distant suburb, in one of my many share houses on the other side of the harbour. I'd turned eighteen picking cherries outside the country town of Young, then worked for a women's union project, as a waitress, as a kitchenhand, as a storeman and packer. I'd sold newspapers from a stand outside Wynyard. On Sundays I crawled out of bed after four hours of sleep to get to my job selling manchester at a boutique in the Eastern Suburbs. I was saving to buy a typewriter. I lived on a shoestring and wrote my unpublished stories by hand.

I was working and studying part-time. My university degree was taking forever. I kept doing other things. I joined feminist collectives, worked in community radio, experimented with collage. Friends lived in squats in Darlinghurst, near the nightclubs and the tiny galleries and the avant-garde, post-punk, post-disco gigs. A friend and I printed a hand-made journal of our writing, which we sold through Nicholas Pounder's Exiles Bookstore at Taylor Square. Nicholas was always charmed by us, two black-haired beauties turning up in our vintage silk dresses with our strange tales. I fell in love with an artist who later became a little famous. In a rage over one of his flagrant infidelities, I tore up the large pastel drawings he was storing at my place in preparation for an exhibition and dumped them in a garbage bag at his mother's house. A feminist herself, she approved of my direct action.

My parents' achievements were far more decisive. My father had earned his PhD in biochemistry a few years after arriving in Australia as a stateless German Jewish refugee. He'd gone from the temporary job at Stanford University to being a professor of biochemistry at the University of Sydney. My mother was a Depression-era child of British and Irish migrants, born in the Western Australian bush, who'd scored a scholarship to Perth Modern School and trained as a nurse. Like my father, she'd lost her mother when she was young. When she'd been a trainee nurse, her mother, Annie, was dying on the oncology ward on the floor below. No wonder she'd wanted to stop nursing after she married. Now, thanks to second-wave feminism, she was underway with her own PhD, in sociology.

True-to-age, I was generally uninterested in my parents' personal histories, their day-to-day concerns, and I felt cramped by their persistent interest in me and angered by their evident disappointment in my lack of measurable progress in my studies, career, boyfriends and manners. I was making my own way, much to their dissatisfaction. They found me completely frustrating.

Despite all that, there was nothing better than one of my mother's meals; a spiced chicken casserole with olives, or a salad with lots of leafy greens and garlic bread, or a roast herbed with rosemary and thyme and squeezes of lemon. Some leftovers to take home. Perhaps the aroma of one of these meals was wafting from the kitchen as I arrived.

My parents and I were standing on the seagrass matting in the airy high-ceilinged living room, near the bookshelves and their store of histories and photograph albums, the memorabilia of our family. William L Shirer's *The Rise and Fall of the Third Reich* sat as a marker of my father Michael's survival, alongside histories of the ancient Greek world, the American, English, and Russian novels in translation, our dictionaries and school encyclopaedias. A small brass menorah was there, empty of candles, a marker of my father's secular Jewish identity. What a tussle it was, between the vivid life he enjoyed now, and the past with its ledger of death, loss and grief.

It wasn't summer, but some cooler month. Through the south-facing windows I could see where the land fell away to the Shell Oil storage tanks, and a tanker that was in dock. Something was up, I could tell. They'd corralled me in the living room.

My parents were in their prime. Not that I saw them like that at the time. But looking back, I remember that Dad was lean and upright, his hair still black, his eyes a bright dark blue, his skin olive. My mother was long-limbed, her hair dark, and beautiful in her late forties.

Dad said, 'I don't think I've ever explained to you, Jane, how my mother died.' He spoke with his usual deliberate, clear enunciation.

What did I know about the Messer family history at that time? I knew Bella had never been sent to a camp, though others in Dad's family had. I knew she'd died when he was in his early twenties, but not how. I knew from what he'd told me that Bella's hair was grey, and her eyes had been blue, like his. I knew many anecdotes, such as stories about the trip through London before he and his sister arrived at the boarding school in Kent. How they'd had a nanny in Berlin who'd take them to the park. That Bella hadn't loved him, that he'd not seen my grandfather from the years 1935 to 1947. There was a bit more that I knew about her then, but not much.

He gave me one of his serious but gentle looks and said, 'My mother committed suicide.'

That came as quite a shock. Very left field.

My parents hovered solicitously, as if ready to physically steady me. I found the moment embarrassing – not because of what he'd told me, but because they were both so focused on my reaction. My parents seemed to believe that sharing this information was to spread some psychic contagion, to pass on the grief and shame.

I hadn't met either of my grandmothers, and my grandfathers I'd met only a few times. Bella and Mum's mother, Annie, were both gone long before I was born, before my parents had even met each other. What I did know from my father, having heard it numerous times since I was young, was that Bella hadn't loved him. He said he was a 'mistake', a pregnancy she hadn't wanted and, he also said, more than once, 'Possibly I wasn't a very likeable child.'

Dad's way of talking was to communicate clearly, but with an economy of words. 'You're old enough now to know,' he said as we continued to stand awkwardly in the middle of the living room. I had reached my early twenties, so they must have decided it was time to tell me that Bella had taken her own life. Having got through my dark teenage years, I was apparently ready to heed the warning.

'We were worried before how it might affect you,' my mother said.

I had long been the problem child in their eyes, though my troubles were of an ordinary nature. It was the 1970s and I was interested in freedom, protest, live bands, love and sex, pot, staying out late, giving cheek, changing schools, and struggling with deep bouts of depression.

'Bella took an overdose of barbiturates,' Dad said, enunciating the syllables of the word 'barbiturates' almost too clearly. He explained that his father had returned home to their Elwood flat as usual one evening in December 1949. Bella had been in Melbourne for two years after leaving Tel Aviv. She was fifty-six years old, Willy fifty-nine. Willy had been in Australia ten years, since early 1939. They had not been happily reunited in Melbourne. They slept separately in the second-floor flat: Willy in the main bedroom, Bella in the larger living room with the frosted glass doors that divided it from the hallway, my father in the little bedroom next to the kitchen. She was lying unconscious, on the bed or the floor,

I don't know. It was a cool, dry summer's day; I know this because, in trying to imagine that day, I sourced the local paper's weather report via Trove. Willy called an ambulance, and Bella was taken to hospital.

Dad had been on a working holiday in Tasmania, then flew back to Melbourne (his first plane trip) to see her. He went alone to the hospital and found her in a coma. 'Tubes and wires running around and in and out of her,' he said, gesturing the tangle with his hands. She'd lain still and very pale, and it was frightening to see her like that. She died within a couple of days. She was cremated without a ceremony, no sitting shiva, or a gathering of any kind. (Who did they know in Melbourne who would have come?)

I liked my father and was sensitive to him being hurt. I was the daughter who observed well and felt acutely but was yet to understand. When I stood with my parents in the living room, I didn't know how brutal suicide is.

'It was terrible,' my father assured me, still with his diffident, matter-of-fact voice. 'And I was so immature. I felt it was my fault, that I was to blame, that I could have helped her but hadn't.'

I needed to give some acknowledgement of the event's importance for him, but I was completely unprepared, and was too young to understand. I can't recall what I said. I hope I didn't disappoint. It's likely I gave him a hug. The conversation had begun out of nowhere for me, whereas they'd practised it, and felt relieved to have told me.

By now, surely, we'd sat down and were no longer standing in the living room. Perhaps my mother went to make a pot of tea, or maybe Dad poured us a wine or opened some of his home-brewed beer, cloudy like harbour water after rain.

Then Dad added that his grandmother Doris, Bella's mother, had killed herself too. 'So we were worried there was a pattern.'

I was mightily perplexed. How could these distant women, who in the photographs looked nothing like me, have an influence on my destiny? My parents seemed to think I could be on a precipice, that there was a genetic inheritance that would lead me to take my own life. First Doris, then Bella, then who knows, maybe Jane.

Oy vey! I might have said, if I'd known any Yiddish. But Dad had come from an aspirational, bourgeois German Jewish family. A family that post-migration grew almost hydroponically in the new country, without old people around to share the memories or the language.

On that warm afternoon I was embarrassed by my parents' intensity.

'Suicide,' said my mother firmly, 'is a very selfish act.'

The long-dead can be blamed for everything – and Bella was.

I feel for them now, this fragment of my parents that I remember, how horribly awkward it had been for them that day. They'd been worried. They cared. I'm a parent now. I get it.

*

On the last page of the History, Dad wrote of Bella:

> In Melbourne she had no work and no friends and found that she was completely estranged from both her husband and her son, with whom she had to live in a small 2-bedroom flat.

He's the son. He wants to remain factual, naturally enough. But facts are never enough. They're the frame of the window you still need to push open and climb through. Was it Bella who felt estranged from him, while longing to feel close? Was it Michael who felt estranged from her, and after the war had been unable to respond to a mother he'd not seen for twelve years?

For years I didn't give a second thought to how 'The History of My Family' ended, until one day it struck me how truly brutal and eloquent the last paragraph is:

> Bella eventually arrived in Melbourne from Palestine in January 1948, 10 months after my own arrival. As is evident from the letter she wrote to Ruth in the days before her death, her departure from Palestine – which became Israel only a few months later – to come to Australia, was a tragic mistake. In December 1949 she ended her life with an overdose of barbiturates while my father was at work and I was away in Tasmania during the Christmas holidays.

*

Bella's death shaped so much of what was to come between Willy, Ruth and Michael. They'd lived apart for years across three continents, had already lost most of their family to the Holocaust. And here, in their bruised hands, was their mother, and Willy's wife. Silence riveted around each of them, separating one from another for the rest of their days. And it shaped me, too, the stain that can't be shifted, that you don't even know is there for the longest time. The knowledge that my grandmother had taken her life was strangely connected to her not loving my father. The knowledge of both these things felt hidden but present, like a thread tied around my finger. But there it was, a discomforting, tensile knot.

It's strange, isn't it, how you can feel uninvolved during the moment of being told of a death, and yet recognise years later how deeply affecting the telling was. There was a long trail of aftershocks, which I only felt as they accumulated. After hearing about Bella's last days, she travelled with me for many years before I realised she was there. She wasn't present as someone whose death I had any desire to imitate, but as an unspeakable question, a vast sadness and shame. She was my melancholy grandmother-ghost.

Telling me how she died meant a great deal to my father, Michael. We have gone over it many times since then. It was a threshold he'd crossed, but I couldn't immediately figure out why telling me mattered so much to him. It has been the work of years, figuring it out: why she chose to end her life, and why they'd held back telling me. Was it only their worry about me? Or also the guilt that she'd taken her life? So many wounded silences surrounded Bella.

At least a decade passed before Bella's suicide was spoken of again. But Bella was there in me, along with the dark sensation of my father's hurt that he'd been unloved, that he had been unlovable. There was so much to later unfold, to nourish my curiosity and sadness.

In a series of numbered paragraphs titled 'On the Concept of History', Walter Benjamin talks of 'blasting a specific life out of an era or a specific work out of the lifework'. He'd never intended the essay for publication because a public reading, he said, would 'open the door to enthusiastic misunderstanding'. (Reader, you are warned.) In looking for Bella, I was trying to push through the miasma of a past as seductively lit as any galaxy of myriad events, gestures, or words can be. My aim: to make fragments of Bella and my father cohere, to create a kind of guardianship, to try to make the fragments into a whole. Benjamin's urgency was mine too; I wanted to blast Bella's life out from the silences in my family – and the homogeneity that so often describes the lives of women and mothers, even from out of the sometimes-homogenous Holocaust narratives. 'Theses on the Concept of History' was Benjamin's last work, before ending his life in September 1940 at the Hotel de Francia in Portbou, as he escaped the round-up of Jews in authoritarian France.

Memory is its own beast. It wants to push to the front or draws itself back into the dark. Over the years of my conversations with Dad about Bella's death at Melbourne's Alfred Hospital, and the days that followed it, new elements emerged that he remembered very clearly, yet had never mentioned. Is there something about our older minds, that we find new recollections while also losing others? Only in 2023, after years of focused conversations about Bella, did he tell me that Willy had sent him to the morgue to identify her body.

'The morgue!' I exclaimed, gobsmacked. In the many conversations we'd had over the past decade, he had not once mentioned the morgue. What blasted that open?

In the long unwinding spool of our conversations, he was ninety-six years old when he told me this. It had taken that long for the cold room with her body lying on the stainless steel bed to be spoken about. When we reached this point in the conversation, Dad was downcast, and I was, too. There we sat in the Balmain house my parents had moved to in 2001, missing my mother, who was now living alone with advanced dementia in her aged care home. The past was so close, so present.

I was shocked that he'd been sent to identify her. He was the youngest in the family. 'Why didn't Willy go?' I asked. '*He* should have gone, or Ruth.' She was young, too, at the age of twenty-seven, but she was still five years older than Michael.

Dad didn't share my certainty. 'Well,' he offered, 'they were probably too shocked and upset.'

'You mean,' I said, 'you went back to the hospital to see her a *second* time, but this time you had to find your way to her at the morgue?'

Dad nodded. 'It was somewhere downstairs in the building.'

At this point I remembered that he had indeed mentioned seeing Bella twice in the hospital. I'd always assumed he meant that he'd seen her *alive* twice.

It was kind of him to say they were too shocked and upset, I thought. Possibly too kind. For my grandfather to send such a young man – I couldn't fathom it. Except that in his distress and shock, Willy wasn't thinking clearly.

One of the letters my cousin Lisa showed me when I visited her in the Blue Mountains was a letter to Ruth from a long-time family friend, Henry Una, Ruth's 'Uncle Henry'. He'd fled Germany for New York, and the letter arrived in Melbourne months after Bella's death. He wrote that Willy was a broken man, who had not been strong to begin with.

Dad continued, looking away, shaking his head, remembering how speechless he had been. 'I walked in a daze out of the hospital back to the street. I wanted to get home as soon as possible. A film club friend spoke to me at the tram stop. He said hello, stopped to have a chat. But I couldn't answer. I just turned away.'

Pestalozzi-Fröbel Haus

Bella was, of course, so much more than these desperately sad stories. To find information about her that illuminated her, or at least something approximating her, has been work. Much of it, material work: gathering documents from various family members, asking my father for translations, translating documents myself with apps; reading innumerable histories and oral narratives, peering at archival photographs and grainy birth and death notices in old-world fonts. The Holocaust victim databases and survivor archives are vast. The deciphering of pre- and postwar maps with their changing names, borders and alliances is finicky, invaluable, but also often fruitless. War reports in the regional Australian newspapers held by Trove have been remarkably helpful. The price of oranges in Palestine in 1937, those fabulous, sweet oranges, reported on in tiny regional Australian newspapers. When Bella got to Palestine, she could drink as much orange juice as she liked. The wholesale price of oranges and where the groves were harvested was a part of my effort to uncover the stories of community and cohabitation between Palestinians and Jews decades earlier during the OttomanEmpire. The oranges are just one part of a culture and history now distorted and, worse, erased. I saw howthe disaster of the Holocaust, which had brought Bella and thousands of other Jews to Palestine, had led to the disaster of the Nakba (1948 and 1967), the Palestinian Catastrophe, after which only a small Palestinian population of Muslims and

Christians was left, lacking its former social institutions and political power.

It has only been through this material work that I've been able to confirm anything about Bella's life beyond the bare details of my father's History; to create a chronology and from that chronology to see what the shape of her life might have been, or even the meaning she gave to her life.

And to be able to confidently write this, for instance: that after finishing high school, she trained as an early childhood teacher at Pestalozzi-Fröbel Haus in Berlin-Schöneberg and took this training with her into her war work during World War I, into the postwar world, and then again into World War II. Who knew that in our family? The fragments of information were there, if one paid attention and properly looked at them. No one had, and even putting aside the complications of Bella's life and death, she was just a woman. And women's histories disappear. They go unrecorded or become trivialised.

Following World War I, during the years of hyperinflation and the Depression, millions were starving in Germany. Public welfare assistance was only provided by philanthropic organisations, many of them women's organisations. Pestalozzi-Fröbel Haus was already internationally famous as a training institution when Bella started there circa 1909, aged sixteen. The institute integrated the training of teachers with on-site practicums in its kindergartens and elementary school. The children were local, and most of them from the poor working-class families of Schöneberg, many of them with no breadwinner.

The Pestalozzi-Fröbel Haus philosophy of child education placed the child as an individual at the centre of the learning experience, and along with its approach to teacher training, this philosophy was revolutionary, and influential worldwide. The institution was frequently visited by educators from the USA, Britain and Europe. American women were especially interested, with the American kindergarten and early childhood education movement well underway there.

It's hard to convey just how radical the initiatives of Henriette Schrader-Breymann and Alice Salomon were, founding the Pestalozzi-Fröbel Haus and the Social Women's School, the first college of social work, and for a young woman such as Bella to have studied at either of these innovative institutions. No one before her in her family had gained a tertiary education. University study was out of the question for Bella; laws had only recently been enacted permitting German women to enrol in full programs at university. Well-off German women had been going overseas from the 1880s to other European countries, the USA and Britain for their university education.

For Jewish women who needed and wanted to work, their options outside of family businesses were limited, not least because of antisemitism, and a reluctance by younger Jewish women especially to work in potentially hostile and culturally unfamiliar environments. Education led to employment and financial independence, and it also developed your *bildung* – a very specific German notion that expresses all the complexities of being educated, not just through formal study but also through the conscious development of the self. The historian Marion A Kaplan describes *bildung* as 'the belief in the primacy of culture and the potential of humanity, with notions of character formation and moral education'. Until the revolution in women's education began in Germany, the gendered notion of *bildung* had 'left women out'.

Pestalozzi-Fröbel Haus, with its educational, humanitarian, social and international focus, offered women such as Bella the possibility of developing their *bildung*. The institute regularly hosted eminent visitors from Europe and the USA. Even a few Eastern European Jewish women from the early migrations to Palestine trained at Pestalozzi-Fröbel Haus and then returned to Palestine (then under the rule of the Ottoman Empire, and understood not as a nation but as a number of administrative districts) to teach using the new methods. For some German Jewish women, their education at the Haus and at the associated Social Women's School enabled them to later leave Germany as professional migrants to England and the USA. At least one Jewish graduate, Dora Peyser, was sponsored to come to Australia – and thus escaped deportation.

The Spirit of 1914

With her Pestalozzi-Fröbel Haus training completed, Bella had skills to offer when she volunteered at the outbreak of World War I. My father notes in the History that Bella was issued a certificate by the Prussian Red Cross which stated that from August to September 1914 she had completed 20 hours of training as a nurse's aide.

She'd have fronted up to the enlistment office with that certificate. Her sister Minnie may also have trained at Pestalozzi-Fröbel Haus and then, with the outbreak of war, as a nurse's aide. Photographs from one of Bella's boxes show them both in what look like nurses' uniforms. That they volunteered wasn't unusual. With few exceptions, most of the German Jewish population – Reform, Orthodox, Zionist and socialist – responded at the outset in support for the war, in large part because of the widespread belief it was a war against the violently antisemitic Russia.

And the Kaiser had included them in his rallying cries. On 31 July 1914, Wilhelm II warned of an imminent war, claiming he had no choice: 'A fateful hour has fallen for Germany. Envious rivals everywhere force us to legitimate defence. The sword has been forced into our hands.' The following day he declared war on Russia. He was no longer concerned about his nation's various parties, denominations or past internal disputes: 'Today we are all German brothers and only German brothers.' Jews implicitly understood they were included as Germans in these declarations. The Kaiserin, Auguste Victoria, addressed the nation's women on

4 August, the day after Germany announced it was also at war with France: 'I call upon you women and girls of Germany, and all to whom it is not given to fight for our beloved home, for help. Let every one now do what lies in her power to lighten the struggle for our husbands, sons, and brothers.'

This new civic truce (*burgfrieden*) raised morale among German Jews more than anything had since Napoleon Bonaparte's radical emancipation of the Jews of France and the French Empire a hundred years earlier. After Napoleon's defeat in 1815, Jews had rapidly lost the rights he had granted them: they were once again prohibited from certain professions, and throughout most of the pre-unification German states, their rights to work, settle and marry were again restricted. In most states, Jews were excluded from posts in public administration, the army, and secondary and tertiary teaching positions.

Banned from so many professions, Jews were often impoverished as tenant farmers on tiny plots, or worked as peddlers, street sweepers, laundresses, and the like. Expensive registration certificates were required to marry, and the numbers of Jews allowed to marry in a particular city or county was highly restricted under a law known as the *matrikel*. The result was that many marriages were not legally recognised. Jewish people were also heavily taxed. During the Mediaeval period, many Christians had come to believe that Jews were responsible for the death of Christ because it was a Jewish man, Judas Iscariot, who betrayed Jesus to the Romans. This misconception persisted for centuries.

There was also the accusation of blood libel: that Jews use the blood of murdered Christian children in their rituals, such as in the baking of the *Pesach* (Passover) matzos. This idea was popularised during the mediaeval period, despite being denounced as false by at least two popes. It is present in Geoffrey Chaucer's 'The Prioress's Tale' (though as Jews had been expelled from England in 1290, the prioress could not have met one).

I don't know how aware my father was as a young man of the details of this long history of antisemitism or its main features. (From a young age Willy had believed that as a Jew he'd never be fully included in German society.) I find it excruciating to read through these histories of persecution. My family was born out of these persecutions and expulsions, but now the racism has turned, and Israel has been slaughtering Palestinians in retaliation following Hamas's savagery of October 2023, and to expand its territories.

Excluded from the skilful and respected professions of law, the military, the public service and teaching, the Christian church's prohibition on Christians practising usury effectively pushed Jews into moneylending, tax and rent collecting. Tensions between (Jewish) creditors and (Christian) debtors exacerbated antisemitism.

For three months in 1819, pogroms known as the Hep-Hep riots (*Hep Hep* being the rioters' rallying cry) took place throughout German states. Poorer Jews especially were physically attacked. Homes, possessions and shops were damaged in large numbers.

In Russia, whose winter snows had in part defeated Napoleon, discriminatory decrees were proclaimed by the antisemitic tsar of Russia. Pogroms in the early 1880s worsened in 1881 and 1882 with over 200 taking place in Kiev, Warsaw and Odessa. The frequent pogroms led to poverty and a constant stream of Jewish emigration away from the Pale of Settlement to Europe, Argentina, Uruguay, North Africa, Palestine, America and Britain.

*

It's not possible to underestimate the eagerness of German Jews, given the opportunity to do so in 1914, to actively and ardently identify with their Fatherland through participation in the war effort. Acknowledged as Germans at last, Jews shared in a powerful sense of national belonging, what came to be known as the 'Spirit of 1914'.

As the summer continued, the recruitment depots were inundated with enlisting men. The *Berliner Tageblatt* described the crush of volunteers at Schöneberg, near the Riess family home, as 'unremittingly large'. The streets were filled with men, women and children, everyone on edge, excited and fearful and wanting to know what was going to happen next. Within weeks, over 8000 men had enlisted at the Schöneberg depot alone.

German men were routinely drafted into the army from the age of twenty for two or three years of peacetime training as part of their compulsory military service. And so within two weeks the German army expanded from around 800 000 to 3.5 million soldiers. Bella's brother, Julius, was among them, with the rank of an officer it seems from the photographs I have of him in uniform. Within a year, the army had grown to 9 million men, with over 90 000 volunteer military nurses. These women made up around 40 per cent of the medical personnel attached to the field and reserve armies.

Drawing upon the Schlieffen Plan, the war cabinet expected Russia would focus its army on the distant Western Front, the 700-kilometre stretch of land weaving through France and Belgium from the Swiss border to the North Sea. While the German army was looting, raping, shooting men, women and children, and burning Belgian villages, the Russian army was committing its own war crimes in German territory. Russian troops invaded East Prussia, the region north-east of Berlin that borders the Baltic Sea. The province's many small undefended towns were burned, livestock stolen and killed; homes, crops, barns, bridges and schools razed. Hundreds of women and girls were raped, and over a thousand civilian men and women slain. Over ten thousand Jews were living in East Prussia at the time, and many were among the victims. More than 13 000 men, women and children were deported to Russia as prisoners, a third of them never returning to Germany. Two critical battles, one the famous Battle of Tannenberg, culminated in a decisive victory for the German army.

Once the Russian armies had been defeated, Bella made her way to Rauschen (now Svetlogorsk, in Kaliningrad) in East Prussia. She had completed her training as a nurse's aide and now boarded a steam train to travel 800 kilometres north-east from Berlin to Rauschen. Very likely she travelled with Minnie; there are photographs in which Minnie seems to also be in Rauschen. What must it have been like to leave Berlin during the first months of the war, passing through a battle-ravaged countryside and burned and looted towns? I imagine a feeling of absolute necessity, the compulsion to act, and perhaps the exuberant audacity of youth.

With its picturesque lakes and freshwater lagoons and sea-frontages, Rauschen had become popular in the 1800s as a spa town. In the early 1900s the beach areas had been added to with timber promenades and a funicular to take visitors from the train to the beach. The artist Käthe Kollwitz, the writer Thomas Mann, and philosopher Wilhelm von Humboldt (after whom the university in Berlin is named) would stay there. Of all the places to be sent in the ruins of East Prussia, Rauschen was not too bad an assignment for Bella.

Now the town was playing a role in the post-invasion recovery of East Prussia. For Germans, the invasion of East Prussia was a shock that was felt viscerally. There was extensive newspaper and newsreel coverage, and soon, letters home from soldiers, and stories told by evacuees. The invasion affected Germans profoundly and mobilised the nation. German businesses and individuals donated millions of marks to rebuild the East Prussian communities. Funds flooded into the stricken province. Over the next couple of years, films, memoirs, histories, bestselling novels, and even books for children about the invasion were broadcast and published.

Another document my father translated described how Bella had worked as a kindergarten teacher in a 'rest home' in Rauschen. The children were some of the many affected by the invasion. For women like Bella, already involved in educational organisations,

Bella with children in her care, Rauschen, 1915.

the mobilisation offered them the possibility of having impact and influence. A reference from her employers that Dad also translated for me, states that, 'With her first-rate training and fortunate bent for her profession … Fräulein Riess has excellent character traits, so that I can strongly recommend her.' The 'first-rate training' referred to her time at Pestalozzi-Fröbel Haus.

Half a dozen Rauschen photographs lie in a jumble in Bella's sewing box. In one she is visible on a grassy area near the sea, a beach flag waving behind the gathered children. In another, she and the children are outside the rest home. She wears a pale-coloured shirt and tie, the shirt tucked into a long skirt of darker fabric. Some photos show her with a pinafore over her shirt and skirt. She was still a Victorian-era young woman, her hair halfway to her waist, her skirts long. She was not yet the postwar New Woman with cropped hair and ambition that she was to become soon after the war's end. In all the photographs she appears plump-faced, relaxed and confident. She's not camera-shy, she beams and seems happy.

Bella's own adult children, Ruth and Michael, would come to have only the faintest sense of what she'd done before her marriage to Willy. My father always passed over this period of Bella's life, just as Ruth had too, neither of them knowing much about it. Being apart from them for over a decade, there'd been no opportunity for her to tell her children stories about her life. Neither were aware, except in the vaguest ways, of what she'd done in the next war, either, World War II. From the day she died, she was rarely spoken of. For years all physical traces of her were kept out of sight; these documents and photographs were stored in cupboards and sheds. They were never discussed, never brought out to look over, as we do when we want to remember.

Another document states that she did further volunteer work for a year with children back in Berlin, from September 1915 to June 1916. It seems she moved between Rauschen and Berlin for the first two or three years of the war. She was highly praised for managing, 'quite rapidly', to 'tame some rather wild children with her love and understanding', demonstrating 'outstanding pedagogical talents'. In a photograph of her with a group of cheerful boys and girls, the group stands in front of what looks like a city building with large windows that seem to be barred. A couple of the children do indeed look boisterous, with cheeky poses and broad smiles.

At some point she was awarded a '1914' commemorative brass pendant for 'meritorious military aid'. She kept it in its original box lined with purple velvet. The phrase *für verdienstvolle Kriegshilfe* – 'for meritorious war aid'– is inscribed in relief above an image of two stags facing each other, horns entangled below the twisting branches of a tree. On the other side is the figure of a demure woman in Grecian-style draped fabric, standing with her hands opening towards a pedestal, and the year in the top corner.

Knowing that I was writing this book, my second cousin Lisa Morgan, Bella's great-granddaughter, rang me sometime in 2022 to tell me she had a box of letters and photographs Ruth had given her that related to Ruth and Bella. I drove up to Katoomba in the Blue Mountains west of Sydney, an easy journey of an hour and a half, where she'd recently bought a home. She was now unpacked, and the box of Bella's and Ruth's stuff had surfaced.

We sat at her kitchen table and picked our way through the box, trading what we each knew. We found some of Ruth's school reports from Bunce Court, a scarce few letters from Bella to Ruth dating from the 1940s, and the 1914 pendant. It had travelled a mighty long way over those one hundred years, from Berlin to Tel Aviv, then Melbourne, and finally the mountain town of Katoomba. I've scoured the internet looking for information about this war pendant; blogs and historical sites about war medals, and online auction sites such as eBay. I've used search terms in German and English. There are medals for every war, all of them traded online, but this pendant awarded to German women has remained invisible. Like so much about women's war efforts, the facts of the pendant's introduction, how it was awarded and to whom, are now gone.

As more of Bella's life revealed itself, she was emerging anew. I was getting a picture of her as a young woman who'd been affable, efficient, patriotic and even courageous in her early twenties.

It was not all work for Bella during the war. Photographs show her out and about with Minnie, swimming, boating and picnicking. Aside from Russia's early invasion of East Prussia, this war was fought outside of Germany. People could move about. In 1915 the sisters were photographed wearing the decorous swimsuits of the day (the tops of their thighs are covered), lounging on a lakeside jetty. Their long hair is tied up in loose buns. A white-suited

Minnie and Bella at lake, 'Wannsee II Pfingsten (Pentecost) 1915'.

lifeguard stands behind them some twenty metres away. It must be a sunny day, for they're both squinting.

Bella's months in Rauschen among the children and local community, and being a part of the mobilisation of women through the Prussian Red Cross, had surely lent a new focus to whatever she'd previously imagined she'd be doing until she married. I think it is likely that Bella's war years were for her an opportunity to grow her *bildung*. The Riess family were bourgeois Germans, and she took the patriotic stance that this was a war for the defence of the Fatherland. Even after the terrifying years in Berlin before the children went to England and she and Willy fled, she carted her complete works of Goethe from Berlin to Tel Aviv to Melbourne.

In later photographs, before the terror comes, some of the pictures capture her confidence and fearlessness. There is a photo of her on a yacht, it must be the late 1920s or very early 1930s,

Ruth distributing Communist Party of Australia newspapers in Bourke Street, Melbourne, September 1946. This photograph and an article about her in the CPA's *Guardian* prompted ASIO to open a file on her.

perhaps taken on the trip she and Willy made to Palestine when they visited her best friend, Elli Preis. She is leaning against the mast, face averted, half smiling, the wind is whipping her bobbed hair loose; her wide trousers flap, and she is lost in the pleasure of the sea and the wind and the sun.

The kind of woman Bella showed herself to be during World War I and the postwar years, and how it prepared her for what was to come in Nazi Germany and then in Palestine, was not known even by her daughter, Ruth. My aunt Ruth had been a staunch member of the Communist Party of Australia for decades, was watched and has an ASIO file. She was a feminist especially active in her advocacy for other migrant women, and an active member of the Nuclear Disarmament Party for many years. She once said her proudest moment came when she was arrested for protesting at an anti-uranium march. Did she not realise that some of her *chutzpah* came from her own mother?

Fighting for Germany

In Bella's sewing box with its faded embroidered lid and hook-and-eyelet closure, I found two photographs of her brother, Julius in his military officer's uniform. Only with the Kaiser's declaration of the 'civic truce' could Julius have become an officer. Jews had been barred from holding senior positions in the courts, universities, and military as officers. Until World War I, Jews were not promoted to officer rank unless they had converted to Christianity. Julius could have been mistaken for one of the Kaiser's handsome sons: his hair is oiled and parted in the middle, and in one hand he holds cloth gloves, in the other a sword with a tassel. The buttons on his cuffs and chest gleam.

In response to his pristine appearance in this studio portrait, I remind myself that Julius then left to fight in the trenches alongside horse cavalry, using rifles, trench knives and bayonets, with the infantrymen literally dragging the cannons forward when they didn't have horses. Julius was one of 100 000 German Jews who fought, representing about a third of the total male Jewish population.

Rather than recognise their contribution, many Germans retained the long-held antisemitic prejudice that claimed Jews were reluctant to self-sacrifice for the Fatherland. Jewish soldiers were commonly described as *drückeberger*, 'shirkers'. The Military High Command conducted a *Judenzählung* in October 1916, a detailed census of Jewish soldiers serving in the German army;

Julius Riess.

the majority served at the Western Front, which had the highest number of casualties. The *Judenzählung* was completed by officers, who answered questions about their soldiers, including whether the Jews under their command were fighting at the front, or in the less dangerous rear. Though it had been designed to confirm a lack of Jewish patriotism, the 1916 census failed to uncover evidence of Jewish shirking. The War Ministry didn't, however, release the findings. Germans knew it had been undertaken but weren't told its conclusions. Despite the demoralising effect the census had on German Jews, it didn't impact their patriotism. In fact, Jews contributed equally to the war's wins, and to its destruction and terror. The historian Tim Grady shows that Jewish men were enthusiastic and 'active participants in the German military', and Jewish women active patriots as military nurses and on the home front, 'long before they became its victims'.

Bella was still a few years away from meeting Willy, who meanwhile had been conscripted into the Austro-Hungarian army. And he *was*, quite possibly, a *drückeberger*. Though born in Berlin, Willy was not recognised as a citizen, his father having been born in Krakow. (He wasn't naturalised until 1921, and was stripped of his citizenship in 1933.) The Austro-Hungarian Empire was vast and diverse, made up of ethnic Austrians, Hungarians, Poles, Croats, Bosnians, Serbians, Italians, Romanians, Czechs, Ruthenes, Slovaks and Slovenes. Embassies as far away as the USA set about notifying the empire's male citizens that they were required to enlist, deploying posters and newspaper advertisements in multiple languages. The polyglot army that Willy joined spoke more than eleven languages. A pidgin language was devised, 'Army Slavic', a set of about eighty words, that combined elements of German and Czech. Willy was serving in a Polish legion (or, possibly, a Galician regiment), but didn't speak Polish. He told my father how, instead of fighting, he moved between various camp hospitals on suspicion of typhoid, helped by 'doctor friends', rather than going into the field of battle. Willy had survived tuberculosis as a child and lost a finger to it. I remember the stub of bone on his hand, which you'd think would have exempted him. Later, in the early 1950s, he had a serious recurrence of tuberculosis and was hospitalised. Its return was caused, he said, by the shock of Bella's death. (Was even that remark an accusation?)

What he didn't tell Michael was how violently antisemitic the Catholic Poles were, who comprised most of his regiment.

It's hard to know what to make of Willy's war story, given that he intended it to make light of his experience. Many years later, when he was corresponding with the young woman who was to become his second wife, Erica Wolff, he said that although he'd been raised 'in the Jewish tradition', he was not a believer and had found no sense in 'mechanically imitating predigested customs', and that living in Germany's 'Christian environment' as a teenager he was:

> ... forced into the conclusion that, as a Jew, I was different from the others and that the solution or part-solution of the Jewish problem could be achieved only through Zionism.

Secular Zionism was a relatively new idea; the word based on Orthodox Jews invoking a return to 'Zion', named in the Old Testament as the two hills east of ancient Jerusalem. Willy was very likely familiar with Theodor Herzl's political pamphlet *The Jewish State*, published in 1896, and Herzl's newspaper *Die Welt*. Willy had wanted to be German, and certainly became a bourgeois German Jew and hardworking manufacturer – but he knew he could never pass.

He was a few years older than Ernst Toller, a Jewish writer, war veteran and activist who wrote his autobiography in 1934 in New York – he'd fled Germany after attempts on his life and five years in jail as a political prisoner. He opens *I Was A German* with the intentionally ironic story that his maternal great-grandfather had received permission from Frederick the Great to settle as the only Jewish family in the Prussian town of Samotschin. Toller recalls how very proud he was as a boy of his great-grandfather's elite status, and that he 'used to brag about it to my school-fellows, and dreamed of advancement and ennoblement'.

Perhaps having become aware of the persistence of antisemitism, Willy was sceptical of the hyper-patriotism of other German Jews, and the rush of men signing up to volunteer. The journalist and novelist Arnold Zweig, for instance, spoke for many when he said that the war heralded a new German Jewish symbiosis. He volunteered immediately: 'In my inherently Jewish way, I will make Germany's cause, my cause,' adding that he was 'not going to stop being a Jew'.

Among the chaos at the recruitment depots, Willy's brother Arnold enlisted with the German army. Perplexed by how the two brothers could have fought in different armies, Willy for the Austrian-Hungarian and Arnold for the German, I wrote to the military historian Alex Watson at the University of London, whose research I'd already drawn on for insights into the Russian invasion of East Prussia. He promptly responded that at the outset of the war, the situation at the enlistment centres was chaotic. Arnold's presentation at a centre to enlist was most likely simply accepted, no questions asked. 'It's entirely possible,' Watson wrote, 'that your great-uncle went along to the offices with German Jewish friends or colleagues – the population was well assimilated into Germany, and Russia (the principal enemy) was the most antisemitic great power in Europe at this time.'

Berlin was one of the centres of Jewish immigration for the Russian Jews leaving the Pale, and Bella would have often encountered such families and individuals in her welfare work. Jewish organisations, many of them women's organisations, supported the migrants, whether they were settling or transiting to other countries. Bertha Pappenheim, a feminist social pioneer and writer, had co-founded the League of Jewish Women (Jüdischer Frauenbund or JFB), the largest charitable Jewish organisation in Germany for many years. (It is not so well known that she is 'Anna O', the young woman at the centre of Joseph Breur and Sigmund Freud's famous case study. Fortunately, Pappenheim recovered.) Pappenheim saw Jewish women's education, including religious education, as key to reinvigorating Judaism in Germany, arguing that Jews were turning away from Judaism because its women, the transmitters of culture, were alienated from patriarchal Jewish life. Bella may well have known Bertha Pappenheim during these many productive years.

Pappenheim's best-known book, *Sisyphus Arbeit* (*Sisyphean Labour: Travel letters from the years 1911 and 1912*, first published in 1924), exposed the problem of Jewish prostitution and the traffic in women in Eastern Europe and Palestine. Among her many campaigns, Pappenheim worked to end this trafficking, which was later seized upon as grist for Nazi propaganda to demonise Jewish men.

*

In Berlin, bread rationing was introduced in early 1915, and was worsened the next year by the *Seeblockade*, Britain's naval blockade in the North Sea. The blockade led to shortages of food and agricultural fertiliser and starvation in Germany. Food imports Germany had long relied on were not able to get through the blockade. The country had not prepared well for war. Very quickly, supplies of food and raw materials became a critical problem. Prices rose and food queues lengthened. People were starving. In Austria, civilians rioted, demanding they be fed. All homegrown foodstuffs went first to Germany's soldiers. There were shortages of fruit and meat, butter, cooking fat, sugar, potatoes, coffee, tea. Civilian and military hunger worsened every year and reached extreme proportions in 1917 when there was a poor potato harvest. At some point in late 1916 or early 1917, Bella returned to Berlin from Rauschen and started paid employment as a district welfare worker. She'd also most likely have joined her mother and sisters in the food queues.

With the USA entering the war in support of the Allies in 1917, Germany's failures began to multiply, and on 9 November

1918, Wilhelm Kaiser II sheathed his sword and abdicated. The following day, 11 November, after four years of a horrific war and millions of deaths and injuries, Germany surrendered to the Allies. By December the two questions Berliners asked were, 'When are the Allied troops coming?' and 'Will they give us food?' They did begin food distribution, but even three years later, in 1921, a million children a day needed to be fed at thousands of food kitchens across the country.

The war had ended at last, but for German Jews the nation's resounding defeat was worsened by the postwar 'defeat accusation' that the loss was caused by Jewish and communist shirkers and traitors. German Jews' initial experience of inclusion was soon overtaken by the National Socialist Party's antisemitic rewriting of history. But Julius Riess was still alive and, given the massive numbers of deaths and the daily sight of maimed soldiers, his return must have been a huge relief to his mother and sisters. He was in his prime, aged thirty. What he did for work or where he lived on his return we don't know. However, we do know that in November 1916, against the trend of fewer marriages taking place during the war, he married Cornelia Susana Lader from Utrecht. Both thirty, his mother, Doris, and sister Minnie were their witnesses. Whether Cornelia's Christian heritage was a concern for Doris or others in the family, we don't know. It couldn't have been too strong as Doris and Minnie were the couple's witnesses. In 1921 Julius and Cornelia divorced. In 1925, he married a second time.

For Bella, the return to peace, with its many wounded, its fatherless families and food rationing, demanded she apply herself in Berlin. She continued to work in the poverty-stricken area of Schöneberg, working for the district welfare office.

Spring arrival in Berlin

I had arrived in Germany one hundred years after the start of that first world war, during months of summery light and warmth. On this first trip I was with my teenage son, Louis. While Louis attended one of the local high schools, I explored East Berlin, getting to know our ancestors' city. I was on long service leave and had rented out my townhouse in Sydney to pay the mortgage while we were away. My daughter was living with her father in Sydney while studying at university, and my partner, Martin, who had his own apartment, stayed behind, busy with work. I'd found our Berlin apartment through Airbnb (this was well before the City of Berlin introduced restrictions on rentals to protect locals). In my Airbnb searches I'd selected the Prenzlauer Berg district because the area was central, not too expensive, and Messer family friends, Suzi and Micha Kossack, and their sons, Stefan and Jan, and Jan's wife, Elke, lived there. The neighbourhood was also reasonably close to Louis's high school, and not too far from where my younger 'cousins' Katharina and Simon lived in Kreuzberg and Schöneberg. (We call each other cousins; they are the grandchildren of Dad's cousin Helga. Helga lived then in Munich, and their father and mother, Rolf and Anne, were further north in Lübeck.)

A couple of months before we left, I told Dad I'd secured a place to live.

'What's the address?' he asked. I couldn't remember the name of the street, so was looking it up on my phone, while telling him I'd seen its name on a street sign that was part of a scene in a German film; it could have been *The Lives of Others* ... I was distracted as I tried to recall the name of the film.

'Hufelandstrasse,' I said, enunciating it awkwardly, hoping I had it right.

'*Hufelandstrasse?* Are you joking?' He looked very surprised. 'What number?'

'Twenty-four, fourth floor.'

'I was born there, at number twenty-two, second floor!'

I don't believe in omens, but it seemed a very good omen indeed.

The street's brick and stone apartment buildings still stood, with the same narrow balconies and wide timber doorways. The *wohnung* (apartment) at number 22 had first been home to Willy's parents, Adolf and Emma, and their children, after they'd left the barn quarter, and then home to Willy and Bella once they married.

And now here we were, living next door, passing their former home each day, walking the same footpaths that Bella, Willy, Ruth and Michael had last walked upon in the 1920s and 1930s. A few times I knocked on the dividing wall in our apartment, imagining my father as a boy hearing my faint knock all those decades ago. A few times I just placed my hand on the walls, as if I could feel the past through the cold plaster.

Our Airbnb host was an artist and photographer called Sabine. The apartment's owner, another photographer, had decamped to Mumbai with his partner. The ceilings were high, the windows tall, the floors were the original timbers. From the narrow balcony I would look down at the bright green canopy of the oak trees below, and the awnings and café umbrellas that lined the footpaths. Berlin was known as one of the hippest, most on-trend cities in Europe. For me, it was also an estranged city. I was living in it across two timeframes, the Berlin of my family and the Berlin that followed, emptied of Jews, Sinti, gays, dissidents, the disabled and infirm. I would stop on my walks to study the small brass Stolpersteine hammered into the cobblestones outside the homes of deported Jews. But the Stolpersteine aren't only for those like me searching for a past I hadn't lived through, or history tourists; they're done by and for the people who live in those homes now.

Dad had asked me to check if a carved owl was still there at the foot of the banister in the lobby of his former home. One day as a resident opened the front door, I slipped into the foyer behind them. The owl was still atop the first post of the darkened timber banister at the foot of the stairs, worn by a thousand hands and barely discernible as a bird. I ran my hand over it, as Dad said he'd liked to do.

At the ground level our street was populated by cafés, a bakery, cosy Italian, Vietnamese and German restaurants, a bookstore, a vintage Bauhaus furniture store across the road from a contemporary Danish-style homewares store, a shop just for water filters, others for vintage clothing, bicycles, flowers, a Vietnamese-German corner store, the childcare centre, and the asylum seekers' hostel. The neighbourhood was a microcosm of a successful, gentrified East Berlin, one that was also encountering a new wave of asylum seekers and migrants. A street away and around the corner a swingers' club could be identified by the neon sign that lit up at night and a solid door, never open during the day.

A few of the local shopkeepers displayed photographs of their store's prewar days in the shop windows. I'd stop, examine the images, wondering if there was anyone from my family among the figures. When Willy and Bella lived here, this part of Prenzlauer Berg was densely populated with the new immigrants, the better-off *herrschaften* Jews, as well as the working-class Jews. The buildings and streets had been far grimier, the footpaths treeless, but animated, lively and bustling.

Prenzlauer Berg had been part of the communist German Democratic Republic (GDR) only twenty-five years earlier, and the soot from the coal heaters that some residents used even now was visible on these buildings. Many of the external walls were still painted with the dull GDR hospital-grade yellowed whites and browns: chipped, unsexy, 'authentic'. The graffiti on many of the entryways and front doors merged with wall art, with street art, with street posters and flyers. People here remembered the GDR days, but no one remained from when my grandparents called the place home.

In the mornings our corner shop was usually busy with parents and young children buying bread, milk, croissants or other pastries for breakfast, and returning bottles for cash. People in this area of Prenzlauer Berg were financially safe, employed or studying, though there was a small apartment block given over to refugee housing up beyond the corner store. There was little mingling between the locals and those I later recognised as the first of the Syrians fleeing their country's civil war. The next year, 2015, they became the world's largest refugee group. The German chancellor, Angela Merkel, was determined that Germany would assist, announcing, 'I put it simply, Germany is a strong country,' and '*Wir schaffen das.*'

Our Airbnb host Sabine was the first to tentatively ask me about my family's story. She was the first German to tell me they'd never met a German Jew before, as if I was one. My connection to Germany was filled with absence: of family, of known history, of silences between those who survived. What I did know was that we had arrived in August, one hundred years after the start of World War I and the cascade of catastrophes that would lead to the Nazis and the Third Reich.

We had also arrived a few months before the twenty-fifth anniversary of the fall of the Berlin Wall, which led to the reunification of Germany in 1990. Flags and banners bearing the number '25' fluttered on walls and from lampposts. The mood of the city, if one can talk of such a collective experience, seemed buoyant. It was summer still. The long dark months of winter were far off.

The monkey out of her cage

When Bella married Willy and became Frau Messer in October 1921, she wore white, he wore a top hat, and in the photo they are very happily stepping out of the Muenchener Strasse synagogue. Their rabbi was Dr Arthur Levy (who I'm pretty sure was sent to a camp and murdered). Bella had turned twenty-eight in May that year; only a couple of years older than the average age Berlin's Jewish women married. She had been working as a kindergarten teacher, living still with Doris, as was usual for an unmarried daughter. Julius and her older sisters were all married. At thirty Willy was now marriageable; among middle-class Jews it was expected that the men didn't marry until they had established themselves in their profession and could provide a home and income. Bella was also pregnant with their first child, Ruth.

They moved in circles of work and friends that were mostly Jewish, but Jews who were assimilated, bourgeois. The two of them met when they were each holidaying in Austria. Willy's story was that his friends referred to Bella as 'Schöne Beine', 'nice legs', and encouraged him to say hello. This is the only trace of eros in Willy's story; this and the fact that within a fairly short time, Bella was pregnant. German women could access contraception, but most often used the withdrawal method. Baby Ruth was born 'premature' in early June 1922.

Willy told Michael much later that in 1920 or 1921 Bella had sent him a postcard with a drawing of a monkey in a cage. She was

Bella and Willy leaving the synagogue after their wedding ceremony.

the monkey, her mother, Doris, was her cage, and she wanted to escape. Like most women, Bella had to wait until marriage to leave the family home. Bella had told Michael, when she was miserable in Melbourne, that she'd married Willy to get away from her mother. Dad puts a great store in these two stories, the one that damns Doris, the other that damns his mother. While I think, *of course* she would have wanted to leave – she was the last child left, working, a grown woman – did that make Doris a horrid person? What's more, she was pregnant when she married. Who got her pregnant? My grandfather did.

Once they were married, Bella moved to the Messer apartment in Prenzlauer Berg. It's unlikely that she contributed a dowry, in this era they were on the wane and there probably wasn't much left for her as the youngest daughter of a widow in postwar Germany. She did have a trousseau, however, which she would have started many years earlier. I have remnants of her hand-embroidered table linen, and when we had dinner guests my mother would always get out Bella's silverware, engraved with her maiden initials, 'BR'.

After her marriage, Bella worked in the office of Willy's cap factory, a short walk away at Heinrich-Roller-Strasse. To begin with Willy was still in partnership with his troublemaker brother Arnold (often drunk, late and unreliable) in their late father's cap and hat-manufacturing business.

They both came home for the midday meal, had a sleep, and then Willy would return to work. Bella spent mornings with Willy in the business, though he was often on the road in other towns and cities, taking orders from the retail outlets. The school day ended at 1 p.m. and, while my father, Michael, doesn't have any recollection of this, Ruth does remember going to the park each day with young Michael and their nanny, where they'd meet up with other friends and their nannies. In her autobiography, Ruth recalls that the family employed both a nursemaid and a kitchen maid. Bella supervised the cooking and was a good cook but, according to

Bella and a nurse at the balcony window,
Hufelandstrasse apartment, circa 1926.

Ruth, didn't like cooking. Then Ruth writes, 'We seemed to have a lot of changes with the maids. According to my father, Mutti sacked the nursemaids if we became too fond of them.' While Willy might have said this, I wonder how true it is. There is one nursemaid, Kati, who Bella was clearly friendly with, writing very warmly to her about the children and her travels from a trip abroad in 1932.

A family of two children was typical of Jewish families during this period. There is a five-year age gap between Michael and Ruth, so perhaps Bella and Willy's efforts at contraception had become more effective. Condoms, pessaries and other 'abortifacients' were advertised in all the women's magazines. My father claims, however, that it was *his* conception that was the accident, and that the gap between Ruth and him is evidence of that. His birth being an accident is a key element of his narrative of Bella's abandonment of him. He was the unwanted baby. Yet it was Ruth who was the original unplanned child.

In preparation for marrying Willy in October 1921, Bella had resigned from her post as a district welfare officer. Her employer, the Juvenile Board of the Municipality of Berlin Schöneberg presented her with a certificate, which explains that from 1916 to 1919 she was employed by Pestalozzi-Fröbel Haus, then from 1919 to 1921 she worked for the Juvenile Board. Her first 'sphere of action' was the war relief work.

> Her main functions were the introduction and development of school welfare work in two elementary and secondary schools, supervision of the municipal foster-children and obtaining of adequate trustee education places, supervision of the single wards and the wards of the professional guardian, welfare work for all the other destitute and exposed children, co-operation with and superintendence of the children's welfare institutions of her district ... as well as guidance of pupils and voluntary assistants.

Bella with Berlin children and teens.

She had important and broad responsibilities. The certificate praises her work in detail, and describes her as 'extraordinarily talented for dealing with children ... gaining the great confidence of those families entrusted in her care' and that she is outstanding in her welfare work.

In her autobiography Ruth writes that she vaguely remembers her mother telling her of this work in the 'Berlin slums', and the terrible poverty the families lived in. The overcrowded tenements, called *mietskasernen*, 'would have as many as six courtyards, the poorer you were the further back you lived,' Ruth recalled. 'The living areas had no running water or toilets, these were down a flight of stairs between each storey.'

Over the next decade Willy and Bella built a profitable business together. Profitable enough to move to a larger apartment in Charlottenburg in 1933.

The slap

The move wasn't propitious and it was brief.

In May 1933, the young British writer Christopher Isherwood fled Germany after living in Berlin as a gay man. Isherwood had been in Berlin for four years, during the collapse of the Weimar Republic and the ascendancy of the Third Reich. He recalled the 'self-important' SA men who'd casually block the footpath as they chatted, forcing passers-by to walk in the gutter. In his novel *Goodbye to Berlin*, the narrator observes of one character that, 'Like everyone else in Berlin, she refers continually to the political situation, but only briefly, with a conventional melancholy ... It is quite unreal to her.'

In fact, the situation was tremendously real to many German Jews, who began to leave in their tens of thousands the same year as Christopher Isherwood, if they could. Bella and Willy's friends Elli and Max Priess, with whom they had shared a skiing holiday in the Giant Mountains in Czechoslovakia, emigrated to Palestine in 1933. Willy's cousin Edith and her husband, Kurt, left for Bulgaria, and then the USA. The visa offices were daily full of German Jews. People sat in them for days, hoping for an appointment. Others scoured international phone books, writing to fourth cousins and even people they'd never met, pleading to be sponsored. The Jewish assistance organisations were inundated with inquiries.

Ruth had started at her local school in 1928. But after Hitler became Chancellor, Jewish children were increasingly persecuted in the public schools. The schools were inculcating Nazi ideals and adoration of Adolf Hitler. One school primer began, *My Führer, I know you well and love you dearly, Like father and mother. And when I grow up, I will help you, Like I will father and mother. I want to always be obedient to you.* As a German you belonged not to yourself, nor even to your family, but to the *Volksgemeinschaft*, your racial community, and its father, the Führer.

Ruth now attended a Jewish school in west Berlin, travelling there by bus. She remembers Bella telling her not to get off near Alexanderplatz because of the street fighting. For years, until 1932 when the Nazi party became the largest political organisation, the Weimar Republic had been characterised by political instability, with dozens of parties vying for the votes of the German citizenry. Germans were used to paramilitary groups; following the country's defeat in World War I, the government had established volunteer troops known as Freikorps to maintain its authority. But with the country in post-defeat economic ruin, many Freikorps members shifted to the right, joining the paramilitary groups created by the parties vying for power. The infamous Sturmabteilung (aka SA, Storm Troopers, Brownshirts; later superseded by the SS) was formed by Hitler in 1921. The left-wing Communist Party (KPD) had the Roter Frontkämpferbund (Red Front Fighters' League), then, after it was banned, the Kampfbund gegen den Faschismus (Fighting League against Fascism) and Antifaschistische Aktion (Antifascist Action). With half-a-million members, the far-right Der Stahlhelm, Bund der Frontsoldaten (The Steel Helmet, League of Front-Line Soldiers) was the largest of the paramilitary organisations until it was integrated into Hitler's Sturmabteilung (SA).

The role of these paramilitaries was to protect members at party meetings, to march and rally, and to harass, intimidate and harm opponents. Street clashes frequently led to injuries, sometimes deaths. This was the context of Bella's warning to Ruth not to walk about at the large Alexanderplatz square and train station.

At the Jewish school Ruth was learning Hebrew and meeting children from observant families; very soon she requested that the family become more religiously observant. Thus it was that one Friday evening, when she was on her way to the bakery to get the braided challah bread for the evening's Shabbat meal, she was accosted by a girl shouting, 'Jew, Jew go to Palestine.' Ruth ignored her but decided that if the girl taunted her again on her way back from the bakery, she would slap the girl's face. The girl *was* there again, and again she yelled out. Ruth stepped up to her and slapped her face as hard as she could, saying, 'That's how Jews can hit!'

I was shocked to read Ruth's account, having never slapped a girl's face at age ten, or at any age. But I could also imagine her being that fired up; she'd been physically strong and agile – and righteous and feisty as an activist.

She hadn't understood at the time the context of the girl's taunts, and the grim irony of the girl telling her to go to Palestine. The British, who had controlled Palestine under a mandate from the League of Nations since 1920, had given the delegated Jewish Agency strict and narrow quotas for the numbers of immigration certificates it was allowed to issue. Between 1932 and 1938, just over 34 500 German Jews immigrated to Palestine from a population of half a million.

As a child, Ruth was confident and naïve about how Jews could hit back. She had taken retaliation as her right. This feistiness continued well into her fifties, when she was arrested for leading a march for the Nuclear Disarmament Party in Melbourne in the 1970s. Ruth had been proud to be not just a woman in the cells, but a *migrant* woman in the cells. I remember her at my parents' dinner table, saying that her arrest was one of the highlights of her life, then laughing.

Though Bella had moved Ruth to the Jewish school and warned her to be careful, my grandparents weren't talking to her in detail about antisemitism and the Nazis, perhaps not wanting to frighten her. (Michael, five years younger than Ruth, was too young.) But with so much public violence, it was inevitable that Ruth would sooner or later experience more of what the girl had flung at her.

On Judenboykott, the day a boycott of Jewish businesses was proclaimed (1 April 1933), Bella and Willy, not knowing what was to happen, were underway with the move to the larger apartment in Charlottenburg, west Berlin. Ruth and Michael had been sent to a friend's place for the day. Ruth recalled watching from a window as Brownshirts smashed the windows of Jewish shops up and down the street, defacing the storefronts with racist slurs.

'What my parents kept from me,' she wrote later, 'was that the Brownshirts came to our factory, interrogated Vati's staff, went through his stock and took some of it away.'

Ruth doesn't write about this, but my father did in his History: that it was in 1933 that Bella heard a troop of what she and other Jews called the Braune Pest, the 'brown plague', singing the 'Heckerlied'. The 'Heckerlied' was a revolutionary song of the Baden Revolution in the previous century, which even now has been adopted by contemporary far-right extremists. The line Bella remembered, recorded by my father in his History was, 'When Jewish blood sprays from the knife, things will go well again' ('*Wenn das Judenblut vom Messer spritzt, es wird wieder gut gehen*').

Now, whenever the Nazis staged a rally, the family stayed at home. Ruth remembered seeing their maid pull on her good white gloves before leaving the new apartment to hear Hitler speak. Soon after it was forbidden for 'Aryans' to live and work in Jewish households, and the maid left.

*

In March 1933, the Nazis had used physical intimidation and imprisonment of over a hundred Communist Party and Social Democrat parliamentarians to ensure the men were not present in the Reichstag building to vote against the anti-democratic *Law to Remedy the Distress of the People and the Reich*, commonly known as the *Enabling Act (Ermächtigungsgesetz)*. The kidnapped parliamentarians were detained in camps by the SA and SS. The *Enabling Act* was passed, allowing the new Chancellor, Hitler, to sign legislation into law without obtaining parliamentary consent. The Third Reich was now a legal dictatorship. The Supreme Court didn't challenge the kidnapping and detentions, nor the legislative outcomes. A plethora of laws and administrative changes followed: now the public administration, judiciary, security apparatus and armed forces all acted in accord with the 'Führer principle'; political parties and mass organisations other than those in accord with National Socialists were banned; and freedom of the press was abolished. The persecution of individual opponents including communist and pacifist writers and artists was systematic and brutal.

The *Enabling Act* was followed in April by the *Law for the Restoration of the Professional Civil Service* (commonly known as the *Civil Service Law, Berufsbeamtengesetz*). It limited Jewish employment in the professions and rendered them unemployed. Naturalised Jews, Sinti and Afro-Germans' citizenship was revoked; Willy and his mother and siblings became state subjects. By 1938 the *Civil Service Law* had led to over 40 per cent of established and junior academics in universities losing their jobs: anyone deemed non-Aryan, a member of the Communist Party or individuals affiliated with the opposition parties.

In May 1933 book burnings, led by university students, professors and members of the National Socialists, were witnessed by tens of thousands of Germans across the country. Works of philosophy, art history, history, novels, plays, science, anything at all progressive was burned. Tens of thousands of books were destroyed. The night was the culmination of the months-long 'Action against the Un-German Spirit'.

All these changes affected Willy's wholesale cap business: increasingly, German retailers wouldn't buy from him, and he was barred from accommodation in hotels. There were fewer Jewish regional stores to sell to or stay at, as Jews in the towns and villages were closing shop and fleeing local persecution for the comparative safety of the larger German cities.

It was around this time that the relationships Bella had formed with other women at Pestalozzi-Fröbel Haus became critical once again. As I went deeper into the histories of German education reform, I realised there was a network of women connected through friendship, philosophy, and work, and that Bella had been on the periphery of that network. I was becoming confident that it was her time at Pestalozzi-Fröbel Haus and the various friendships forged there that led her to contact the remarkable Dr Anna Essinger, who had established a German Jewish school in England, in 1933.

After university training in the USA, and with the assistance of some of her family, Anna Essinger had established a boarding school near Ulm, south of Germany, the Landschulheim Herrlingen. Its methods were based in part upon the revolutionary Maria Montessori program.

Anna Essinger had then established a boarding school in Kent, England. Now called New Herrlingen, it was best known as Bunce Court. And this was where Bella sought a safe haven for her children.

The family had to leave the Charlottenburg apartment in 1933 within months of moving in; Willy's business income was plummeting. They shifted further west to Stülpnagelstrasse near the Kaiserdamm boulevard. Ruth and Michael's Jewish school had also moved, and was close enough that the children could walk there. When Ruth and Michael arrived each day, they'd see a new

Bella alone (*left*) and again Bella with Michael (*right*) at Schierke health resort, August 1934.

empty chair, another child gone. Families were leaving overnight, clandestinely and suddenly.

By 1935 Ruth had her own secret to keep: that she and Michael were leaving, going to Anna Essinger's Bunce Court boarding school, the news of which, in her excitement, she'd shared with a schoolfriend. One of her last recollections of her life in Berlin was learning English at high school. The teacher warmly praised her pronunciation of the line, 'Simple Simon met a pieman'. Her friend Lily Soberski then spoke up, telling the class excitedly that Ruth was leaving for England.

The children's war

Here is where Ruth and Michael part ways from their mother and father. Michael was eight and Ruth thirteen when they arrived at Bunce Court in September 1935. Bella had taken them by train, possibly via the Netherlands, to the port of Calais, crossing the Channel by ferry to Dover, then a train first to London and on to a local line to Kent. They had a couple of leather suitcases with their clothes, perhaps some of Michael's favourite toys and a book. And that was the end of their German lives. When Ruth and Michael next returned, more than fifty years had passed.

In London they stopped a day or two. While they both remember Bella taking them to see Charlie Chaplin's anti-fascist film *Modern Times*, they can't have, as it wasn't released until the following year. It's possible they saw it the following March, in 1936, when Bella came to the school to celebrate Michael's ninth birthday or in June that year when she and Willy visited the children together. *Modern Times* had opened in February 1936 in London cinemas. Perhaps during that first time in London, they'd seen Chaplin's older *City Lights*, which along with many other films and filmmakers had been banned by the Nazis. A generation later, Dad would enthusiastically sit my brothers and me down to watch the midday movie when a Chaplin or Laurel and Hardy movie was being screened. The grainy grey film palette that is so quaint and visually perplexing to us today was still exciting to us then.

The original school, Landschulheim Herrlingen, had been based in Germany, but Anna Essinger had realised that it wasn't possible to teach safely or ethically after Hitler became chancellor and brought in discriminatory changes to schooling for Jewish children, along with the requirement that all schools promote a Nazi curriculum. Willy and Bella's friends Lili and Max Rosenberg had sent their children to Landschulheim Herrlingen before the family left for Palestine, and they'd have shared what they knew, including the school's daring escape from Germany to England in 1933.

Anna Essinger had close contacts among the Quakers from her university study in the USA. She was keenly aware that Germany was no longer a place in which children could be educated with freedom and integrity. Many hundreds of teachers and educators were leaving Germany, either because their education practices made them a target of the Nazis, or because they were Jewish, or being Jewish, had been sacked. She searched for alternative countries for the school, and it was through her American and British Quaker contacts that she received the sponsorship needed to establish Bunce Court.

Ruth kept a copy of the school prospectus:

> The school wants to give the children, as far as this is possible today, a happy childhood and youth, enjoy a healthy and beautiful environment under the guidance of German and English men and women who believe in the natural and undisturbed growth, in the developments and demands of individual talents in spiritual, artistic and practical fields. To this effect we wish to let the boys and girls take part in building a world in which there is growth in spiritual life, mutual respect, helpfulness and responsibility for their community, pleasure at a well done job appreciated by

> everyone for its worth. Where there is a busy active life full of interest for everything that makes life worthwhile and where creativeness is valued above all other possessions.

From 1933, twenty 'exile' schools were opened worldwide, most of them aligned with the German progressive educational reform tradition that had shaped Essinger's first school and then Bunce Court: the *Landerziehungsheime*, the 'countryside educational homes'. As with these other schools, Bunce Court embarked upon the immense task of supporting the children who'd been uprooted, separated from their parents, often without preparation, now living in unfamiliar environments and some of them discovering, as the years went on, that they were orphaned. The teachers aimed to protect the children from knowledge of the many atrocities taking place, though news of the war was followed closely and some of the children were in letter-communication with their parents.

To begin with, the school was situated on the outskirts of the small village of Otterden in the Kent Downs. The closest train station was at Charing, six kilometres away. For my shy eight-year-old father, his lasting impression was of being enrolled at the school because he was unloved, that his mother had abandoned him with no hint of what was to come as she left with a bright wave. It's hard to know quite what happened: it's unlikely that there was accommodation for her to stay at the school, as the older children had been tasked with constructing new beds under the supervision of one of the teachers for the steadily growing number of children arriving. She may only have stayed for the day. 'She left,' my dad tells me, 'saying she'd be coming back.' He pauses for emphasis. 'But she didn't come back.' Even now this angers him. At ninety-seven years of age, he tells me that he lost his trust in her with that false goodbye. 'She abandoned me, and she lied to me. She said she'd be back, but she never came.' No matter that eight decades have passed, the hurt is still there.

Michael, Ruth, Bella and Willy all together, Bunce Court, 1936.

It's the truth of his experience that he felt bereft, abandoned and lied to. But which parent can claim they've never said, 'I'll be back soon,' or 'You'll be fine,' about school or vacation care, knowing full well it's not true? Perhaps Bella felt anguish that she was leaving both her children in a safe but foreign country, possibly anticipating his feelings of loss? She'd have known that Michael was the sensitive type, unlike her boisterous older daughter. She returned to visit the children twice the next year, in March when her 'J' (Jew) passport was issued, and again in June 1936 with Willy, her passport showing she had visas for one month maximum for each visit. That she returned on these occasions didn't change his experience of that first leaving.

The older and younger children lived in separate areas at the school, and so while Ruth ran off to meet her friends – she knew girls and boys who'd left Germany and a few were already at Bunce Court – Michael struggled with the sudden absence of his parents and home. Ruth had been excited to be going to Bunce Court and never questioned why her parents weren't keeping the children in Berlin with them. She'd been living through the persecution, and though ignorant of the larger meanings of the Nazis' intentions, she'd seen the violence for herself.

The cottage where the younger children slept and took their classes was situated across a small field from the main school building. This is where Michael lived when he arrived. His cohort would then join the older students for the main midday meal.

There's a photograph of him among a group of about twenty seated children in a garden. He's one of the youngest, and sits among them shyly, not exactly unhappy looking, but uncertain and careful. His shirt is carefully buttoned to the neck. Has he just arrived? Will he always be that neat? Some of the children are smiling happily, others seem lost in their thoughts. It is summer, everyone is dressed lightly. A few girls and boys wear just their cotton bloomers, their chests bare. Michael and Ruth had arrived in early autumn, in September 1935, but the big kids are not in this picture. Ruth isn't there. There are two teachers, youngish women. Both have thick dark hair, and they're smiling happily. I found the photograph in one of Bella's sewing boxes, among dozens of other pictures. When I showed it to him, Michael was surprised to see it, wondering where I got it from. 'From you,' I said, 'in one of Bella's boxes.' He recognised no one in the picture. Barely recognised himself.

Everyone's portrait is so clear in this photograph that I decided then to create a Facebook page in the hope that descendants might come forward and identify the other children and the teachers. In the years since that the page *@buncecourtstudents, Bunce Court*

New Herrlingen School has been in existence, I've learned nothing new about the children, though I've had contact from all sorts of readers from the UK, Israel and the USA. I've translated posts into Hebrew and German, but no one is yet to see the post and recognise their parent or grandparent.

As mentioned earlier, the school's prospectus began, *The school wants to give the children, as far as this is possible today, a happy childhood and youth.* Anna Essinger was cognisant of what was to come, although in 1935 there was no certainty when or even if Germany would go to war, no certain foreknowledge that the life skills the children were practising at the school – building the furniture they needed to use such as beds and desks, growing vegetables, cutting wood for the heating, tending to fruit trees and poultry – would become essential to their day-to-day survival through the rationing of six years of war and the postwar years of hardship that followed.

Soon after Michael arrived, he began to sleep in the cottage known as the 'isolation hut' with Tante Paula, Anna Essinger's sister, who was a trained nurse and had been integral to both the original German school and the new school, Bunce Court. Franziska (Fanny) Essinger, Anna and Paula's mother, also lived in the cottage with Paula and Michael. The cottage had been built in 1934 by the teachers and older children during an outbreak of polio. One of the boys had died. Apparently, my father experienced seizures in his first days or months at the school, so while he'd spend the morning in class or playing with the other children, he would return to the cottage for lunch. This was another of his dinnertime stories that I found sobering as a child – no, far worse than that, frightening – to imagine my father having fits. Did he bite his tongue? Froth at the mouth? I'd only seen this happen in movies. I felt sorry for my dad as a child, and for him as an adult telling us. I felt vaguely guilty, burdened by these sadnesses I didn't understand.

The teachers felt that a less noisy and stimulating environment would benefit him. But away from the children for half of each day and at night after classes, he was very lonely.

I met Tante Paula in 1974 when our family was living in London. We drove down to Bunce Court where she still lived in the same cottage that Dad had lived in with her and her mother, Fanny. Tante Paula was very wrinkled and tiny sitting in her armchair, thrilled to see Michael, smiling and shaking her head in wonder at him and at us.

Over the course of 1936, when Michael and Ruth were settling into their new life at the school, Bella and Willy reported monthly to the local police station to have their papers stamped. Bella's 'Jew' passport contains page after page of these Polizei stamps, dates and official signatures. Her sister Minnie was moving back and forth between England and Germany, and during one of the periods she was in England, sometime in 1936, my father remembers that she visited him and Ruth at Bunce Court. There is a photograph of her in the garden, and Michael has a recollection of her being there. That was to be Minnie's last contact with anyone in the family.

Ultimately, the plan was for the whole family to live in Palestine once the children had finished their schooling; that is, if they could obtain the necessary approvals.

The price of escape

Between 1933 and 1937, Bella's 'Jew' passport shows that she was repeatedly applying for visas to make short trips to England and Palestine. I had been intrigued by these frequent 'holidays' until learning that the point of them was for Bella to both visit the children and to take cash out of Germany. Initially, the Third Reich had a policy of encouraging German Jews to emigrate, though finding a country to go to was challenging. The international refugee convention was many years off. Few countries had refugee policies; not the UK, not America or Australia. The USA's first refugee policy wasn't devised until 1948 (the *Displaced Persons Act*), and in any case, it didn't distinguish between immigrants forced to flee their homelands and others who were migrating for economic or family reasons.

The Reich government was imposing extreme financial obstacles, including the punitive Reich Flight Tax. Originally introduced in 1931 to stem the capital flight of wealthy individuals from the Weimar Republic due to Germany's hyperinflation, the Nazis used the law to confiscate Jewish assets. By 1937, the tax on Willy's earnings from his wholesale business was over 90 per cent. Post-tax funds had to be placed in controlled German accounts, which could be used to buy foreign currency at very unfavourable exchange rates. Bella repeatedly smuggled money out of the country. Ruth recalls Bella's seamstress sewing binding around a brown rug and money being inserted into the binding:

> Fraulein Döbler came to do our mending for many years and was obviously not a Nazi sympathiser to be trusted with this job. Mutti took this rug with her to Czechoslovakia on one of her cure trips. On arrival she sent Vati a telegram saying she, i.e. the rug, had arrived safely. All this was still possible, though illegal, [and] after 1937 or '38 it was very dangerous, [for] by then the Nazi authorities had been alerted to these devices.

In September 1935, the same month that Michael and Ruth safely arrived in England, the *Reich Citizenship Law*, and the *Law for the Protection of German Blood and German Honour* were proclaimed by Hitler at a huge rally in Nuremberg, a city in Bavaria with good rail lines and infrastructure where the party had long had a strong base. The laws essentially stated that Jews and Sinti were 'enemies of the race-based state', and legalised their segregation, persecution and imprisonment. The reintroduction of compulsory military service for racially 'pure' German men was also announced at the rally, communicating to Germans and the world that Germany no longer accepted the terms of the Versailles Treaty, which included German disarmament. The laws facilitated the boycotting of Jewish businesses, which had begun with the Judenboykott in April 1933 that had such an immediate impact on Willy's manufacturing business.

In October 1935, Hitler declared a prohibition on the publication of material by journalists and writers who were not 'Aryan'. Sales of his 1925 manifesto, *Mein Kampf*, reached over 850 000 copies that year.

The legalised political violence first launched in 1933 was terrifying for everyone targeted, especially the Nazis' political opponents, who included vast numbers of communists and social democrats. They and other dissidents were beaten, imprisoned, sometimes murdered. Dachau, and the Osthofen camp in the

Rhineland state of Hesse, were among Germany's first concentration camps. Situated on the outskirts of Munich, Dachau opened in March 1933 with capacity for 5000 prisoners; an incredible number to have planned for. Political opponents, trade unionists, and later, Sinti, homosexual men and other 'asocials' were arrested and sent there. The much smaller Osthofen, built for 2000, usually held just a few hundred at a time: political opponents, non-political Jews, Jehovah's Witnesses, and Seventh Day Adventists were detained there, beaten and tortured.

There were other, less violent, persecutions – the hours during which Jews were allowed to shop for groceries were restricted, and they were only allowed to use designated seating in parks. Discrimination and persecution governed marriages, work, education, food, housing and citizenship. The experience of Nazism was ever present when Jews were out in public. This was their 'social death', as the historian Marion A Kaplan has defined it. Brownshirts and other paramilitaries frequently assaulted Jews on the street.

The requirements for emigration made escape very difficult, even though between 1933 and 1939 Nazi policy ostensibly encouraged Jewish emigration. To do so, Jews had to pass a medical test and pay the flight taxes. But countries worldwide were limiting the number of immigrants they would accept.

*

My father, Ruth, and many others have said to me how prescient Bella was to have taken the children out of the country in 1935 and to immigrate to Palestine in 1937, along with the decision to send the two children to Bunce Court in Kent. Hearing this, I've always been pleased by her exceptionalism. But in fact, despite the obstacles, in the years between 1933 and 1939, more than half of Berlin's Jewish population emigrated. They left for neighbouring countries such as France, Belgium and the Netherlands, from which they were later deported to camps. Eastern Europe was limited in its options for Jews, who had been fleeing pogroms and persecution for decades. Others immigrated to Latin American countries, until these too closed their borders. Some returned to Germany after failing to establish themselves, and would once again apply to leave for another country. America at this time had a quota of just under 26 000 German immigrants per year. But with the requirement for citizenship papers (which many German Jews no longer had, as they were now stateless), and immigrant and transit visas, only 1241 German Jews were admitted in 1933. This left 82 787 German Jews on the waiting list.

Immigration to Palestine continued to be difficult and highly restricted, as it had been from the first days of the Balfour Declaration of 1917, when Britain announced its support for the establishment of a Jewish homeland in Palestine, then part of the Ottoman Empire. The Palestinian and allied Arab-nations' opposition was to changing the power relations between the indigenous populations and the immigrant population, and to the fact that Jews are named in the Declaration as Jews while the Palestinian Arabs (the majority in the land) are referred to as 'non-Jews'. Essentially, they opposed it from fear of losing Palestinian indigeneity and Palestinian primacy in the land, which is indeed what happened. Britain initially enacted policies that ostensibly aimed to ensure that Palestinians continued to be the majority population in Palestine, at least for the time being. Until 1939, all Jews needed to apply to immigrate to Palestine competitively, the criteria including the applicant's ability to be financially independent, or to possess much-needed manufacturing or agricultural skills. Persecution or the threat of persecution was not a criterion. For the Jewish Agency, it was a difficult 'zero-sum game': the immigration quota was constrained by Britain, and for each Jew given entry, others were denied.

The most sought-after destination was the USA, but after

World War I, the USA had restricted immigration, based in part on the belief that new migrants would add to the already many millions of unemployed and become 'public charges', an economic and social burden. This policy was broadly supported by most Jewish leaders in the USA, whose communities were already providing extensive support to their own poor and unemployed during years of worldwide economic hardship. The majority of applications from German Jews in the years 1933 to 1939 remained on waiting lists. From 1933, those visas that were granted were, in the main, to people who were 'non-labourers' and 'exceptional persons'. In the 1930s and 1940s the Emergency Committee in Aid of Displaced Foreign Scholars (EC) was the most significant refugee organisation working to resettle Jewish science and humanities researchers, and it lobbied for many. Among the exceptional persons was Albert Einstein, who arrived in 1933 and lobbied for expanding immigration opportunities and provided affidavits for individual Jews. Thomas Mann, along with his wife, Katya, and their adult children, all vocal opponents of the Nazis, arrived in 1938, having fled Germany for Switzerland, where they'd lived in Zurich for five years. Thomas Mann lobbied the president to expand entry to persecuted Jews. Their efforts were mostly unsuccessful.

*

Many Jews were unable to escape. The murder-suicides of Hitler and other Nazi leaders and their families in the days immediately prior to Germany's defeat are well known, but for years before their deaths, many thousands of Jewish – and non-Jewish – Germans who found their circumstances intolerable under the Third Reich had been 'voluntarily' ending their lives. Suicide during the years of the Weimar Republic and the early years of the Third Reich was assumed by many to be a 'sign of the times'. Everyone knew someone who had died or knew a family who'd lost someone to suicide. A sense of crisis – perceived in various ways as a sign of modernity, or arising from the erosion of religion, or the loss of jobs and the means to make a human-scale living – was pervasive. The constant discourse around crisis, especially in the cities and in Berlin, fuelled a 'widespread sense that everything was in flux and urgently required a transformation' (Moritz Föllmer). So prevalent was it, providing so many gripping human stories – and able to be used in so many divisive debates – that it was routinely discussed in newspapers of all political stripes. Between 1929 and 1932, the German suicide rate rose by 11.9 per cent, undoubtedly symptomatic of mass unemployment and the cuts to welfare.

Since before World War I, the rate of suicide in Austria and Germany had been significantly higher than elsewhere in western Europe (Austria continued to be significantly higher). It was higher among German Jews than German Catholics or Protestants, and men took their lives more often than women. During World War I, suicide in Germany fell to its lowest levels (typical during war), then with defeat it rose among all groups, with twice as many men than women suiciding, especially older men. To put these many individual incidents of grief and trauma into numbers: in 1917–1918 the rate was around twenty male deaths per 100 000 (fewer for women); by 1941 and through to 1943, the rate of suicide among German Jewish women reached a peak of sixty suicides per 100 000. Among the Jewish population (and other groups targeted by the Nazis) incidents of suicide rose with each new proclamation and brutal event: with the Nuremberg laws of 1935; the terror of the *Anschluss*, the annexation of Austria by Germany in March 1938; and the *Kristallnacht* pogroms in November the same year. The Nuremberg proclamations were witnessed by the hundreds of thousands of Germans present, filmed by Leni Riefenstahl, and news of the laws was widely distributed.

Initially, the regime welcomed these *Freitod* 'voluntary' deaths. The Nazis were aware of the impact of the annual Nuremberg rallies, but claimed the deaths were the consequence of individual weakness and Jewish racial degeneracy, not the Nazis' own racial policies.

Many of those who took their lives left notes for their families. They wrote of their desire to choose the time and place of their death, as far as was possible. The Berlin police diligently collected these documents, interviewed families and spouses, filed their reports, archived everything. As the persecution, arrests and deportations steadily increased during the 1930s, people made plans for their ends, often 'paying an exorbitant price' for veronal or other chemicals with which to kill themselves. In Vicki Baum's bestselling 1930 social realist novel *Grand Hotel*, a character asked himself, 'Good Lord, has everyone got a teacup of veronal ready to hand?'

Some suicides were in fact murders: Nazi officials would classify the deaths of political opponents or Jewish civilians as suicide. Self-annihilation and lawless disappearances: the fortunate escaped, emigrated, and surfaced somewhere else with whatever tokens of self, family, profession and speech they could salvage.

Postwar, in Melbourne, Willy never spoke to Ruth or Michael of the deaths of friends and family. The survivor's tactic of silence is another kind of erasure.

A bad time to be in Berlin

Things get worse before they get better, goes the old adage. After settling Michael and Ruth at Bunce Court, Bella returned to Berlin in the winter of 1935–1936 and all the anguish that the Third Reich and the loss of friends and her children must have given her. Many friends had fled Berlin. Her mother was suffering in ways that are only understandable within the limits of what's possible to understand when a person ends their own life, and within the broader story of the epoch's epidemic of suicide. Doris ended her life by suicide in January 1936, soon after Bella returned from England. The death notice published in one of the newspapers stated that the cremation was held in silence, 'in accordance with her wishes'. And silence most certainly followed Doris Riess's death. If my great grandmother left a note, it is long gone.

Perhaps she wanted as little said as possible, to resist the daily spectacularising of suicide. These very personal experiences were fodder for news copy and were daily harnessed to divisive political debates in the newspapers. German conservative nationalists, far-right Nazis, and left-wing communists equally used their newspapers to 'combine sensationalism and agitation by creating and fuelling scandals' around individual suicides and the collective problem (Moritz Föllmer). For instance, Joseph Goebbels' newspaper *Der Angriff* regularly published the names of people who had taken their lives, claiming that their suffering was caused by the daily hardships of the reparation payments demanded by the Allies under the Treaty of Versailles. These vivid and gruesome narratives served Goebbels' anti-Weimar Republic propaganda. The communist newspaper *Die Welt am Abend* also printed stories about suicides on an almost daily basis: accounts of proletarian men and women beaten down by the system, a suffering that would continue until capitalism was defeated.

This was some of the context of Doris's last three years. Aged seventy-eight when she died, Doris understood she'd end up alone and vulnerable to the Nazis. She had ended her life within the context of the persecution of Jews all around her, of suicides all around her, and the exodus of her family and many of her friends. Depression, despair, fearfulness or terror, whichever of these emotions she felt, each was a logical response to her situation. Older Jewish women were the most vulnerable of all. Gender made a difference to what was possible for one's future. Foreign countries did not offer visas to older Jewish women. Many were widows, without independent financial means, surviving on their German pension, which many lost when they became stateless. From 1940 to 1944 more Jewish women committed suicide than did Jewish men. These older women remained through force of circumstance. It was hard for them to go into hiding. Their families had already emigrated, gone into hiding, been sent to prisons or camps, or were too poor to protect them. The elderly needed a foreign sponsor. Many were too frail to travel. Between mid-1941, when the 'Final Solution' deportations began, and 1943, there were over 3000 suicides in Germany, most of them in Berlin, most of them Jews, and in the last two years, most of them older Jewish women.

One by one, each of Doris's children had either left Germany or was making plans to leave. Bella and Willy were well underway with their efforts to sell the business and emigrate. Her grandchildren Michael and Ruth were in Britain. Her son Julius was in the process of applying for a visa to Ecuador or had already left. Her daughter Minnie and husband, Kurt Fuchs, were in Britain; photographs of

Minnie and Kurt show them travelling a great deal, and Minnie had visited Michael and Ruth at Bunce Court sometime in 1936 or 1937. Doris's second eldest child, Lotte (Charlotte), had immigrated to the USA years earlier, but didn't have the funds to sponsor Doris to join her. Doris's first-born, Hedwig, was already a widow, and her daughter, Susanne, was married and living in the USA but was not able to sponsor Hedwig.

The historian Christian Goeschel analysed the vast archive of suicide letters collected by the Berlin police, an archive that survived the bombing of Berlin in the last months of World War II. Goeschel argues that suicide was very often the only way out of a desperate situation. It allowed Jewish men and women to retain their dignity and assert some agency in the face of the looming Nazi threats and ever-present violence. When I think about Doris now, it's not just as the depressed woman whom my father told me about all those years ago in the living room when I was in my twenties, but as a woman who asserted herself and decided to end her life on the day of her choosing.

Later, with the end of the Third Reich and the war came the persistent trickle of postwar suicides by Jewish survivors and diaspora. Some suicides, such as Bella's, which came four years after the end of the war, had other causes, as she'd written in her letter to Ruth: a sense of hopelessness in an unhappy marriage and a new country to which she felt she had nothing to contribute. But I do not believe that Bella's death can be completely disconnected from Germany's history of suicide during the Weimar and Nazi epochs. The long tail of her exile from Germany, of the family and friends she'd lost, and the horror of the Holocaust had harmed her.

My father knew nothing of this. When I shared what I had learned about the epidemic of suicides and the reasons for them, he was shocked. Like me, he had to recalibrate everything he'd assumed about Doris. All he knew about his grandmother, other than some key birth and marriage dates, was the little that Bella and

Willy had told him in Melbourne. He says that one evening when they were doing the washing up together, Bella told him that she'd not liked her mother, and the only reason she'd married Willy was to get away from her. This isn't quite true though, because she was already two months pregnant with Ruth when they married – but she didn't tell Michael that.

And so, with Doris's death in January, and three years into Hitler's dictatorship, 1936 began badly for the family. It then worsened: in February, Willy's cousin Felix Messer was murdered. He was grabbed on the street by the Berlin police, accused of the crime of *Rassenschande*, 'race disgrace', for being in a relationship with a non-Jewish woman. He was taken to Plötzensee prison in Charlottenburg. A few days later his brother Walter was informed that Felix had been 'found hanging' in the prison cell, and to come collect the body. That same year, Bella's brother, Julius, divorced his German second wife, possibly to save them both from persecution.

Then in August, Bella's visa for Palestine (and most likely Willy's too) was cancelled. She resubmitted her application. They were fronting up each month to the local police station to have their documents stamped. Willy persisted in trying to find a buyer for his business, a process that the regime called 'voluntary Aryanization'. The equipment, the stock, the retail outlets he'd been selling to, his inventory, the goodwill built up over two decades; he wasn't able to find a buyer who would pay a decent price. The Reich was squeezing German Jews of their rights, freedoms, economic independence, their professions, their businesses, killing off the opposition, driving the brightest and most creative talents away. His business was officially liquidated along with thousands more in 1939, two years after he and Bella had left the country. This stage was called 'forced Aryanization': the state took over any property not already stolen and redistributed it to Germans.

In March 1941 the *Hamburger Fremdenblatt* newspaper reported the first mass auctions of possessions of deported Jews.

The port city became the clearing house for the possessions of Jews from across Europe. After individual Jewish citizens were deported, their apartments were opened, and private auctions held. Jews had good reason to fear that deportation would lead to death; Hitler had repeatedly articulated his desire to be rid of the 'race-tuberculosis of the peoples'. Newspaper articles discussed the progress of deportations and deaths and labour issues in the camps, as did published government reports. Germans and German Jews were becoming aware of the deaths of Jews, communists, Sinti and other 'undesirables'. By 1942 it was well understood among German Jews that what the regime described as 'evacuations to work in the East', 'resettlement' and, for older Jews, 'perpetual care' in 'the East' in exchange for their property, were in fact deportations to concentration camps, enslavement in labour camps, and likely death.

Willy's cousin Edith had left Germany in 1933 with her husband, Kurt Friedlaender, and their young son, Klaus, going first to Bulgaria, where they established a business. When Germany annexed Bulgaria in 1941, the family took the last ship out to the USA, from Odessa to Osaka, San Francisco and finally New York, a journey of two months. Their entry had been sponsored by Kurt's great-aunt Elsa Friedlaender. Willy received a letter from New York sometime in the early 1940s when the deportations and murders of Jews and the regime's political opponents were escalating. It was from his cousin Edith, using the lightweight airmail paper that was such a precious commodity then, typing right to the edges of each page. Then, in a fine cursive, she penned a last-minute note into the slip of space still available in the margin of one of the pages. She handwrote the names of people in their family who had died in the camps, writing 'these are feared gone'.

In an email to me, Edith's daughter Pamela commented that, 'my mother's inability to get Oma Rosa [Edith's mother] to America was very painful and I think it haunted her to her dying day'. Pamela's words remind me of my own question: how much Bella and Willy were haunted by having to leave behind sisters, cousins and Willy's mother.

In the US Edith and Kurt Friedlaender not only changed their surname, Friedlaender, to Frazer, but Kurt became Ken, and Klaus became Claude. 'Edith' was Anglo enough to stay as it was. It was by these names that I met them in Newark in 1993 when I travelled to see them from Baltimore, where I was studying for an MFA at Johns Hopkins University. Edith and Ken must have been in their eighties by then, both gracious, welcoming and happy to see me there with my father, Edith's cousin, and my mother.

In early 1939, Minnie, who'd now been widowed for two years and was soon to turn fifty, returned to Germany from England to collect some belongings. She transported small pieces of furniture, mementos, books, clothes, as much as she could, to Britain. Maybe she said goodbye to Hedwig, her older sister and the only immediate member of her family left in Germany. In May 1940 Minnie was interred at the Rushen women's camp on the Isle of Man, a civilian internment camp to detain 'enemy aliens' such as Germans and German Jews, who were considered a potential security risk to the UK. Meanwhile, Bella was in Tel Aviv and young Michael at Bunce Court, and Willy and Ruth were moving between a series of Melbourne boarding houses.

It's as if I've dropped a porcelain cup onto the floor and here I stand, looking at how far the pieces have scattered. I think of the sorrow felt by the American Jewish writer and academic Daniel Mendelsohn when he writes in his book *The Lost: A search for six of six million* about his mother saying something to him 'urgently, something important, although it would be another forty years before I was finally reminded of what it was; a complex emotional yearning and fear and shame ...' His American Jewish family had lost all trace of six of their Polish family in the Holocaust. The purpose of the book was to find and tell the story of those lost six.

Our family diasporas are like multiple spills on a fabric: the fallen glass, the leaking jug, the scalding coffee, each stain spreading its own way, widening across the folds and wrinkles, until each of them at last exhausts itself, and comes to a stop.

Rubble women

In Berlin in 2014, I'd often take a book or my laptop downstairs to a café and work there for an hour or so. I'd never stay at a table if the place got busy, would re-order drinks as often as I could, practising my limited German language skills with the patient staff. A waiter I got to know a little asked me about my father's childhood here in the street. What was Jewish life like back then? I couldn't tell her much; my father had very few memories, I said. She was a local, an East Berliner, a child born in the GDR. I asked her about living in the divided city, and what she remembered of 1989 when the Wall came down. She'd been in primary school then, and what she recalled most was how excited her parents were that at last they could take a holiday outside the GDR. At the border, leaving for Czechoslovakia, they were apprehensive, concerned that they'd be harassed or arrested by the GDR border guards. Older East Berliners talked of the anxieties they'd had in those first hours and days after the *Mauer* came down, worried about the possibility of a new war, more privations, or Stasi repercussions.

Our family friends Suzanne and Micha Kossack lived just a couple of streets from us and their presence was one of the reasons I'd chosen to live in Prenzlauer Berg. Messers and Kossacks had a decades-long friendship.

With the celebrations for the twenty-fifth anniversary of the fall of the Wall and then unification so present that year, I asked Suzanne what it had been like, seeing the *Mauer* come down. The fortifications had divided the city of Berlin since 1961, and extended a further 120 kilometres around West Berlin, separating it from the rest of East Germany. Would-be escapees had been deterred by watchtowers, shoot-to-kill orders and anti-personnel mines.

Had Suzanne and Micha gone out onto the streets and watched the Wall being knocked down for themselves?

'No! We stayed indoors, watching the television news.'

'Were you excited?' I asked.

She shook her head. 'Not at all, we were worried. We didn't know what might follow. A revolution, a crackdown, maybe emergency curfews? We were anticipating the worst as the Wall was demolished. We were too afraid to be happy.'

One day when Suzanne and Micha took Louis and me sightseeing, we drove along Karl-Marx-Alle. Its GDR name had been Stalinallee. Suzanne pointed out the grand 'wedding cake' style buildings and told us she'd cleaned the bricks that had built those buildings. As we passed the imposing apartment buildings that lined this section of Karl-Marx-Allee, Suzanne told us that her mother had volunteered to chip mortar from the bricks of bombed buildings, which during the war the *Trümmerfrauen* – 'rubble women' – had piled up before them. She'd take Suzi, who was around seven, with her, and she'd chip away too. Along with other East Berliners, they cleaned the bricks from bombed buildings to build grand multi-storey apartment blocks on this most socialist of boulevards.

From my back seat in the car, I leaned forward and asked, 'Was your mother allocated an apartment after working on the bricks for all that time?' As soon as I spoke, I thought how foolish I was to ask: East Berliners such as Suzanne were probably sick of hearing West Berliners and foreigners like me pointing out the injustices of GDR socialism.

She shrugged my question off. 'The first apartments were given to the Trümmerfrauen and best workers. Later on, the VIPs.'

One evening I was lucky enough to spend time inside one of these Karl-Marx-Allee apartments. I was visiting a playwright and radio drama producer, Jean-Claude Kuner, whom I'd been put in touch with by Jane Ulman, who'd directed my two radio dramas. The foyer of his tall building was grand, beautifully tiled in granite and marble, the large lifts fitted with ornate gleaming metal. Inside his ninth-floor apartment the ceilings soared. Except for the tiny kitchen, the rooms were luxuriously large, far larger than Suzanne and Micha's apartment. In one room there was a grand piano and divans strewn with cloths from Morocco and Türkiye. From the tall windows I could see for miles over the flat city. I'd brought bottles of good wine from the boutique wine store around the corner from Hufelandstrasse. We talked about books, radio, art, history, and then I pedalled away around midnight, safety lights blinking blearily, weaving and wobbling along the empty footpaths feeling like a true Berliner, drunk on a bike. I felt that I was reclaiming something of the joy of the city my grandparents had known, the city many thousands of Jews had once known as their Berlin.

Finding Goethe

The first thing of Bella's that I ever touched, the first tangible connection to something she herself had handled, came to me after Erica, my grandfather's second wife, died in 1994. We had gathered at Erica and Willy's townhouse in Brighton, Melbourne, and were making a huge mess of the place; we being my parents, my brothers and our spouses, and Ruth. Nine of us in the small townhouse, tripping over each other, hurrying to sort what to keep, and who should have it, what needed to be sent to Erica's sister and nieces in Tasmania, what was rubbish or should be donated. Our methods were chaotic: open, move, untie, exclaim, put to one side. Erica had remained in the townhouse for many years after Willy's passing. At some point she'd started to use the second bedroom to store tins and packets of food of the kind that you serve to guests, a guest such as myself, her step-granddaughter Jane, when I came for a visit. She'd serve me an aperitif with crackers, fish paste, oily tinned oysters, pickled gherkins and baby onions. Two or three hard-boiled eggs topped with Black Sea caviar. Toothpicks. I loved this food, it was familiar and homely, just like she was herself.

We were short on time. The Brighton townhouse in its retiree cul-de-sac was to be sold, and all of us except Ruth needed to fly home to Sydney and return to work. We found a diamond ring in one of Erica's coat pockets, even though Erica had not worn rings for twenty years. Her bank book surfaced from the back of a drawer, showing a healthy balance of $150 000. Who'd have known? My grandfather evidently had no nostalgia for the European furnishings of his past – there were 1950s Douglas Snelling chairs and footstools with their distinctive webbing, a teak dining table and side tables. Snelling's designs were a radical shift from the heavier, more ornate prewar styles. There were also Max Liebermann drawings Willy had brought from Berlin, where Liebermann had been a famous painter and printmaker. Max Liebermann had died of old age, but his wife, Martha Liebermann, took her own life the day before her scheduled deportation to Theresienstadt Ghetto. By 1943, Jews had been banned for two years from leaving Germany, other than on a transport train to a concentration camp. Germans of standing, including Walter Feilchenfeldt, an esteemed art dealer, the art collector Oskar Reinhart, and even Prince Eugen of Sweden, had attempted to get an exit visa approved for Martha, but their efforts had been rejected. Like many others living through Nazism, she chose to end her life in her home, alone.

In the good-crockery cupboard, we found white Meissen dinner sets, and the silverware from Bella's trousseau, each piece initialled 'BR'. And somewhere the 'Jew' passport issued to her by the Third Reich surfaced. Had she kept it as evidence? *This is what they did to us.* There were photograph albums and sewing boxes filled with loose photographs. Where did Bella's wedding ring go? As I write this today, it's only just occurred to me that I have no idea.

Willy and Erica had travelled a great deal across Australia and in Europe during the twenty-three years of their marriage (though Willy had never returned to Germany). Erica travelled with friends for a few more years after she was widowed. There were many hundreds of postcards from European art galleries along with flight and berth tickets, travel agents' printed itineraries, menus from restaurants, ships, trains and planes, city and country maps; gallery, theatre and film programs, vintage Qantas and Ansett accessories. Everything was more-or-less sorted if you knew what was in the box, but a lot less sorted once we'd picked through it all.

There was vintage Bakelite kitchenware, and packets of expensive never-used single-bed sheet sets in white; single because Willy and Erica had slept in twin beds. I found an olive-green suitcase that we had used when my parents and I and my baby brothers sailed to America in 1964, with its P&O *Oriana* stickers still in place. Erica and Willy had been very interested in Aboriginal and Torres Strait Islander culture and especially art. We found photographs and tapes they'd made on their trips; super-8 home movies, one of an Arnhem Land ceremony sometime in the mid-1960s.

Erica possessed a keen intellect and a gentle nature. She and Willy had married five years after Bella's death, in 1954, just three years before my parents met and married. Willy must have heard about Erica before they were properly introduced by their Jewish matchmaker, for in 1948 Erica Wolff had been the first person in Australia – not only the first woman, but the first person – to be awarded a PhD by an Australian university: Melbourne University. It is a little-known fact that Australia's first PhD was written by a Jewish migrant (though she didn't identify as Jewish), and from an Arts discipline. Her thesis topic was the French-Australian writer Paul Wenz. Her achievement was well covered in the newspapers. Then, all knowledge of it disappeared.

During one of my examinations of Bella's address book, when I was attempting to decipher the entries of former Tel Aviv, Haifa and Jerusalem friends with the idea I'd try to contact their grandchildren, I noticed that Erica was there, under 'W' for Wolff, at her parents' address in Taroona, just south of Hobart, Tasmania. Yet Erica had not met Willy until they were introduced by the matchmaker in 1954. It is a doubly strange entry, for there are so few Australian people recorded in the address book. For a person who'd had so many friends, Bella seemed friendless in Melbourne.

Among all this stuff in the townhouse, was Bella's thirteen-volume set of the works of the revered German Enlightenment writer Johann Wolfgang von Goethe. The title of each volume was embossed in gold on the spine. I was seeing Bella's handwriting for the first time, penned in a spider-fine ink on the flyleaf: *Bella Riess*, and holding the books she had held in my hands. She had been a reader. I hadn't known that. There is no doubt that such artefacts have power; they touch you – literally and emotionally. I was drawn to her, with the weight of the volumes in my hands.

They had been packed away in the second bedroom. There we also found a three-volume set of Goethe and his friend Friedrich von Schiller's letters, boxed in red cloth, the box small enough to hold in one hand. And *Briefe Von Goethes Mutter*, a 1908 edition of Goethe and his mother Anna Maria's correspondence. Much later I realised that Bella had carried these books with her from Berlin to Tel Aviv and then on to Melbourne. They had taken up precious space in her luggage. This was one of the first new things I learned about her.

On the day, I was given the Goethe and Schiller because I was the writer and no one else wanted to carry them home.

The worst of mothers

My father was in his mid-eighties when he said, 'I have to tell you something more.' I was always ready to hear more. I was eager to hear more! I'd not yet gone to Berlin, though twenty years had passed since I'd first been given Bella's collection of Goethe's books in 1994, and thirty years since he'd told me about Bella's suicide. Perhaps five years had passed since he'd first told me about Bella's affair with another man, although we still didn't know much about him, such as where he'd lived, or what his profession had been. Perhaps my father felt compelled to speak on this particular day, before I took off with Louis to Berlin.

We were sitting at my parents' oak dining table, which had been the site of so many conversations. Dad still looked youthful, like he was in his healthy seventies. He had a particular posture I was alert to, that all at once combined fear, an awareness of the irony of the moment, with a chin-up bravura and the wish to be listened to. Followed by the pause.

'My mother was a nymphomaniac,' he said with a look that was worried if also amused.

This was not what I'd expected at all. 'A nymphomaniac? What is a nymphomaniac even?' I exclaimed. The whole notion of nymphomania was so very Victorian-era, but had persisted for decades longer to the mid-20th century. A term that was shaming, that invited disgust and condemnation. Hearing it as her granddaughter, it was especially creepy.

'They don't even exist, Dad.'

With a quizzical tilt of his head, he laughed. Perhaps he was relieved. Who wouldn't be?

'William told me after she died,' he said.

My father quite often used his father's anglicised name, William, rather than the German 'Willy'. He'd been 'Willi or Willy' on his birth certificate, until his parents changed it to Wilhelm, like the Kaiser; but then the Kaiser became unpopular after the defeat of World War I and his abdication. My grandfather was 'Willy' on his immigration application to Australia, but I usually called him Grandfather William (seeing as 'willy' in English is slang for a boy's penis).

I can be a bit abrupt at times. 'So, all you're saying really, is that she fell in love with another man. That's all. That's normal, that's what happens in marriages! People have been doing that forever.' But of course, women's erotic and romantic desire outside of marriage has most often been represented as self-harming, delusional, pathetic, suicidal even; and certainly not normal.

Like hysterics, nymphomaniacs are only ever women. My father and I were so very far apart at this point; he came from another world in which men used ugly language for women. But language can also be a bridge, so here we were, trying to understand each other.

'Your father must have been very angry to be talking to you about her like that,' I said, a little nervously because I'd almost never heard a word of criticism from my father about Willy.

He nodded slightly, considering this new possibility.

'People have affairs, Dad. That doesn't make you a sex maniac.'

The terrible secret that was even more unspeakable than suicide had been said aloud. A new way for him to think about her opened. I had said that nymphomaniacs don't exist, and he seemed to believe me. What he'd believed about her had shaped his feelings about Bella for *decades*. What my father believed was knotted in thick with the many questions he didn't have answers to. Such as, why didn't she come to get him from England in 1938 or 1939 and take him to Palestine with her? Dad had said to me a few times that it was because she'd been too busy having affairs. Only now did I see that this narrative had begun with his father.

When Willy told Dad that Bella was a nymphomaniac, the term still carried pseudo-medical meanings. Even for those who'd lived through the experimentations of the Weimar period, in twentieth-century Europe women could be 'diagnosed' with nymphomania for any slight against the patriarchy: for being adulterous, flirtatious, divorced, for feeling more eager for sex than their husbands.

Willy was very conservative about sexual matters, according to my father. Although he also rather liked or needed sex; this was gleaned from his second wife, Erica, who had asked both Ruth and my mother how often was 'normal'. *Willusch*, she'd said, wanted it very often. Was she simply curious, wanting to know what 'normal' was? Or was it a problem for her of it being too often? That Erica had asked her daughter-in-law about this revealed how close my mother and Erica must have been. They spoke on the phone and wrote each other letters; wherever we were living, in Australia or overseas, there were frequent letters between my mother and Willy and Erica. I can remember my mother sitting at the kitchen table writing in her looping longhand on the pale blue aerograms.

*

With Dad telling me that my own grandmother was a nymphomaniac, I was now even more interested in the man she'd had the relationship with. Who was he? And the others, if they were there to be found. Had Bella had a few lovers, or many, or just one? The only name my father came up with was that of Walter Strauss – a name that, even after all these decades, he had no difficulty recalling. One of Willy's best friends, my father said, though much later he told me he had no idea if that was true. From the moment he said the man's name, 'Walter Strauss', I never forgot it.

We didn't know what Strauss looked like, or who he'd been. Dad said he'd had a mentally ill wife; but then men often describe wives they've fallen out of love with as crazy. Dad also said that Bella and Walter had immigrated to Palestine together. This seemed quite incredible, that she would have travelled to Palestine with Strauss and not my grandfather. I looked online for him but only found a brief Wikipedia entry about an American mathematician born in 1937. Not him. I needed help with German and Hebrew language searches but was yet to get it. In the meantime, I searched for him in Bella's photograph albums and boxes. Dad said Walter was his father's best friend. Was he one of the men skiing with Willy, at a fancy-dress party, at those dinners? I examined all of Willy's male friends. I searched for him in her address book and found nothing.

Adulterous women's stories all end badly. After Dad told me about Bella having this hypersexuality disorder, to use a non-gendered contemporary term, I turned to European histories of sexuality and women, and picked through novels that Bella might have been reading, or might have heard about from friends, or read about in the papers. After all, it is through fiction that a culture speaks of its discordant fears and desires, and can explore the private thoughts and actions of individuals within and against their class or gender. I found novels of the day in which women showed individual agency, such as Effi in *Effi Briest*, by the popular writer Theodore Fontane, whose novels had sold in the millions; Anna in *Anna Karenina* by Leo Tolstoy, Emma in *Madame Bovary* by Gustave Flaubert, and Emile Zola's novels *Nana* and *Thérèse Raquin*. Is there something about an eponymous novel with a woman's name that dooms her to suffer from romantic delusions and a great capacity for self-destruction during and after the adulterous affairs? The century was fascinated by adulterous women.

These women's transgressions had begun within marriages that lacked intimacy, friendship and mutual respect. There were reasons why these fictional but very realistic women were susceptible to extramarital desires. They were in the main middle-class and were required to keep themselves interested in life somehow, to raise their children, to manage themselves within the constraints of what was expected of women of their class. Without other means to broaden their sense of life-satisfaction, each of them finds relief, pleasure and despair in relationships with men outside of their marriage.

Translations

Many years passed after learning that my grandmother had ended her life, before Dad showed me his translation of Bella's suicide letter, written to Ruth. He showed it to me sometime after my step-grandmother, Erica, had died in 1994, but fortunately before Ruth's death in 2001. If I'd not read it, I'd not have understood my dying aunt's plea to me, to take action, to perhaps absolve her of some guilt. There'd not been a letter from Bella for him, only for Ruth. Bella's goodbye letter to Ruth mattered a lot to my father; she had received a goodbye, and he had not. Ruth had given him Bella's letter to her, or a copy of it. All I have is my father's translation of it and my scan of the original letter. Maybe the original letter from Bella to Ruth was scooped up with bills, statements, torn-open envelopes, discarded printouts of emails and dropped into the blue-lid recycling bin. His study is quite messy. I sometimes think I can remember holding the letter in my hands many years ago: a few pages written with the blue ink of a fountain pen on a letter pad, the kind of lightweight paper no one uses any more. But where is it now?

Elsewhere, Ruth had written that Bella died on 15 December 1949; but that date is wrong. It was 23 December. Why did Ruth make this error? It wasn't like her to be wrong like that. Her own autobiography is very exact and, I've always assumed, correct about dates.

While the original letter is lost, I recently found my scan of Bella's letter, made many years ago. Her cursive fills three pages. My scan begins with an image of the Australia Post airmail envelope Ruth placed the letter in. She had gathered the original letter together with a few others into this new envelope, writing on the front:

> Mutti's letters
> 2 written when I was pregnant
> The other the day she committed suicide 15/12/1949.

Were these the only letters Ruth treasured? There were many written between Bella and Ruth over the years of separation, but they're long gone.

Around the 15 December Ruth was leaving Melbourne with her son Leigh and second husband Clem for their summer holiday. The original envelope, if there was one, is no more. Bella wrote to Ruth on the elegantly lightweight paper used then to reduce the cost of international postage. It had been folded into sixths; the fold marks are visible in the scan. The letter begins with her usual greeting to Ruth, whose pet name used by Willy and Bella was 'Hasi':

> My beloved Hare ['*Meine geliebte Hasi*'],
>
> You have just gone away and in retrospect you will understand why I have been behaving somewhat strangely. I did not want you to come, out of cowardice and worry that I would lose my resolve. After all these awful months of tension, sadness and despair this was justified and the strain on my nerves has been a bit much for me. The decision for this step was made a long time ago. You will now understand – though you must have been surprised and hurt – that I did not immediately offer to look after Leigh. Now you know why.

The letter explicitly said that Ruth was not to blame herself, that she had in no way contributed to Bella's decision. Each of the siblings carried their own guilt about Bella's death, and Ruth's was that she'd been close to her mother, so why hadn't she paid more attention? Shown her more care? Given her more of her time? She'd said as much to me when she was dying, but had never shared these feelings with Michael. My father carefully translated Bella's short letter to Ruth from her German into his English, so he could share it with others – with my mother, and then, much later, with me. Perhaps my brothers, too; I don't know. It was a sad and hurtful task for Dad.

Bella wrote that she had chosen to end her life now that her debt to Willy for the passage to Australia had been paid off through her housework and cooking. She had calculated her worth in shillings and pence per day. She set down the number of days and the daily rate. She said that there was no life for her here in Melbourne, as Willy would not socialise with her, was stingy with money as always and as Ruth knew him to be. She was stuck in the flat, and there was, as Ruth knew, no love between herself and Willy any longer. She could see that Ruth had made a full and happy life for herself. She reassured her that there was nothing Ruth could have done to make a difference. She listed some of her possessions, and who they were to be given to.

If she regretted coming to Melbourne, she didn't say. There was nothing about her son, Michael. I think this is what hurt Dad the most. It was a wound that never healed, that there was no mention of him in the letter to Ruth, and no letter for him.

But what if Bella had left a letter for her son that Willy had destroyed or hidden? What if he read it, and didn't like it, or simply disposed of the unopened envelope? It is certainly possible that Bella wrote a letter to my father; this was my persistent wish. When she was still in Palestine, and Michael was a boy living at Bunce Court school in England, she wrote a strongly worded letter to Ruth from Tel Aviv, to say she was shocked and disappointed that Ruth had not been writing to her brother 'Micha', and hadn't sent him a birthday gift though she easily could have, even a small and inexpensive one, and that she expected Ruth to be less self-centred. I told him about this letter after I read it – it is among the documents Ruth's granddaughter Lisa has. He was surprised that Bella had castigated Ruth on his behalf. He almost didn't believe me.

Surely then, Bella wrote something to my father? Of course, this was me being hopeful. I'm the one who wants to redress my father's grievances about her.

In *A Tale of Love and Darkness*, Amos Oz writes about his mother's suicide, and how it affected him:

> All mothers love their children: that's the law of nature. Even a cat or a goat. Even mothers of criminals or murderers. Even mothers of Nazis ... The fact that only I couldn't be loved, that mother had run away from me, only proved that there was nothing in me to love, that I didn't deserve love.

Oz's words resonated for me; they seemed to express my father's experience exactly.

Meeting his mother again in Melbourne after twelve years apart, there was the feeling of abandonment, and then her death, with no note, leaving him feeling he was to blame, in part or wholly – all of this makes for a heavy heart. Thank goodness for my mother, Judy, who loved him tenderly, thoughtfully, only once driving off and leaving him – leaving us all – at a campsite on the coast for a day and a night! If Dad was worried, he didn't show it.

When they first met, she'd shown him what a cuddle was, as if he'd never been cuddled before. Told him to kiss her goodbye when he left for work, a gentle sign of affection he had never thought to offer. She'd tell my brothers and me stories about Dad's quixotic ignorance of signs of love and affection as a young man, pulling Dad into a hug as she spoke, and he'd laugh a little sheepishly.

Berlin Porn Film Festival

In Berlin, an academic I knew was chairing a panel at the annual Berlin Porn Film Festival (Pornfilmfestival Berlin). This was a feminist, LGBTQI alliance of filmmakers, with speakers who questioned normative definitions of gender and sexuality, critiqued the porn industry and challenged sex slavery. The venues were various; the one I attended was in one of Humboldt University's statuesque auditoriums. I reached the room after walking up two-metre wide marble staircases busy with film-goers, then stepped through tall carved doors and found a seat among 500 tattooed, punk, vegan, pink- and blue-haired, denimed, and sometimes earnest young Berliners and others from all over Germany – maybe from all over Europe.

Berlin, then the 'it' city in Europe for transgressive culture, was also a city famous for its prewar history as a home to queer and fringe cultures, and for its progressive research into sex and sexuality. I was intrigued to read somewhere that Walter Benjamin had rented a room for a few months in Charlottenburg at the Institute for Sex Research (Institut für Sexualwissenschaft), founded by physician, sexologist and LGBT advocate Magnus Hirschfeld. Benjamin hadn't been the only writer there. Other artists had lived in the repurposed mansion, in rooms let out by the Institute at affordable rents, including Christopher Isherwood, Anita Berber, Francis Turville-Petre, and Ernst Bloch.

In 1897 Hirschfeld had founded the world's first LGBT rights organisation, the Scientific-Humanitarian Committee

(Wissenschaftlich-humanitäres Komitee), which was based at the Institute. The Institute undertook the first gender-affirming sex-reassignment surgeries. It provided public health services such as marriage counselling, gynaecology and contraceptive advice, and alcoholism treatments, and undertook sociological and medical research. Who knows, perhaps Bella or her friends or family used its clinics. The Institute's records were destroyed by the Nazis.

Scientists, researchers and policymakers from Europe and America were frequent visitors, and Hirschfeld toured and spoke internationally. In 1931, he toured multiple countries, including Palestine, where he attracted hundreds to lecture halls in Tel Aviv, Haifa, and the kibbutz Beit Alfa. Learning that he'd spoken at a kibbutz intrigued me. Why had he made a special trip to this kibbutz? I discovered it had been established in 1922 by mostly young Galician and Polish Labour Zionists (left-wing, socialist, secular), members of Hashomer Hatzair, which later (unsuccessfully) advocated a binational solution, and equality between Palestinians and Jews.

Back in Berlin in the late 1920s, one of the members of the Institute for Sex Research was the Dutch physician Theodoor Hendrik van de Velde. Van de Velde was filling halls and theatres throughout Germany and Europe, and with his focus on sex and marriage, Bella and her sister Minnie may well have attended one of his lectures. They were both married by the time van de Velde's 1926 book, *Ideal Marriage: Its physiology and technique* was selling in the millions, just one of many marriage manuals published amid an explosion of advocacy for marriage, sexual health and contraception reform. He was keen for women and their husbands to take an interest in women's sexuality. His description of foreplay techniques a good husband should employ with his wife was over ten pages long. Van de Velde was convinced that men needed to make more of an effort to satisfy their wives sexually. Even if a man wasn't, in van de Velde's words, an 'erotic genius', he should at least have some 'explicit knowledge'.

Van de Velde wasn't advocating sexual pleasure as an end in itself, but to support heteronormative marriage, and thus a flourishing society. For a principally Protestant country (with Catholics the next largest grouping), his recommendations would have been shocking if also intriguing for many Germans. But for observant Jews, perhaps less so. The new emphasis on a woman's sexual pleasure was congruent with traditional Jewish teachings on marriage, riven though they were with restrictions and procreative purpose. The twelfth-century *Iggeret Hakodesh* (The Holy Epistle) subtitled *Sefer Chibbur Adam ve Ishto* (The Book of Joining of Man and His Wife) described sex in which only the man takes pleasure as animalistic. Reciprocity of pleasure was required for sex in marriage to be an expression of humanity and holiness.

The dissemination of modern 'sexology' came to an end with the collapse of the Weimar Republic. From 1933, the new Nazi government targeted the medical profession. In April that year, non-Aryan doctors and any suspected of affiliation with opponents of the National Socialist German Workers' Party were dismissed from municipal and communal health institutes and were made ineligible for health insurance, thus removing their major source of income. Germany's public health system was decimated, losing half its personnel.

*

Following the Berlin Porn Film Festival and my day-long immersion in discussions of queer and feminist sexualities, diverse bodies, and a great deal of erotic filmed nudity and sex, I didn't want to think about whether my grandfather was an 'erotic genius' or merely functionally literate in bed. I'd been dunked in contemporary 'deviance' and the immersion had certainly made me aware of my own inhibitions and false certainties.

In the absence of facts about her private life, I sensed that I

Bella with dapper army captain at Teplice, 1932.

had a bias towards a Bella who tried to embrace fidelity; that is, in love with her husband, and then in love with Walter Strauss and no one else. I realised that deep down, despite my feminism, I wanted my grandmother to be a Good Woman and Mother. Every guilty lust I'd felt was amplified, it seemed, by her possible past. Yet I also wanted her to have been a part of the Weimar Republic's exploration of new ideas, sexuality, its revolutions in education, welfare, philosophy, and so on. In fact, Bella may have had an affair with Walter Strauss and with other men as well. So be it. That's what men and women have done for eons.

I thought back to my teenage years and how my mother had driven me to the Family Planning clinic in Lane Cove when I was fourteen and was spending inordinate amounts of time with my boyfriend. Very worried about pregnancy, she wanted me to go on the contraceptive Pill. She was sensible and brave to make the appointment, but at the time I didn't appreciate that. I was daunted and felt sick with worry that someone from school might see me and that I'd be talked about and slut-shamed – not that we had that phrase to hand then. The movement to reclaim shaming words about women was a few years off.

At some point a couple of years later, perhaps when I was seventeen or so, Mum was angry with me. I'd probably been rude to her; I was often dismissive. I think we were talking about my future studies or career, something I had absolutely no clarity about. Something prompted her to say that I was like my father and grandmother, telling me, 'You're like them, more physical than intellectual.' We stood on a threshold, literally: she was on the wide back deck with the bushland and the bay below it. I was at the doorway to the deck. I could see how furious she was with me. Was she worrying that I was genetically disposed towards promiscuity?

At the time, I knew nothing about Bella's infidelity; knew much less about Bella than Mum did.

Was I now, as a woman older than my mother had been back then, researching my grandmother's life and its impact on my father, willing to discover that Bella might have had two or three or more lovers, and learn that her absolute focus couldn't have been on her children or her youngest child, my father? In the sewing box that held the jumble of photographs, I found an envelope containing half a dozen prints of her with men at some kind of conference in

Teplice, Czechoslovakia, dated 1932. She turned thirty-nine that year. The conference had something to do with medicine or health; the names written on the back of the prints showed the men were doctors and professors. Why was she there? Was she working still in some capacity, or representing an organisation back in Berlin? Also in Teplice was a dapper army captain who sat close to her on some steps, just the two of them, knees almost touching. Or were their knees most certainly touching?

My cousins Rolf Verleger and his sister Hanna insisted their knees *were* touching. This was part of a sometimes hilarious but also disturbing conversation with them when I brought out a range of photographs that I was perplexed by – the Teplice conference photos were among them – during a few days we spent together at a resort in Cyprus in November 2019. From Germany, Rolf and his wife, Anne, had made this their regular summer holiday haunt, and others had joined them that year: Katharina and Nico, Simon and Leonie and their two boys, and Hanna and Noam from Tel Aviv. I took a weekend break from my research and zipped across to make the most of our once-in-a-lifetime proximity.

And then I'd return to my grandfather's name-calling. Willy had been wrong to tell his only son that the woman who'd borne him was a nymphomaniac – and when I've talked about it with Dad, he agrees. He even wrote on my manuscript, 'I agree.' It's important to him too.

But then, don't we all say unreasonable things, speak out of turn at some point in our lives? Who can claim to have always been good? The only reason I was now suspicious of her standing next to other men in Teplice, of touching knees, was because of what Willy had said to my father. Their suspicions had become mine.

My Germany

During that first visit to Berlin, I hadn't been able to reconcile my attempts to make sense of the past Germany with the fact that I had a present-day Jewish family and a network of friends living there, which should have, logically, made the place imaginable. My Germany had been populated by the ghosts of murderers and their accomplices drinking beers and cheerily rowing on lakes, their faces souring with laughter that turned to hatred. One day, when Louis and I went to lunch in Munich, I had an encounter with the ghosts. We were with my father's cousin Helga, Rolf and Hanna's mother, who as a teenager had survived a series of labour camps and returned on foot to Berlin in 1945. Now aged in her late eighties, as she stood on the Munich street, Helga was so frail I feared a gust of wind could lift her from the earth and scatter her before lunch. The Munich restaurant we went to had once been popular with Brown Shirts and the SS, and I felt their presence around us. Although Helga's parents had been murdered by the Nazis, she had selected this place for us. Perhaps it was her way of banishing their ghosts. Or perhaps she just shut down those thoughts. Sitting in that Munich restaurant, I felt the bombastic, stone-hearted revelry of men at the timber tables with their tall jugs of beer and tumblers of schnapps.

Helga had chosen to stay in Germany after the war, though she was encouraged by American relatives to leave. Instead, she accepted the hand in marriage of an older Jewish man, a lace manufacturer,

Ernst Verleger, whose wife and children had not survived the camps. After the war he'd been able to reclaim his lace business, and chose to stay.

In Berlin, I didn't have the same sense of the Nazi otherworld of past lives I sensed in Munich. Many of the old venues I frequented had been sites of political resistance and artistic dissent. When friends from Australia visited, we'd danced at Clärchens Ballhaus. I'd seen films at the Babylon Ballhaus, and Martha Wainright perform at the Roter Salon at the Volksbühne. The Berliners I met were like our Airbnb landlady Sabine, interested and deeply sympathetic.

The subtle and not so subtle trail of crumbs that made up what I knew about the country had been shaped by my father's stories of the war and the Holocaust, along with the endless Third Reich and Hitler documentaries that screen on SBS, year in, year out. I intuited that Germany was the cause of his loneliness as a boy growing up in England during the war, of the breaking up of his family, the murders of his extended family and of millions more. It was the reason for his wariness, along with adult night terrors – he'd tell us about his nightmares the following day; not every day, but often enough that I can remember. My father's histories of himself and his family seeped into me as a Jewish stain, a worry, a lurking. Dad's talk of antisemitism and the Nazis' use of racism was clear; we were a loathed people, people to be eradicated. Our father didn't say 'be watchful', though he himself always was. We read Anne Frank's journal at school. I felt shocked and estranged, aware of feelings of sympathy and revulsion. She had the dark hair, the eyes, the same as I had. Jewish people seemed able to spot me a mile off.

Amos Oz writes about his parents' glee that he, their only child, had blond hair, and then of his own desire as a young man who joined the Kibbutz Hulda to be born anew as a muscular and sun-tanned 'Hebrew Jew' (his words) – to leave behind the weak, complaining, nervy, dark-haired character of his European

Jewishness. The new state of Israel had been inundated postwar with the damaged survivors of the camps. With the defeat of Germany and the liberation of the camps, approximately half a million Holocaust survivors made their way to Palestine and post-1948 Israel, arriving either directly from camps or via the Displaced Persons camps in Germany, Austria and Italy. Encounters between this traumatised but frequently determined population and the resident Jews were complex. Many Jews in Palestine were impatient with what they (mis)perceived as the survivors' passivity under Nazism. The cultural historian Liat Steir-Livn put it like this:

> Shock was mingled with anguish and a desire to help the Holocaust survivors, but, both during and after the war, questions and doubts began to arise as to the response of European Jews to the Nazis during the Holocaust.

These doubts were put aside once the full extent of the brutal regime was made public: the Nuremberg trials were a significant part of that process. But at first, the Nazis' victimisation of the Jews struck those in Palestine, and indeed in much of the world, as too incredible.

These were my father's people, and thus my own. This was a story of his origins, of the brutalities his immediate family escaped, and of the kindness of others – which he often did not remember without effort. Yet he'd achieved so much already by the 1970s: a PhD in biochemistry, work at the best universities (I still encounter doctors who took his nutrition and biochemistry lectures at the University of Sydney all those years ago); a loving wife and children, a home, interesting friends – but the bad dreams still woke him, the persistent pessimism continued, the drag and lumber of abandonment.

In the years I'm thinking of, we were living in Greenwich in a 1930s Californian bungalow that had been extended by the previous owners to include a back deck. The open-plan dining room overlooked bushland that led down to a small bay, Gore Cove, in Sydney Harbour. Across the water was the peninsular suburb of Wollstonecraft, with bushland below the houses and then more bushland on Berry Island, which was no longer an island, as a field now connected it to mainland Wollstonecraft. Our back garden ended with a sudden, small sandstone cliff, a three-metre drop that you could manoeuvre down via steep steps. Below, the bush reserve sloped down to the water, the muddy beach rimmed with sharp oyster shells and remnant mangroves. When there was a very low tide, enough mud would be exposed that you could walk across to Berry Island.

We had set places at the dinner table. My younger brothers sat together on one side, looking across the bay to Wollstonecraft and pulling faces at their reflections in the wide timber-framed windows. I sat opposite, facing the wall of bookshelves in the living room either side of the unused fireplace. The collection that included William L Shirer's *The Rise and Fall of the Third Reich*, published the year I was born. Thinking about those books now, I realise that my father didn't read the famous German writers like Thomas Mann, Hermann Hesse or – Bella's favourite – Johann Wolfgang von Goethe. Maybe there had been a Günter Grass on the shelf. Germany for him was not playful, not a work of fiction, but world history and difficult memories. He had books of analysis and history. The Russians could do fiction – there was Tolstoy, Dostoevsky, and Gorky and Turgenev in small volumes bound with dark red cloth; and the modern Americans – Miller, Roth, Hemingway, Mary McCarthy's *The Group*, and Ogden Nash, whose witty limericks my father enjoyed reading aloud, animatedly jumping from one foot to another to amuse us.

We'd regularly eat the foods of his brief German childhood, which he was able to enjoy again when he began living with his father in Melbourne: rollmops, liverwurst, pumpernickel, Polish-style dill pickles, sauerkraut, and Philadelphia cream cheese, the closest he could get to *frischkäse*. His Limburger and other aromatic cheeses lived in solitary containers in the fridge and were taken out when none of us were at the table.

Perhaps Dad and I were both cleaning our teeth, or one of us was entering just as the other was exiting, but somehow one day we were crammed into the tiny main bathroom together and Dad pointed out to me that the bathroom scales were made by Krupp, and that Krupp had manufactured the gas chambers for the Nazis. He'd been debating with himself whether he should have bought these scales, he said. Krupp profited hugely from their contracts with the Nazis, using slave labourers – concentration-camp prisoners and prisoners of war – to produce armaments, including guns, tanks and submarines. Topf and Sons manufactured many of the ovens.

Both my parents were 'weight conscious', carefully managing their food intake, analysing the nutritional value of everything we ate. When I anxiously weighed my teenage self, I'd think of Krupp, Germany and the camps. My eyes glanced down my flat but well-filled stomach and down my toned legs – legs I wished were slender-boned like one of Nabokov's nymphets, Lolita or Ada, instead of strong – to my feet on the scales. I'd recall the photographs of the bone-thin survivors pressing up against the camp fences as the Allied liberators came. Was this Dad's perverse expression of his guilt at surviving, by having what he believed were Krupp scales in the house? A daily reminder of what he didn't suffer. He's said he has often felt survivor's guilt that he never suffered like others did in the camps.

When I was hungry or cold, I'd think of how very much hungrier and colder the camp prisoners had been. I'd imagine the cold, the lice, the dysentery. I still do, and decade after decade I 'remember' something I've not myself experienced. Linda Kinstler speculates that we remember because:

> These stories – these inheritances, really – come with demands. To receive them is also to inherit a set of obligations and dilemmas: how much to preserve? How much to expose ... How much to reclaim?

These objects we had in the house, the bathroom scales, *The Rise and Fall of the Third Reich*, the empty menorah, were reminders of my father's obligation to remember and preserve. The obligation was passed on to me, the eldest, the daughter, and the writer in the family.

My parents during those years were friends with Alice and Herbert Beauchamp, who lived in nearby Lane Cove. They were conservationists as well. In my first non-waitressing job after leaving high school, I started work with them as a storeman and packer, getting out stock and filling the orders for the shops they sold to. Alice was originally from Mannheim in Germany, and Herbert from Hungary. Both were Jewish. Lovely, kind people. They had a business importing clothes and giftware from countries along the old silk roads of Afghanistan, Pakistan, India and Indonesia, then wholesaling to retail stores across Australia. Everything 'ethnic' was fashionable then; the thick woven jackets that smelt of alpaca and goat, the summer cheesecloth dresses and shirts hand-dyed in India, amber beads that were too expensive for me, patchouli oil and sandalwood incense.

I can no longer recall what Herbert and I were talking about, but something led to this: he gently put his arm forward and pushed up his sleeve. He showed me his number, tattooed onto him as a child in Auschwitz. Still visible on his warm, living forearm. The tiny cold arm of the boy had grown, and the numbers had grown with him. Herbert is gone now, but his smooth-skinned brown arm and the green-grey-blue ink of his tattoo have transferred into my memory. The fact of the tattooing embedded itself in me.

*

Recently, I discovered that my father had been mistaken. Our scales were made by *Krups,* spelled with one 'p' and an 's'. This other Krups had been manufacturing scales since the mid-1800s, not weapons. In that way of finding correspondences between unrelated events, I realised the company began in the same decade that the German writer Heinrich Hoffmann wrote a book that Dad had read to me many times, known in English as *The Story of the Thumbsucker.* As a boy himself, he'd had Hoffmann's vividly illustrated *Struwwelpeter* read to him, and he in turn read its English translation to me and my younger brothers. In 'The Story of the Thumbsucker', Konrad ignores his mother's commands to leave his thumb alone. He keeps on being a naughty thumb-sucker. (I was a thumb-sucker!) A tailor comes to the house with long, sharp scissors and cuts off Konrad's thumbs. The colour illustration shows blood spurting from the stumps. Most of these tales end badly for the misbehaving children. A girl plays with matches; she burns to death. A fussy eater won't eat his soup; he wastes away and dies. My father was gleefully astounded by the cruelty of these stories. His eyes would gleam as he read them, and he'd chuckle at how awful the punishments were. Perhaps we laughed too, I think we did.

In another story, a 'true' one from the past that I remember only the bare bones of, one of his aunts was with her husband and children in their car. I can recall how avidly I listened to this story. There was an accident, and the car drove off a bridge and went into the water. His aunt and uncle managed to save themselves and the children, and their passports and identification papers. Without documentation, 'you were a goner', Dad said, a nobody who could be thrown in prison or disappeared and murdered. They had to save the passports. When I asked him about the incident a couple of years ago, wanting to know which aunt this had happened to and when and so forth, he couldn't remember.

Did I feel that there was a connection between being Jewish, the Holocaust, the broken family, the punishments that the *Struwwelpeter* children endured? The saddest story, the first time I heard of a child taking their own life, came from Bunce Court school. Dad was seventeen when a younger student hanged himself from a tree. The war had been raging for four years, and many of the Jewish children knew their parents had died. This boy's parents had survived and were safe in America. His two sisters were at the school. But for whatever reason amid the fundamental mystery of taking one's own life, the boy ended his. This was another story I asked my father about in recent years. He remembers the incident, that it was shocking and grim. Then, in case it wasn't true after all, I searched for the boy in Holocaust archives. And yes, it was true. The boy was Martin Solmitz, originally from Hamburg.

The point Dad had been impressing on us through these dinner-table stories was that life had been uncertain and terrifying. These stories, large and small, swirled about me, became entangled with others. They dragged me in, and they fascinated me.

Reading Goethe

I've looked many times through the collection of Bella's books on my shelves, so beautifully produced with their fine skin of leather. Bella carried them for so long and so far, surely they had a message for me. I turned to Goethe in English translations to find out more.

But it was too enormous a project to try to recover something of her from the great man's writing. If she enjoyed reading Goethe, well and good, but I certainly didn't. Johann Wolfgang von Goethe, whose books Bella had carried across the world, had never even been to Berlin, so was no use at all as a source on the city that had made her. I tried to read him, to sense what it was that she had connected with in his writing as a German Jew, a woman, and a Berliner. I started on *The Sorrows of Young Werther*, published a century before Bella was born, in 1774. Goethe's expression, considered modern in his own day, was now too congested, his ideas too Romantic, his vision too male. It was insufferable, yet he'd been an icon for German Jews. (Young Werther also ends his life, for reasons of unrequited love and social alienation.) By the 1930s, Goethe was no longer an icon for those who identified with the revolutionary artistic and political spirit of writers such as Bertolt Brecht, Lion Feuchtwanger, Heinrich Mann (Thomas Mann's brother), and many others. Bella was perhaps like other German Jewish refugees, who at first had seen themselves as German, with an identity that had previously offered both a home and habitat.

This effort by Jews to view themselves and, through their contributions to German society, *to be seen* as German, is present in Gabriele Tergit's 1951 epic intergenerational novel, *Effingers: A Berlin saga*, recently translated into English for the first time. Most of the characters are Jewish; in Tergit's words it was a Berlin novel in which very many people were Jewish, until Nazism. While writing the novel, Tergit shared with a colleague her hope that when reading it, 'every German Jew says, "Yes, that's how we were, that's how we lived from 1878 to 1939," and that they give it to their children so that they may know what it was like'.

When one of my PhD students was writing about the Gothic Romantic genre in Australian literature, I read up on European Romantic literature so I could competently supervise her project, but everything about it annoyed me. I disliked the often lurid exaltation of emotion over pragmatism and the turning in upon the (usually male) self.

'Don't you find these misanthropic men like Goethe complete bores?' I asked her at last. She laughed and said yes, as if it was a revelation that such a thing could be uttered out loud.

I much preferred the Russians I'd read growing up: Dostoevsky, Turgenev, Tolstoy and Gorky, the poets Anna Akhmatova and Alexander Pushkin. I found Anton Chekhov in my twenties. Chekhov was humanist and egalitarian; his writing was informed by his work as a doctor meeting people from all walks of life. In 1890 Chekhov lived for months on the frontier prison island of Sakhalin, north of Japan, researching the appalling conditions that the thousands of prisoners and their families endured. He met with every destitute, starving, ruined person there and his final report, serialised between 1891 and 1893 and published in full in 1895, changed Russia's prison system. (In the mid-2000s, I wrote the radio drama *Dear Dr Chekhov*, based on Chekhov's months on Sakhalin Island, which was produced by ABC Radio National.)

How could I possibly expect to have an affinity with Goethe? I couldn't. I was struggling with *Young Werther* when Louis and I were living at Hufelandstrasse. Sometimes Louis would come into my room if I was working late, and tell me it was time to take a break. And then I'd allow myself an episode of the TV series *Breaking Bad*.

I dared not say to my German language teacher, Sven, that I preferred watching American serials about moral degeneracy and drug trafficking to Goethe. I was learning German with him in private classes at the Goethe Institute. I needed all the help I could get. I'd had too many humiliating hours in group language classes where all the other students' vocabularies were twice as large as mine. The Institute was situated on the commercial Neue Schönhauser Strasse, a twenty-minute bicycle ride away from our apartment. Sven was lean, black-haired, gracious, articulating a perplexing combination of liberal politics and a belief in a German 'character', a particular German connectedness to the land and to the project of developing one's *bildung*. He found Australia's multiculturalism fundamentally strange: that something called 'Australian' should be so diverse.

German Jews in Bella's day had celebrated Goethe's works: intent on acculturation, some even read Goethe aloud at the dinner table to feed their *bildung*, their German *embourgeoisement*. The writer Ernst Toller recalls in his autobiography, *I Was A German*, that, as a boy growing up in southern Germany, 'The Jews looked upon themselves as the pioneers of German culture, and their houses in these little towns became cultural centres where German literature, philosophy and art were cultivated with pride ...' With postwar, post-Holocaust hindsight, he adds that this acculturation 'bordered on the ridiculous'.

Had Bella simply kept the books out of respect for the Germany she'd once loved? Or perhaps they recalled memories of her birth family? Don't we all hold on to talismans of what we have lost?

Childhoods, homes, lovers and friends ... I came to see that I could learn little about her perspective on life from her volumes of Goethe. This one line of his would have to do: *Knowing is not enough; we must apply. Willing is not enough; we must do.* She was most certainly a doer.

Perhaps she read Thomas Mann's novels of the day, *Death in Venice*, or *The Magic Mountain*? Or her contemporaries, younger writers such as Irmgard Keun or Gabriele Tergit? Walter Benjamin was being published widely in some of the liberal newspapers she'd have read. He made his living from writing, as many of these writers did. Quite possibly my father and aunt had listened to Benjamin on German radio's *Enlightenment for Children* program, which he wrote and presented from 1927 to 1933. He has a nice reading voice, well intonated, warm and even gentle at moments. He was fascinated by natural disasters, and lawlessness, and shared these exciting stories with the children: the Lisbon earthquake; the eruption of Vesuvius and death in Pompeii; smuggling and bootleggers. In other radio programs he wrote and presented play readings, book reviews and fiction.

She may have read Alfred Döblin: his 1929 novel *Berlin Alexanderplatz* is populated with people and places that would have been familiar to her and Willy. There's a scene in which the ex-prisoner Franz is finding his way about the streets after being released:

> Traffic hooted and honked. The facades were never ending ... He drifted down Rosenthaler Strasse, past the Wertheim department store, then swung right into narrow Sophienstrasse. He thought: less light, and the darker the better.

So many of the passages in *Berlin Alexanderplatz* are about the city my grandparents knew; this was the point of Döblin's novel, to record with hyperrealism the Berlin of his day.

I read Margarete Böhme's racy novel *The Diary of a Lost One,* first published in 1905 when Bella was twelve, then republished countless times over many years. The heroine, Thymian, tells of losing her mother at a young age and then being raised carelessly by her drunken father. Exploited and abandoned, without work, she turns to prostitution. Very racy. In 1929 it was adapted to film starring Louise Brooks, the beautiful and internationally famous American actress. Had Bella read *The Diary of a Lost One* as a teenager, perhaps, to find out about sex and love? Surely Bella and Willy would have seen the film; it was a box office hit.

I read Gabriele Tergit's *Käsebier Takes Berlin.* The novel brought Tergit fame but also the attention of the Nazis. She was well known as a journalist, and the satirical novel relates how an ageing singer, Herr Käsebier, is discovered performing on a shabby stage for shopkeepers, typists and labourers, and through a flurry of news reports and inflationary reviews becomes briefly famous. The frenetic novel is set in 1930 at the end of the Weimar Republic, before Berliners realise that Nazism is about to take over. Reading it, I'd catch on to particular lines like this one, which could have described Bella: [an] *unusual woman ... a completely new type.* I wanted to *feel* Berlin as Bella might have felt it; just one iota of her feeling was all I sought.

Like most Berliners, Bella knew Alexanderplatz well; it was a central transport hub, and she would have read the kinds of newspapers that the journalists in Tergit's novel work for. Collectively these were the 'Berlin novels' of her time, recording the latter years of the Weimer Republic and the conflicts between the Nazis and the communists that characterised the end of the 1920s.

In Bella's albums are photographs of her with various friends and family members walking along another of Berlin's signal sites:

the boulevard Unter den Linden, literally, 'under the lindens'. The linden is a tall tree with bright heart-shaped leaves. The first of the boulevard's thousand trees had been planted in the 1670s and it was the city's celebrated central street. When Bella lived there, it was the place to promenade, gawp, flirt and pickpocket. Here were the theatres and cabarets, embassies, ministries and banks. She'd be waiting for a friend to arrive or reading one of the city's hundred newspapers beneath the shade of the trees. There they are, there she is, the women smiling arm-in-arm, pictured in twos or threes, near the majestic trees. When the trees were ordered to be cut down by Hitler to widen the boulevard for his parades, Berliners of all political persuasions protested and grieved.

Rolf and the 5767

On that trip to Berlin in 2014, I made a date to meet my second cousin Rolf for the first time. This is the Rolf who, with his sister Hanna during the later family holiday in Cyprus, would be so sure Bella was touching knees with her officer friend in the 1932 conference photograph. Louis and I were to stay the weekend with him and his wife, Anne Verleger, at their home in Lübeck, a small city on the Baltic coastline north of Berlin, a few hours away by train. It had been hard to find a weekend that suited us both. I knew Rolf was a professor of neuroscience at Lübeck University, and that Anne was both a psychiatrist and clinical psychologist. He seemed very busy with deadlines for articles and talks, things I didn't know much about. His emails were short and somewhat formal, but I was used to that now with Germans. He didn't provide explanations of what exactly he was so busy with. He didn't say, *You do know about the missiles in Gaza a few weeks ago, don't you?*

That year, Israeli Defence Force missiles had killed four boys playing on the beach in Gaza. I had no idea that Rolf's full calendar of meetings and deadlines flowed from an article he had written that was critical of Germany's support for Israel's missile attacks on Gaza.

I knew about his activism only in the vaguest way when Rolf met us on the platform of Lübeck station and looked so warmly at us both, his bright blue-grey eyes and gentle smile showing how he was so glad to see us – we were family who'd journeyed from faraway Australia. We embraced as long-lost cousins. It was a tremendously special moment of coming together over decades and generations. He and I were of the same generation, our parents had been children during the war and the Holocaust and he and his siblings, Hanna and Peter, had grown up without grandparents. Their mother, Helga, with whom Louis and I had lunched in the old restaurant haunted by the ghosts of the SS in Munich, had been an only child, then orphaned because of the Holocaust; not long after her third child was born, she became a widow.

I didn't know that Rolf had been recalled from his position as a member of the board of the Central Council of Jews in Germany a few years earlier. Nor that he had been removed as chairman of the Jewish community in the German state of Schleswig-Holstein for writing a letter to the local council that was critical in the strongest terms of its support for Israel in its 2006 war with Lebanon in particular, and its unquestioning support for Israel in general. Nor did I know that he'd then initiated a petition called the 'Berlin Declaration Shalom 5767'. News of this event hadn't reached the family in Sydney, though it had reached some Jews in Britain and Australia.

The Declaration stated that:

> The root of the problem is the continuing Israeli occupation of Palestinian territory since 1967. The Occupation humiliates and disenfranchises the Palestinians. It paralyses their economic, political and social life. Moreover, this daily recurring experience of injustice prevents a peaceful resolution of the old injustice done to the Palestinians when they were forced to leave in 1948.

The petition called upon the German government to strive earnestly for the realisation of a viable Palestinian state, 'a state with full sovereignty and freedom of movement'.

At that time, as it is now, German Jews who spoke out against Israel's occupation and attacks on Palestinians were described as antisemitic and 'Jew-haters'. Kurt Goldstein, a Holocaust survivor and honorary chairman of the International Auschwitz Committee, countered these accusations and attacks on the petition, arguing that actually, 'the reality is that there is nothing more that helps antisemites [than] what Israel did in the war in Lebanon'. The trustees of the newspaper *Die Jüdische Zeitung*, which had published the declaration and Goldstein's statement, then issued its own statement criticising the paper's editorial decisions to publish, asking, 'Does this newspaper want to go about as the mouthpiece for anti-Israeli propaganda?'

That was the context for Rolf writing about the IDF missiles killing the four boys as they played on the beach of Gaza. Just before we arrived, he had published an opinion piece in which he concluded that:

> A suspicion creeps over me when politicians make statements like this [about critiques of Israel being antisemitic]. Most Germans were fellow travellers during the Nazi era: they saw the injustice against the Jews, but did nothing about it – because they were stuck in the past with their values and because they did not want to imagine the actual extent of the injustice. Could it be that this follower mentality is the real constant in German politics? I mean, I like living in Germany, partly because today there is an honest general regret about what was done to German and European Jews in the German name. But isn't it rather cheap to leave the blame with one's own deceased ancestors and celebrate it on memorial days while at the same time justifying current injustice? Isn't that a follower mentality?

Later, I began to think harder about my own situation as a writer with a particular Jewish history. Was I now like them, the acquiescent Germans and German Jews? Who were these German Jews, in any case? Few are 'indigenous' German Jews because so few survived the Holocaust to have descendants like Rolf and his children Katharina and Simon. The majority of German Jews are immigrants from Russia, Ukraine, and other Baltic states following the 1991 *Contingency Refugee Act*; they have Jewish heritage but may not actively identify as Jewish; some have ancestors who were murdered in Nazi camps and massacres, others not. I was in part from this multi-historied, peripatetic group: a citizen enjoying my freedom of movement in Germany and Europe. Was there anywhere in the world I could *not* go? My father had arrived in Australia alone and stateless, but now I was so very privileged with my dual citizenship, my protections and freedoms. Rolf and I didn't talk about any of this. I had no idea of his recent interviews and writings, and only a vague idea about his political stance on Israel. Perhaps he was used to being cautious about raising these issues that have divided so many Jews. Yet we were, in fact, in agreement.

What was unique to us was our family history, and that is what we talked about after we'd settled in at the house. Its large first-floor windows overlooked a lovely garden. Slender white-trunked birch trees, trees I've long loved but which don't thrive in Sydney's humidity, were tall against the soft grey sky above. I paused to look at the living room with its furniture pushed back to the walls. Anne noticed and said that she and Rolf liked to dance in the evenings together. Waltzes, a foxtrot perhaps, I can't exactly remember. It was easy being with them, they got on so well, there was so much warmth to them, so much love between them.

Rolf and Anne had met my parents a couple of times and my parents had stayed with them at their Lübeck home and liked them very much. They'd talked at length with Dad about his story of leaving Germany, and were impressed by Judy's work as an environmentalist, and her great energy and capacity for action. They were impressed by how easily she navigated their kitchen, serving up 'unforgettable' fried eggs with tomatoes in the mornings.

Rolf and Anne took Louis and me cycling through picturesque Lübeck. They claimed my mother had ridden a bike, too. I had never once seen my mother on a bike. We rode over historic timber bridges past fast-running water and bright green grasses, over bumpy cobbled streets and down laneways. On the Sunday afternoon, we walked along a cliff path above the Baltic, the sea whipped white by the fierce wind. We were so excited by the biting cold, it was almost funny how Louis and I exclaimed and huddled into our coats, while Rolf and Anne sauntered beside us. We'd not felt anything like it before; we'd been dozing in Berlin's post-summer temperatures.

But my mother had changed because of her Alzheimer's since they'd last seen her, and so I had to say she wasn't as well as she'd been but still very active and interested in the world. I told them about this book, which was then just scraps of notes, and what I had learned so far of Bella's life. I said I'd heard of a man that Bella had had an affair with, a Walter Strauss, but knew little about him.

Not long after we returned to Berlin, Rolf emailed me. He had found a reference to a Walter Strauss in a German social history published in 1994, *Exodus of Sciences from Berlin: Questions, Results, Desiderata: Developments before and after 1933*. From what I read, using an app to translate as I typed in the original German – oh, what a long but eager effort that was, typing in page after page! – I was now certain this was the correct Walter Strauss. He'd been an associate professor in bacteriology and hygiene (i.e. public health) at the Friedrich-Wilhelms University in Berlin until 1933. (He was removed from his university employment along with other Jewish educators; I have not been able to find information on what he did for work until migrating to Palestine in 1937.) It wasn't a great leap to see that Bella and Walter would have known each other, as they both worked in public health and social welfare. *Exodus of Sciences*

Professor Walter Strauss, Head of the Department of Hygiene at the Hebrew University, hands a temporary licence to a student at the University-Hadassah Medical School enabling him to practise medicine in the immigrant camps during his internship, 1 February 1952.

from Berlin examines the impact of the exodus of Jewish scientists from Germany and their contributions to Mandate Palestine. The British hadn't established any welfare or social security systems. Organisations such as the Histadrut, the General Organisation of Workers in Israel, provided resources for the employed and unemployed through a network of enterprises and cooperatives. It's within accounts of this culture of self-help and 'start-ups' that Walter Strauss is discussed for his contribution to founding health centres in Jerusalem and elsewhere. His initiatives were financially supported by the Hadassah, the Women's Zionist Organization of America, which was very active in the British Mandate: 'in the spacious building, built with American donations, a wide range of activities soon developed'. A health education department organised a 'Health Week' for the first time in Palestine. Strauss also founded a new semi-scientific journal called *Hygiene and Health*, which began publication in 1940. Over time, Strauss became 'a major figure in the social-medical field throughout the country'.

It took me years more to get a copy of the book, and then translate the relevant pages, and then get myself over to Israel and the Hebrew University of Jerusalem to view his file archive. But in the meantime, he was at least in a history of German and Palestinian public health initiatives. This told me that he and Bella must have had a deep friendship and not only a passionate love affair, based in part on their shared commitment to public health and child welfare. She wasn't just a sex-mad floozy, or if she was, she'd been a very intellectual one.

The torn page

One affair of the heart makes for a weak indictment. There was only one man that I knew for certain Bella had an affair with: Walter Strauss. And if I seem here to be strangely focused on Bella and Strauss, it's in part because my father has brought him into the family story as the cause – or one of the causes – of his mother not loving him. Strauss has long been the perfect explanation, as neither of us knew much about him, and from what I've learned he had no descendants beyond his one son.

Some of what Dad knew would turn out to be right, some of it wrong. Clues began with Bella's address book, which Dad gave to me along with her passport around 2007 when we first started talking properly about her. The address book is a dark aubergine brown, smooth and slim, small enough for a clutch or coat pocket. The paper is soft yet strong. The book is dense with the names and addresses of people living and working in Tel Aviv, Jerusalem, Haifa, New York, Chicago, Cairo, London, various towns in Britain, Istanbul, Paris, Sydney and Melbourne. Many of the German names and addresses have been struck through. (Did they move house, or die?) There are more Palestinian and British addresses than German. On some pages when she is writing with a fountain pen, her cursive is a style called *kurrentschrift* that dates from the 1500s. The lettering is difficult even for a native German speaker to decipher. A lower case 'S' could be mistaken for an arrow's barb, and in its capitalised form could be the flight of a bumble bee. The letters seem as whimsical yet also as exact as the cavorting of a small bird. 'V' and 'W' are mere suggestions of a letter in lower case. Reading her address book becomes easier when she relaxes into a more modern style, which she seems to do once she is living in Tel Aviv. But none of it is easy to read. I struggle through each word.

Bella's sister Minnie Fuchs is shown living at half a dozen addresses around London and southern England where she worked as a live-in housekeeper after her husband, Kurt, died in 1937 – all of them crossed out. Dad's History stated that she and Kurt Fuchs immigrated to South Africa with her two stepsons, the children of his first marriage. Yet there was no South African address for Minnie. It made some sense to me that she and Kurt had gone to South Africa, where there was economic growth – alongside exploitation and oppression of black South Africans – and a vigorous anti-fascist movement. The movement included organisations such as the Jewish Workers' Club, which was active against right-wing, antisemitic organisations such as the Third Reich's global NSDAP groups (Nationalsozialistische Deutsche Arbeiterpartei). But once again, immigration wasn't straightforward for Jews. South Africa's 1930 *Immigration Quota Act* aimed explicitly to restrict Jewish immigration. It also selected immigrants from 'desirable' and 'undesirable' countries, and preferred skilled professionals.

I set about looking for a record of Minnie's presence in South Africa. I attempted to access the few digitised South African databases I could find. I checked the passenger lists of ships she and Kurt and their sons might have boarded from key ports. Having found no trace of her, I finally engaged an Israeli historian who specialised in Jewish South African genealogy, Paul Cheifitz, who told me she'd never been to South Africa. There was no immigration entry for her, no death certificate or record of residence. Instead, he had evidence that she'd been interned on the Isle of Man off the coast of Britain in the Irish Sea.

The question Bella's address book raised – why there was no current address for Bella's favourite sibling – I've still not fully answered. With the assistance of the generous and thoughtful historians and archivists at the Isle of Man Library and Public Record office, and the German genealogist Claudia Stock, I learned that Minnie's fate was far grimmer than I'd imagined. When she left Germany in May 1939 to work as a housekeeper in Britain, she was already a widow. Kurt Fuchs had died in his birthplace of Liegnitz, Silesia, in 1937. Who cared for the two teenage sons from his first marriage, I don't know. Perhaps his Silesian family took them in. Whether or not they or the boys survived the war, or died in camps, again, I don't know.

In May 1940, she left the last of the addresses Bella had recorded, before being interned on the Isle of Man. Minnie's Isle of Man entry records include a photograph of her on arrival. Her lined face shows a startlingly beautiful, intense woman in her forties. With her large eyes and direct gaze, she could be a sister of Frida Kahlo. Her expression is vibrant, alert, strangely bordering on hopeful. Her hair is dark, and held back in a bandana, not as neat and manicured as the photos of her when she's young.

In the women's camp she began to experience depression and paranoia. Her medical records stated that she was imagining that men were coming to get her in the night. There's no comment that this fear had a basis in fact: she had fled Germany and now Jewish internees had to share dorms with German Nazis in both the male and female camps on the Isle of Man.

She was moved to the island's mental asylum, which was caring for over one hundred internees. Some remained there, others returned to their camp when well enough. Her life there seems to have been relatively peaceful, based on the case notes about her that I've read. She seemed well liked by staff. Her English language skills were excellent, and she is described spending time in the gardens, and working on a theoretical/spiritual work, written in English. I've read parts of it that postulate bizarre coherences between electricity, the cosmos and the spiritual. Postwar, she was transferred to a London asylum, then to asylums in Germany, which Claudia Stock told me would have been brutal. The first that she was placed in was a former concentration camp that had been converted to a Displaced Persons camp and then an asylum. Claudia couldn't find a record of her death.

Did Bella abandon Minnie, perhaps shamed by her mental illness? Did they lose contact with each other? Was there something they'd fallen out over, irrevocably? Did Bella even know that Minnie was unwell? Minnie's life came to me in bursts over half a year as the documents and searches slowly revealed her, first to me and then my dad, when I shared what I'd learned with him. It is an immensely sad story, and neither of us could take in the enormity of it.

Willy's cousin Alice Redlich is also there in Bella's address book. Alice had left Berlin as a trainee nurse and was working in London at the outbreak of war. She wasn't interned on the Isle of Man because England needed nurses. Bella records her living first in Sherriff Road, then on the next page, she is with the '110 Jewish Relief Unit' at 'Glynn Hughes Hospital, B.A.O.R. 23'. The hospital is near the Bergen-Belsen concentration camp, and she was working assisting survivors. At Bergen-Belsen she met and married a camp survivor, John Fink (Hans Finke), literally marrying him in the campgrounds, surrounded by medical staff, other survivors and army well-wishers. Bella had crossed out 'Redlich' in the address book and replaced it with 'Finke', and so while she knew what had happened to Alice, she didn't know or didn't record what had happened to her sister Minnie.

Alice and John immigrated to the USA, and Alice lived to the great age of 103 years, dying in 2023. They raised their four children in Chicago. Dad and I are in regular contact with her children and extended family.

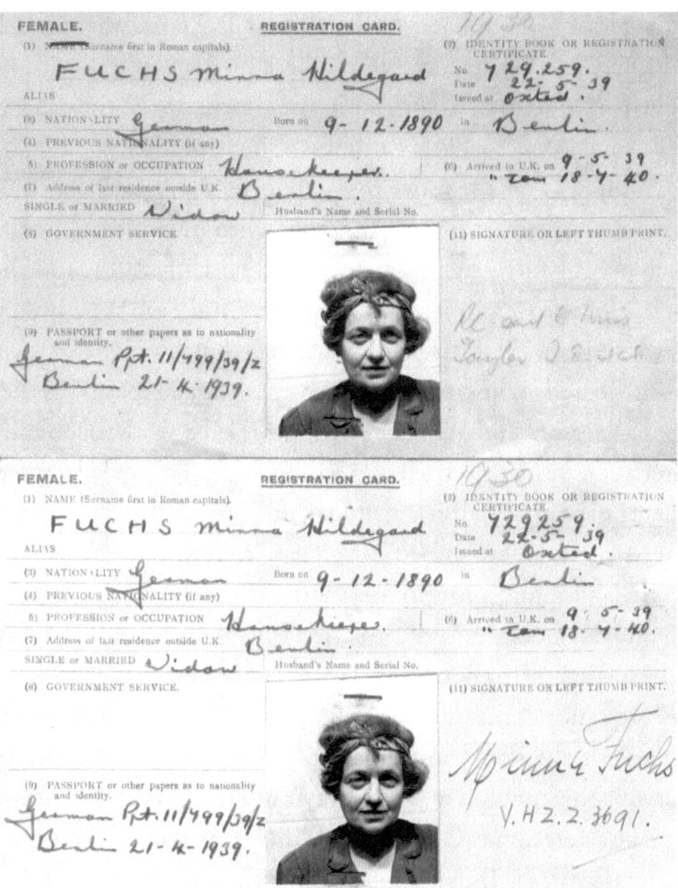

FEMALE. REGISTRATION CARD.

(1) NAME (Surname first in Roman capitals). FUCHS Minna Hildegard

ALIAS

(2) IDENTITY BOOK OR REGISTRATION CERTIFICATE. No 729.259. Date 22-5-39 Issued at Oxted.

(3) NATIONALITY German Born on 9-12-1890 in Berlin.

(4) PREVIOUS NATIONALITY (if any)

(5) PROFESSION or OCCUPATION Housekeeper.

(6) Arrived in U.K. on 9-5-39 / 18-4-40.

(7) Address of last residence outside U.K. Berlin.

SINGLE or MARRIED Widow Husband's Name and Serial No.

(8) GOVERNMENT SERVICE.

(9) PASSPORT or other papers as to nationality and identity. German Ppt. 11/499/39/z Berlin 21-4-1939.

(11) SIGNATURE OR LEFT THUMB PRINT.

FEMALE. REGISTRATION CARD.

(1) NAME (Surname first in Roman capitals). FUCHS Minna Hildegard

ALIAS

(2) IDENTITY BOOK OR REGISTRATION CERTIFICATE. No 729259. Date 22-5-39 Issued at Oxted.

(3) NATIONALITY German Born on 9-12-1890 in Berlin.

(4) PREVIOUS NATIONALITY (if any)

(5) PROFESSION or OCCUPATION Housekeeper.

(6) Arrived in U.K. on 9-5-39 / 18-4-40.

(7) Address of last residence outside U.K. Berlin.

SINGLE or MARRIED Widow Husband's Name and Serial No.

(8) GOVERNMENT SERVICE.

(9) PASSPORT or other papers as to nationality and identity. German Ppt. 11/499/39/z Berlin 21-4-1939.

(11) SIGNATURE OR LEFT THUMB PRINT. Minna Fuchs V.H2.2.3691.

Minna Fuchs [Minnie], 1940 Isle of Man Registration Card.

Bella recorded many Melbourne residences for Ruth, each crossed out as Ruth moved between Prahran, Parkville, Middle Park, St Kilda, Toorak, Caulfield, Albert Park. Some of these places were boarding houses. At one or two she was living with her husband, Frank Morgan, whom she'd married at age nineteen. Letters between them and her own account show him to have been highly intelligent, articulate, neglectful, persuasive, violent and often drunk. During her son Leigh's birth, Frank was stationed in Papua New Guinea. He didn't share his army wages with her, so she had to return to work with a newborn. By the time she was aged twenty-one, in 1943, Ruth was a single mother.

Willy was on the move in Melbourne too, living at various boarding houses. At first on his own, when he'd arrived in 1939 when he was forty-eight years of age, then with Ruth, and then because of their arguments about politics and Frank, he lived on his own again. He focused on building a button manufacturing business based at the Beehive Building in the city. He'd always been a genial person, and he made friends but led a work-focused life. After a few years he settled in a red-brick block of six apartments called Lorne that still stands today in Elwood. This was the flat that Michael, and then Bella, lived in with him.

Bella's fountain pen moves swiftly through various names in the address book, on a diagonal, a line across their name and address – gone. The entries are written on a slant, bits of addresses squeezed into corners, or sprawling across half a page, as if she's pulled out the book on the street, writing in a hurry. She and everyone she knows is on the move, rootless and searching, trying to make a new home. Or murdered. This is the war, the Holocaust, and its aftermath. The struck-out names and addresses are symbolic of so many millions who lost their lives. Some who died remain untouched in the book. Emma Messer, Willy's mother, is still there at Traunsteinerstrasse 6, the apartment she was deported from in August 1942.

Bella recorded a scattering of addresses for people in Australia. There's a 'Noela McFay, 7 Walker St, Moonee Ponds': the house still stands, a quintessential Federation brick bungalow. Under 'A' there are entries for local Australian food producers. A smallgoods firm: 'Kosher! Batagol Bros Melbourne'. 'Asparagus soup, Gordon Edgell and Sons Ltd, Bathurst, Sydney, Cowra'. 'Jam Melbourne Jam Co., 242 Rae St, North Fitzroy'. 'Rabbit in Aspic, Kraft

Walker Cheese Co.'. It's such an odd assortment. Who shared this information with her, and why?

I knew when I packed the address book on that first trip to Berlin, it was foolish to take it. What if I lost it? If it went missing with my luggage? Regardless, I brought it; I needed her tangible presence. The book contained everyone she'd known in her last years in Berlin. One day I was turning its pages, peering closely at the words. I was in our Hufelandstrasse apartment, the light from the French doors streaming in, bouncing off the white walls and the ceiling. I needed that good light, and was bent close to the pages, comparing lettering in words that I could read with letters in words that were a scramble. The differences between her u's, m's and n's were mostly illegible to me. Then I noticed a sliver of ragged-edged paper. The page had been torn. I lifted the remaining triangular fragment with the tip of my finger. It wasn't just a crease in the paper. The address book was divided by alphabet tabs. There was the tab for 'R', but nothing for 'S'. 'R' was followed by the tear, and then 'Sch'. The page that should have had Walter Strauss's details was gone.

My guess is that Bella tore the page out to conceal him from Willy. Or because she was over him and didn't want to be reminded. The tear was a gesture, an act of agency. She'd loved him, and fought with him, and been disappointed by him because he never left his wife for her. The torn page was physical, and irreparable. The discovery felt like a gift from Bella, for it told me how much Walter Strauss had meant to her. I got up and found Louis lying on his bed, sketching. He was the only person around I could tell. I handed the little address book over to him. 'Look, see how the page is missing,' I said in great excitement. He nodded with raised eyebrows and said 'Sweet'; that is, *Good sleuthing, Mum, if that's what gets you going.* But then I was filled with doubt. Perhaps it was Willy who tore out the page? Not Bella? No matter, whoever did the deed was moved in that moment by passion. Holding the book, I felt grief for them, Bella and Willy, and all the dead within its pages.

From Bunce Court to Melbourne

The war ground on, year after year. My father matriculated in 1944 with Distinctions in German, History and Scripture, Credits in English, Art and Biology (but to his shame, just a Pass in Mathematics). Tante Anna, Anna Essinger, recommended that my father remain at the school for another year. Dad believes, perhaps rightly, she and his teachers felt he didn't yet have the emotional maturity to get a job in 'an outside world with which I had had almost no contact, and where I had no relatives'. His aunt Minnie was still in an asylum on the Isle of Man, though possibly he and Bella didn't know that. Alice Redlich, his second cousin, was in England, not yet married to John Fink, but the families were not in touch and most likely had no idea that the other was there. He really was on his own.

These had been happy years for Michael; despite everything, that's how he mostly remembers them, even when he also recalls his own sense of discomfort and awareness of how very unprepared he was for life beyond the school. So, he stayed and worked with the biology teacher and head gardener, Maria Dehn, tending the school's vegetable garden, essential to the school's wartime food supplies, and completed a Junior Certificate with the British Horticultural Society. He read a biography of Madame Curie and was so impressed and excited by her research that he decided he wanted to be a scientist and 'make discoveries'. From there he began to read introductory books on chemistry and biology. Tante

Anna suggested that because of this interest, he could aim to study at university, and become a 'biological chemist', which in fact he did, in the then emerging field of biochemistry. He started as a lab technician in the Pharmacy Department, then completed the first year of London University's Bachelor of Science degree. The war ended, and in December 1946, when a berth became available, he made his way to Amsterdam and boarded the Dutch carrier *Johan de Witt* for Sydney, along with over 700 other migrants and Jewish refugees.

He'd described the ship to me as a cargo ship, but I've seen the passenger list and there were just too many passengers for it to be a cargo ship. I'd found similar lists when writing my second novel *Provenance*. In the novel there's an important regional train journey that comes to a halt in a flood in northern New South Wales. For that book, I'd needed the expertise of obsessive railway historians who knew about 1960s regional trains. Now for *Raven Mother* I found an avid group of online shipping historians. From their website, I learned that the *Johan de Witt* began life as a luxury passenger liner, then at the outbreak of war had been refitted as a troop carrier at the docks on Sydney's Cockatoo Island in 1940. Around 400 men and women had been employed on the island working on Australian, US, British and ally ships throughout the war. By coincidence Cockatoo Island was one of the stops along my ferry route to high school between Greenwich and Woolwich in the mid-1970s. In the mornings and afternoons I'd be on the ferry with the shipwrights, electricians, carpenters, welders and cutters and marine engineers on their way to or from a shift. The one or two women working on Cockatoo Island were secretaries and tea ladies. It was an unexpected connection to have with my father's journey to Australia.

Once it had been fitted out, the *Johan de Witt* departed Sydney in December 1940 as part of a convoy transporting Australian soldiers to Suez. Now, six years later, it was bringing German,

Austrian, Polish and Hungarian refugees to Australia. The Dutch crew was short-staffed and asked for volunteers to help with meals and housekeeping. Michael took up work in the kitchen, being very well trained from his years at Bunce Court, peeling the many hundreds of potatoes required to feed the passengers and crew each day.

Dad had told me that the Australian newspapers reported that the *Johan de Witt* was full of rich Jews. I decided to check for myself and sure enough in Trove's digital newspaper archive, the *Cairns Post* led on Monday, 17 March 1947, with a front-page headline, 'JEWISH REFUGEES ARRIVE AT SYDNEY WITH RICHES':

> Sydney. Mar. 16 – Seven hundred Jewish refugees who arrived on the Dutch steamer Johan de-Witt today brought hundreds of thousands of pounds of personal belongings including jewels, furs and expensive cameras. Customs officers believe it will take about four days to clear their baggage. Most of the refugees came from European concentration camps.

It is incredible that as late as 1947 a journalist could still claim that concentration-camp survivors possessed valuables, and that readers would believe him. Over 150 of the refugees, including my father, were stateless, and the Jewish refugees were required by Australian law to have a sponsor to gain approval for a visa. The sponsor (in Michael's case, this was Willy) and the Jewish community, not the government, was fully responsible for the reception and integration of Jewish migrants.

Michael had not seen his father since 1936, when he and Bella visited the children at Bunce Court. Twelve years had passed since he left Germany. He returned with Willy to his two-bedroom flat, and met Ruth and Ruth's three-year-old son, his nephew, Leigh, for the first time. His memories of his father are that he was kind

Michael, Ruth and Willy with young Leigh, Elwood, 1947.
Michael with Willy, St Kilda, 1947.

and helpful. Willy helped him enrol in a Bachelor of Science at Melbourne University, which he was able to do with credit for his previous studies, and Michael started on a life in science. Some days he'd go into the city and have lunch with his father in Little Collins Street. Crossing the factory floor, the women making the buttons would glance at him – the boss's son. He found it embarrassing. He and Willy started to get to know each other.

He was just one of 40 million people who'd been displaced during and after the war. People had fled combat, conflict and air raids, the destruction of their homes, persecution, genocide and ethnic cleansing. Women had fled advancing armies fearing rape as well as death, carrying their children if they could. These millions had been joined by ex-prisoners of war, freed slave labourers, concentration-camp survivors. Ten million ethnic Germans were expelled immediately after the war from countries including Poland, Czechoslovakia and Hungary, as well as the million who had settled in these invaded countries during the war. There were hundreds of thousands of lost and orphaned children across Europe. Over 20 000 orphaned 'wolf children' were roaming the woods and swamps of East Prussia and Lithuania. Thousands of children had been stolen from their families, taken by force as part of Nazi labour and 'Germanisation' programs. They were now fending for themselves. In the final weeks of the war, these lost, stolen and orphaned children who had been living amid the ruins in German cities, trekked westward, away from the air raids on crowded roads, or were housed in refugee camps. At the end of 1945, UNESCO calculated that 8 million children were homeless in Germany and that many of these children were alone.

It was only in 1951, six years after the war had ended, that the Refugee Convention created a legal definition for refugees, still used today, along with its 1967 Protocol. The last of the European refugee camps didn't close until 1960, the year I was born.

But by this time, a new war had produced Israel, a nation formed of mostly displaced persons; those who had arrived and those who had fled.

Among those who arrived were the Jews who had come in the Fifth Aliyah, the majority during the 1930s and 1940s. Almost a million more migrated after 1948, some of them expelled from Muslim-majority African and Asian countries in response to the formation of the state of Israel. During the Suez Crisis of 1956–1957, when Britain, France and Israel jointly invaded Egypt, half of the Egyptian Jewish population left through coercion and expulsion, around 25 000 of them migrating to Israel. During Iran's Islamic Revolution of 1979–1980, around 650 000 Iranian Jews fled to Israel. Other migrations were facilitated by Zionist agencies over these years.

The Palestinians who fled during the Nakba of 1948 and the years after, totalled over a million, some settling in new countries such as Australia. Up to 15 000 died in massacres and attacks during the Nakba. Approximately 150 000 remained, and became 'Arab Israeli' citizens, but over 30 000 of them were displaced from their original homes. The Palestinians who had fled, expecting to return to their homes, were not allowed to do so. The Israeli government led by David Ben-Gurion decided that the Palestinian expulsion and the refusal of return was essential for the growth of the new Jewish state. By 1950 around 750 000 Palestinians were living in refugee camps in Syria, Lebanon, the West Bank, the Gaza Strip and Jordan. In 1967, a further 300 000 were forcibly displaced from their homes in Israel. Today a population of almost six million Palestinians live as refugees, decades later.

In the novel *The Book of Disappearance*, Ibtisam Azam's character Alaa lives in modern Jaffa. He asks the ghost of his grandmother:

> 'Should I tread lightly? Was I walking over the corpses of those who had passed through and who were decimated? Was I walking over a land that was made of decomposed bodies? ... All my grandparents had died except for you.'

Reading these words, I think of the streets I walked in Jaffa, and recall being in Germany and the shivery awareness of the dead German Jews and the ghosts of Nazis. Alaa continues silently speaking to his grandmother: 'Do we breathe in the decomposed corpses? What are we going to do with all this sorrow? How can we start anew? What will you do with Palestine?'

What are we going to do with all the sorrow?

Part Two

The Land of Promise

The great heft of history had thrown Bella, Willy, Ruth and Michael continents apart from each other. By 1937, the children had been at Bunce Court for two years, living within their own walnut of history, protected by their teachers from the worst of the news of the persecutions in Europe. War was still two years away. In April 1937, Willy and Bella disembarked at the port of Haifa, arriving with a two-year visa for entry into the British Mandate of Palestine. They joined thousands of other Jewish migrants, the majority arriving as a direct consequence of Nazi persecution and before that, persecution and poverty in Eastern Europe. Like all migrants, they hoped that Palestine would indeed become a safe homeland, or a safe point of departure to America, Britain, etc.

In 1935, the film *The Land of Promise* had been released worldwide. Regarded as the most influential Zionist film ever made, the documentary screened for five weeks straight at The Astor in New York. It also screened across Europe, Britain (an abridged version with a British narrator) and the United States in the months and years that followed. Produced by the Palestine Film Company with American funding, *The Land of Promise* was made to promote investment and settlement in Mandate Palestine by Jews. It was viewed by tens of thousands of Jewish Berliners, and Bella and Willy are highly likely to have seen it. Palestine was presented as a deserted land that had waited eons to be colonised by energetic, even zealous, labour.

Young Jewish men and women are filmed as they hoe fields, tend cattle, eat together at a kibbutz. The industrial and manufacturing developments are emphasised, with men and women shown working with machinery in factories making clothes and soap. On a building site, a young woman catches bricks thrown up to her, wearing only sandals, shirt and shorts. Briefly, there's an old man standing high-up on a building's timber scaffolding. He's white-haired, wiry, his mouth toothless and collapsed as he expertly handles a cement mixer. He's an anomaly among the younger immigrants.

Watching the film, I was reminded of the British government's argument in 1788 for the colonisation of Australia – that because there was no recognisable development of the land by Aboriginal people, it was therefore *terra nullius*, a land belonging to no one. Racism takes many forms, and one was Britain's colonial blindness to First Nations people. (It took more than 200 years for Australian courts to recognise Aboriginal and Torres Strait Islanders' rights to their lands: the principle of *terra nullius* was not legally overturned until 1992.)

Forty minutes into the film, Tel Aviv becomes the subject. The narrator in his august Transatlantic accent says that:

> Tel Aviv, with its more than 100 000 inhabitants, stands in the place that was wilderness twenty-five years ago, sands and cactus, where jackals roamed ... it is a city still expanding, still spreading north and south and east, still changing sandy wastes into busy streets.

Now middle-class, middle-aged people like Bella and Willy are seen wearing European dresses and suits, women dining in sleeveless frocks at restaurants, people enjoying the beach in bathing suits and sunhats. It's easy to slip the figures of my grandparents into these scenes, though when I do so, it's with much unease.

Like all immigrants, Willy and Bella needed to make a new life, starting from scratch. They were just two people attaching themselves to some new hope, or already wedded to one which they might, or might not, make good. They were in their late forties now, as energetic as ever, though Bella's hair had turned completely grey, and Willy was inordinately bothered by the heat. Not until 'six o'clock, still an eternity away, would the cool sea-wind rustle across the mountains of Judaea and make it possible to sit on the roofs, in the shade of soaked linen sheets', wrote Arnold Zweig in 1934 in his political novel, *De Vriendt Goes Home*.

Their closest friends lived in Haifa, while they were based in the growing town of Tel Aviv. Possibly they were excited to be participating in the secular Zionism that Willy had believed in since he was a teenager when he'd discovered that, as a young German Jew facing daily discrimination, he'd be forever dispossessed as a German. Perhaps the couple had been able to put aside the problems in their marriage. Perhaps Bella's infidelity with Walter Strauss had been overshadowed by the violence of the Third Reich, and they rekindled some trust or love or hope for a while. I think of them at this moment as the 'doers' they'd always been. I'm sure that to begin with they felt exhilarated to be among others like them, to be following friends who had already arrived, all of them Jewish, feeling free and safe from persecution, though constantly aware of those that remained. I think about the year 1937, when it seemed that the worst they were fleeing in Germany was street violence and police beatings, murder, arrest and imprisonment, and legal, economic and social prejudice and discrimination. All of that was bad enough. But they and the world were unable to imagine what was to come, let alone the scale of the plans first announced in early 1942 at the Nazis' secret Wannsee Conference, code-named *Die Endlösung der Judenfrage*: The Final Solution of the Jewish Question.

The land called Palestine

Most people, I've discovered, are ignorant of the complex history of this tiny tract of land, even those who claim to have a stake in it. Jerusalem and its environs have been a multi-faith place of significance and worship for over three thousand years. The region has been inhabited since the Neolithic Age, when the first settled farming communities evolved. The name 'Palestine' came into use eons ago, in various forms – Plistu, Pleshet, Pleshteem, Filistin (فلسطين), Falesteen (فلسطين) – when the Judeans returned from exile in Egypt, and the Old Testament was completed. In the seventh century, during the Early Islamic Period, Muslim Arabs conquered Palestine, defeating the Christian Byzantines, and Jerusalem, already a site of Christian pilgrimage, became the third holiest city of Islam.

Visiting the holy sites in the Old City, I was moved to see people from all over the world, speaking a hundred languages, with every kind of skin colour, dress and adornment, a festival of peoples of the world, Christian, Jewish and Muslim, finding deep meaning in this sacred place. Even though I'm an atheist, I felt joy at the awe and solace I saw in the people all around me. But heartwarming moments like these have been fleeting when I think about Palestine and Israel.

It's a land that has been invaded many times, the invaders most often coming from the north through what is now Lebanon. Alexander the Great travelled that route, as did the eleventh-century crusaders in the First Crusade. How exhilarating it must have been to reach the heights of the white chalk cliffs above the Rosh HaNikra Grottoes (Ras an-Nakura) where the mountains and the sea clash, forming underwater caves and channels that stretch 200 metres inland. My cousins Hanna and Katharina and I visited the place in 2015. Standing on the rocks above, I marvelled at what shepherds, Bedouins, pilgrims and conquerors before us had seen – the sky wide, the land falling away, valley upon valley, the sea crashing on the rocks, great swirls of white sea foam washing in from the deep blue of the Mediterranean.

Alexander had led the Macedonian army down the coast to Persian Egypt in 332 BCE, razing the port towns so they couldn't be utilised by the Persian Empire's fleet. He was victorious over the Egyptian forces, capturing the Gaza fortress, which stood near the Great Omari Mosque of Gaza (mostly destroyed by Israeli forces in 2023). European crusaders later invaded the lands of Palestine in 1099, besieging Muslim Jerusalem. During this latter period the majority of the kingdom's inhabitants were Christians, Sunni and Shi'a Muslims, with a small number of Jews and Samaritans.

The mostly peaceful coexistence between Palestinians, Jews, Christians and Bedouins during the rule of the Turkish Ottoman Empire was well and truly over by the 1930s. In 1920 the League of Nations gave Britain and France mandates to administer territories of the defeated Ottoman Empire. Britain received a mandate over Palestine, Iraq and Transjordan; France received Syria and Lebanon. Histories tend to focus on Britain's efforts to negotiate between the Jewish and Palestinian claims to the land and its resources. Less discussed is Britain's and France's focus on their own colonial development in the Levant, and Palestine's critical role as a buffer zone between the Suez Canal and potential offensives from the north via Syria and Lebanon.

The traditions, customs and language of the Arab, Bedouin, Jewish and Christian Palestinians had long predominated throughout the area. The Ottomans had governed the differing religious and ethnic minority groups by employing a mostly 'reconciliatory role' during their four centuries of rule. But during the 1800s the empire was seriously destabilised by internal nationalist movements and external invasions, with frequent conflicts and many wars.

The Ottoman government's response to these challenges was not only suppression of independence movements, however. The Tanzimat (*Tanẓîmât*, meaning reorganisation) period of reform and modernisation (1839–1876) was instituted with the aim of creating 'one Ottoman nation out of many Ottoman subjects' (Raja Shehdah). With Western nations modernising and expanding their spheres of influence, the Ottoman government began to establish legal and social equality for all Ottoman citizens. Education, law and government systems were reformed, and codes of representation and secularisation introduced: secular secondary schooling, for instance was introduced for boys and girls. The *jizya*, an ancient head tax on non-Muslim citizens, was abolished. A universal requirement for military service was introduced, which included non-Muslims. Palestine, as elsewhere in the Empire, partook in these reforms, with the modernisation of its economy, structural changes in land ownership, legal reform, schools, and new local and centralised government administration centres.

By 1913, the Empire had lost most of its European territories during the two years of the Balkan Wars. During World War I, the worst of the Ottoman Empire's aggression undoubtedly came with the genocide of Christian Armenians in Eastern Anatolia (modern-day eastern Türkiye). Afraid that invading Entente alliance forces (Britain, France, Russia) might induce the Armenians to join their forces, the Ottoman army deported and massacred between 670 000 and 1.2 million Armenians.

The religious and ethnic pluralism of the previous centuries became a movement towards the shoring-up of an ethnically homogenous community. This was also the period of the first significant European immigration to the area. And as the first Zionist settlers arrived from Eastern Europe, Palestinian nationalism and Islamic movements came into being.

The Ottoman presence in all its historical complexity was still evident when Bella and Willy arrived during the interwar years, and present in the memories of many of the long-settled Jews, Christians and Palestinians. The Ottomans had invested in major infrastructure such as rail lines from Haifa to Istanbul and southwards to Jordan. Indeed, Haifa's network of railways, ports and oil refineries led to it being a major target of Axis bombing in World War II. The rail network serviced the major ports, Jaffa being the largest, and joined cities from Istanbul in Türkiye all the way south towards the holy Muslim city of Mecca. The railroads were evidence of the last ruling sultan's significant investments and governance. The statuesque limestone clock tower that still stands in Jaffa's town square had only just been built in 1900, in celebration of the twenty-fifth anniversary of Sultan Abdul Hamid II's reign.

Many people were bilingual, speaking their family language and that of their neighbours: the principal languages were Ottoman Turkish, Arabic and Persian. Most Palestinians lived on the land as peasant farmers, craftworkers and artisans. Some were prominent landholders. Beginning in the 1920s a working class began to develop as peasants moved to the towns and cities. Some had been impoverished by loss of land or by competition from Jewish producers, others moved with the aim of joining the growing capitalist economy and participating in the expanding local and export markets. Palestinian women were employed as domestic workers in the homes of British officials, and in Jewish and Palestinian middle-class and elite households (as Jewish women were too, but at higher wages). This movement to the towns and cities increased again in the 1930s as more tenant farmers lost their land.

Land purchase laws had changed considerably from the Ottoman to the British Mandate. The British ended the Ottoman's series of prohibitions and restrictions on non-Muslims – including Jews, Christians and foreigners – purchasing land (then instigating restrictions on Jews in the later years of the Mandate). This led to immediate conflict and Palestinians' awareness of the area's vulnerability to foreign money. Well-organised, internationally funded Jewish organisations now bought land from the varied landholders, though during the 1920s the purchases were still only a tiny proportion of the land, and most were uncultivated tracts bought from absentee *effendis*, the elite who lived elsewhere, such as Lebanon or Türkiye. One series of purchases is often cited as being particularly divisive: a large tract of fertile land in the Jezreel Valley (Marj Ibn Amir) had been bought in the mid-1800s by the Greek Orthodox Sursock family of Beirut. Known as the 'Sursock Purchases', the family then re-sold parcels of the land to the Jewish Colonisation Association between 1901 and 1925. The Palestinian farmers, the *fellahin*, had lived in the north of the Jezreel Valley for centuries, some since the Early Islamic Period of 640–1099. Many were now evicted by the new landowners: between twenty and twenty-five villages were forcibly depopulated following one of the Sursock Purchases. As a result of one of the largest group of purchases, the Jewish Colonisation Association evicted over 1700 families comprising 8790 people. These evictions met with increasing resistance from the displaced *fellahin*. In some instances, villagers refused to leave. The resistance of the village of al-Fula was much discussed in the press, and even in the Ottoman parliament. The *qaimaqam*, the town's district governor, supported the villagers in their fight to overturn the sale, refusing to finalise the transaction. The British administration then brought in armed forces and removed the people.

By the 1930s demand for land was increasing, and land prices rose considerably, with the result that more Palestinians were selling to Jewish buyers. 'The damage these sales caused to Palestinian society,' Benny Morris writes in his history of Palestine, 'was material, psychological, and political,' impoverishing thousands of tenant families and feeding Arab nationalism. Only now did Arab identity take on a religious aspect in direct conflict with Judaism, with the conflict linked to religious sites, values and symbols.

Every time I delved into the history, I'd see – as many before me have too – the thousand instances when a different narrative could have emerged. A shared land of coexistence could have been possible, but the historical collision of Western imperialism and German Nazism beat down that possibility. Raja Shehadeh, lawyer, writer and historian, has argued in his 2010 book, *A Rift in Time: Travels with my Ottoman uncle*, that while the earlier Ottoman regime needed reform, 'it was a multi-ethnic system that never attempted to colonise the land', and that this had been a precious virtue of the Ottoman system for over 400 years.

Aliyah

The pre- and post-1930 waves of Jewish migration to Palestine from the late 1800s onwards are known by the word 'Aliyah', a Hebrew expression whose literal meaning is to rise or go up. The word indicates the series of unique migrations that came to be individually numbered, beginning with the 'First Aliyah' of 1882. There's also a personal invocation for the term now: to '*make* Aliyah' which carries more of the Biblical sense of the word, of return. It's not a word I ever heard my father or aunt use, and my guess is that Willy didn't use it either, though he and Bella were part of the Fifth Aliyah. The last one was Aliyah Bet, the groups who immigrated illegally between 1920 and 1948. (In 1950, the Israeli parliament passed the *Law of Return*, which gives diaspora Jews, their children and grandchildren the right to move to Israel and become citizens; a law which has contributed to the massive growth in the settler population that has displaced Palestinians within Israel and has grown to 10 per cent of the Israeli population.)

Jews arriving during these Aliyahs came from many countries and communities. They were religious, secular, socialist and capitalist; Mizrahi (from the Levant), Sephardim (Iberia) and Ashkenazi (Europe). There were ideological and cultural clashes with the established religious communities that lived principally in the Jewish holy towns of Jerusalem, Hebron, Safed and Tiberias, who opposed the formation of a political state in the Land of Israel.

There was no unified religious, ideological or cultural voice, and discord within and between these communities was constant. There were fundamental differences between the Jews who felt themselves forced to immigrate for their own safety, and the committed Zionists, often younger and wholly devoted to beginning a new life in Palestine. These were the secular Zionists who were eager to create a Jewish homeland, an idea my grandparents, to greater or lesser degrees, supported. Who knows, perhaps they thought well of Bit Shalom, a political association formed in 1926 that sought 'to pave the way for understanding between Jews and Arabs for forms of common life in the Land of Israel on the basis of complete equality of the political rights of both nations ...'.

Among the kibbutzim were the strong, outdoorsy Jews that Amos Oz had aspired to become as a young man, in rejection of the pale, dispirited folk he portrays having grown up among. There were also the socialists, who had studied modern Hebrew as part of their pre-immigration agricultural training, including the post-revolution Russian socialists who 'came to this land to build and to be rebuilt in it', as a popular song explained it. The 'new Jews' were being made from the old diaspora Jews.

The Jewish labour organisation the Histadrut aggressively promoted a 'Hebrew [only] labour' policy, which impacted the wages Palestinians earned, but also made cheaper Palestinian labour more attractive. By aligning with Zionist organisations, the Histadrut was sometimes able to subsidise Jewish wages to undercut the typically lower wages that Palestinians worked for. The Histadrut's goal was to facilitate and organise Jewish settlement in Palestine by funding land purchases, infrastructure development, coordinating the establishment of farm cooperatives and campaigning for 'Hebrew labour'. Even so, it worked at points to support a Palestinian Jewish workers' unity in which labour was more definitive than ethnicity or religion – but this aim was ultimately undermined by nationalists from both sides.

Up until the 1930s there'd been widespread intermingling in Palestinian and Jewish communities, businesses, homes, public spaces, shops and on the roads, and a shared knowledge of each other's languages. The German writer Arnold Zweig lived in Palestine for several years; his political murder mystery *De Vriendt Goes Home* (1934), expresses just a fraction of the intense commingling of communities and the fractured politics within and between them. As one reviewer commented about this pluralism, 'Enthusiasts of all parties will not like the novel, neither English nor Arab, nor those among the hosts of Zion. It will be attacked in Israel. But it will be read.' My own secondhand copy certainly seemed well-read when I first bought it, and the book had been reviewed even in Australia. Did my grandparents or their friends read it, talk about it? Quite possibly.

As the Jewish population increased by the tens of thousands, Palestinian communities struggled against the rapid changes to their lands. Zweig draws on these seismic shifts and the many players to build his comic-tragic story. Misunderstanding and distrust pervade everyone's interactions.

As in Zweig's novel, Palestine during the 1930s was populated by Arabs, Persians and Turks from the professional, intellectual and political urban classes. Many of these Palestinians and expatriate professionals came from notable families that had held positions within the former Ottoman bureaucracy. Some had professional and familial connections to families in Lebanon and Syria. Among the political groups advocating for Arab sovereignty in Palestine were men who had studied at European, British and American universities and were in favour of western forms of constitutional government and values such as individual virtue and the right to self-determination. From the Arab peasants and working classes to the wealthy, there was a growing national consciousness. This was the inevitable response to the dissolution of the Ottoman Empire, the presence of colonialist Britain, the land dispossessions, increasing

Jewish migration, and Zionist campaigns for a Jewish homeland.

Ethnically, the Jewish community was diverse. Ashkenazi Jews from Central and Eastern Europe made up the majority of the pre-1948 settlers, along with indigenous Mizrahi Jews and Mizrahi Jews who had migrated prior to World War II from Yemen, Iraq, Iran and Syria. (Roughly half of the 680 000 immigrants who entered Israel between 1948 and 1951 were Mizrahi Jews originating from these neighbouring Arab states, forced to evacuate their communities due to the Nakba antagonising governments and populations in these Muslim-majority countries.) There were Maghreb Jews from North Africa, and Sephardic Jews, some of whom had settled in Palestine during the 1800s; and peasant Yemenite Jews who had voluntarily left Yemen (a predominantly Muslim country, and formerly part of the Ottoman Empire) in the late 1800s, wanting to settle in the 'Holy Land' for religious reasons and hoped-for economic prosperity. Yemeni Jews continued to flee persecution; with the 1947 United Nations vote to create the state of Israel, rioting and pogroms by Yemeni Muslims led to the exodus of some 50 000 Yemeni Jews to Israel.

These diverse communities didn't share a singular idea of what the future for the country should hold. Zionists were one faction among others, and Zionism was not the dominant ideology in the 1930s. There were tensions between the ethnicities, and the differing religious practices, along with different dress, food and marriage traditions, etc. The Ashkenazi and Sephardic Jews, with their European and Iberian ancestries, were suspicious of the Arab ethnicity of the Mizrahi Jews. Tragically, Jewishness was being progressively dissociated from Arabness, erasing a long history of accord and cohabitation in the Levant.

Palestinian Arab communities were fractured in their analyses of how to respond, but their leaders fundamentally rejected the notion that the land was not theirs and ought to be given up to another people seeking a homeland. Edward Said described this period as a 'contest between an affirmation and a denial'. For Britain, both the Jews demanding a new homeland and the Palestinian Arabs demanding their existing homeland be acknowledged were an unwelcome and persistent problem. Britain, France and Italy all competed to maintain or establish their imperialistic presence in the Middle East.

The Balfour Declaration of 1917 had announced Britain's support for the establishment of a 'national home for the Jewish people', along with the safeguarding of the civil and religious rights of Palestinian Arabs. It was 'well-intentioned' insofar as it sought to safeguard Jewish people, but politically opportunistic, and didn't recognise the longevity of Palestinian Arabs in the region. Its impacts are still present today in the continuing conflict and annihilation of Gaza, more than one hundred years later. It was written during World War I, when the Allies were eager to carve up the Ottoman Empire and were considering what they could secure of the Ottomans' resource-rich territories. The case of Palestine was unique because the goal of the Declaration was to state the conditions for the establishment of a Jewish homeland. Though it also set out that 'nothing shall be done which may prejudice the civil and religious rights of existing non-Jewish communities in Palestine', the Mandate document and the actions of the British during their rule discriminated against Palestinian Arabs.

The Declaration was vehemently opposed by the Arab leadership as a violation of international law: it was not an agreement between states, as is required of a treaty, and introduced the term 'national home', which had no precedent in international law. All the subsequent commissions, conferences and delegations of Arab, Zionist, British and other League of Nations representatives failed to reach any agreement on how to divide the Mandate between Palestinians and Jews. The essence of the Palestinian objection was constructed on the basis of possession and history: that Palestinians had lived and thrived in Palestine *before* Zionism and modern

Jewish immigration and therefore a new people could not declare it their homeland. But the Palestinians could not halt the influx of Jewish immigrants, nor deny Jewish history in the region or Jewish need for a safe homeland. The Arab coalition rejected the various proposals for partition and were out-manoeuvred by other alliances driven by national interests. Joseph Stalin, for instance, envisaged opportunities arising from a pro-Zionist policy and reversed Russia's pro-Palestine stance. The two decades of discussion following the unsatisfactory Balfour Declaration, and the many commissions of review and planning, led only to trenchant disagreement. In the words of American Palestinian academic Rashid Khalidi, 'The "Israeli" and "Palestinian" nations came into being simultaneously, and in conflict.'

*

Could it ever have been otherwise? Like many other Jews and Arabs in the 1920s and 1930s, Bella and Willy quite possibly also hoped for a shared Palestinian and Jewish state based on fair land distribution, living wages, and mutual respect and safety. The brutal events that ensued, and which continue today, prove how naïve this hope was. My father no longer supports Israel in the unilateral way he did in previous years, when for me to raise any objection would lead to an argument. Not for us now, the hideous luxury of righteousness.

When Bella worked to help get refugee children off the illegal boats and onto the safe dry land of Palestine, or when she was in Cairo during the war, working with the Auxiliary Territorial Service (ATS) to protect Palestine from a potential Axis invasion, was she thinking of how it might impact the Palestinians in years to come? Perhaps, in the margins of her thoughts, the far margins. It is more likely though, that she simply didn't consider the impact of a new state on Palestinian people, or if she did, perhaps she thought that the needs of Palestinians were secondary to the needs of the Jewish refugees fleeing fascism and antisemitism.

In my effort to see Bella in the British Mandate of Palestine during the decade she lived there, the invitation to minimise the Palestinian Arab presence around her is there. For Jewish people who support the State of Israel categorically, the horror of the Holocaust acts like a tabula rasa or a ground zero. It refuses acknowledgement that the foundation of the State of Israel presented Arab Palestinians with a terrifying and, in places, genocidal situation. Absolutism was born out of the unique horror of the Holocaust.

al-Thawra al-Kubra

Known by Palestinians as *al-Thawra al-Kubra*, the Great Revolt; by the British as the Arab Revolt; and in Israel (in Hebrew) as the Events or Riots of 1936–1939, the insurrection began in 1936 and continued for three years. The Palestinian leadership's initial goal had been to shift British policy on Jewish immigration, to contain it, and to ensure the indigenous Palestinian Arabs remained the majority population. The strikes, protests and violence were mostly directed at the British administration and the huge scale of Jewish immigration, but Jews were also attacked. The British increased their garrisons from two to twenty-two. They seized schools for barracks and garrisons. The country was being inundated with British military. Curfews and pass laws for Palestinians were widespread from the autumn of 1938 along with a ban on vehicle use. The British controlled Palestinians' movements on roads and in and out of villages and towns, with travel to work routes restricted. From that came labour shortages and then vegetable and food shortages for all. The non-Palestinian population was impacted by the rebellion even when it wasn't the target. To begin with there was widespread community support for the Palestinians. This intimidation of the whole Palestinian population eventually succeeded in its aim of eroding what had been bipartisan community support, and the rebellion came to an unsettled end in December 1939. The revolt brought about a new Jewish paramilitary group, the Irgun, which began to bomb Palestinian crowds and buses, killing dozens indiscriminately. Some Palestinian nationalists retaliated, and in Benny Morris's words, it became 'something of a "tradition"'. Over the decades marketplaces, bus stations, movie theatres, and other public buildings have become routine targets.

Bella and Willy would have called it *die Arabische Revolte*. My father believes his parents should have brought him with them to Palestine in 1937. In hindsight, given how very hurt he was by the separation, it would have been best to take him, whatever the circumstances. But aside from the risk of bombings and civil unrest, his parents were middle-class aspirational people who wanted their children to be safe and to receive a progressive education.

Willy and Bella had found a two-bedroom apartment to rent in Syrken Street, Tel Aviv. The Syrken Street apartment remained Bella's home throughout her ten years in the city. It's there still, a modest example of the Bauhaus style of the two- and three-storey apartment buildings that were being rapidly built during those years. When I sought it out, I noticed that the dusty, thick-trunked shrubs at the front gate were old enough to have been young plants when Bella lived there. The low metal gate was most certainly the same gate she would have opened and shut each day. Like many Tel Aviv apartment blocks, the building's entry was via an open-air vestibule. Leaves and grit were gathered on the tiled floor. A concrete path led down the side of the building to the back where there were some washing lines, which Bella would have used to hang her clothes out to dry. The apartments had good sized windows. She'd have had sunlight and breezes, and the building wouldn't have been so dissimilar to those in Berlin; though unlike her former homes, it was newly built and sunny.

I walked down from Syrken Street to the beach, buying a fresh pomegranate juice from one of the carts along the way. Now that I've read histories by Palestinians who were displaced, or by their children, I consider myself very fortunate to have wandered the area freely and seen her former home.

In her book *In My Mother's Footsteps*, Mona Hajjar Halaby describes growing up hearing her mother's stories of her former life in Jerusalem and the home she'd fled in 1948 (first to Cairo then to Geneva): 'stories so robust that listening to them was like inhaling the perfume of an orange the moment you punctured its rind'. In the early 2000s, after a number of trips to Jerusalem, and with the help of George, an Armenian Israeli social historian who was also her translator (Hebrew to English), Halaby at last found her mother's West Jerusalem house and spoke with one of the current owners. During that meeting she experienced the erasure that I was noticing in the histories I was reading: the insistence that before Jewish people came, the land was barren. The owner tells Halaby, 'We heard that this house was so neglected. And it was a desert all around here, and there were no houses. It was like farmland.' Halaby wants to speak out about the families that lived there, their many neighbours, the festivities, the full lives they lived, but feels constrained because the woman had graciously invited them into the house. She mentions to the woman only that the place had not been a desert: 'My mother had an almond tree, a mulberry tree, and apricot tree in the front garden, and pots of jasmine, mint, and basil on the back porch off the kitchen door.' The visit is bittersweet, and she finishes this part of the account with a response to Israel's first prime minister, David Ben-Gurion, who is reputed to have said, 'The old will die and the young will forget.' Walking away from her mother's former home she rejects this, and thinks, 'forgiving is doable, but forgetting is unthinkable'.

Poking around Bella's former home in Syrken Street I wondered who had moved into my grandparents' Berlin apartment. What happened to the belongings they had left behind? Perhaps their furniture was used as fuel in the hard winters that followed. Homes left empty by the fleeing (or massacred) Palestinians during the Nakba became homes for Jewish settlers and camp survivors. Palestinian families left believing that once the political unrest subsided, they'd return. Very few were able to. Ben-Gurion noted in his diary that the foresaken houses had provided accommodation for some 110 000 people:

> 75 000 went to Haifa, Jaffa, Jerusalem and Zefat; 16 000 to Ramleh, Lydda and Acre; 13 000 took over houses and began working in the abandoned villages; 5800 settled abandoned villages and set to working the land.

Most of the 1948–1949 immigrants were survivors of concentration camps, arriving in a new state that had not been able to make sufficient preparations for them. Many of these Holocaust survivors sought out the vacant homes and villages themselves. Often, however, they were following the path of Jewish paramilitary forces such as the Haganah and, after May 1948, IDF (Israel Defense Forces) soldiers who searched homes and waged battles with Palestinian resistance fighters. The Jewish refugees would then move into a home after the paramilitary had evicted the Palestinian family. Some were provided with furniture and household goods that had been 'confiscated' from Palestinian homes and businesses. It is a terrible irony that people who had been dispossessed, deported and enslaved in camps, were now taking the homes of others who had fled or died attempting to hold on to their homeland.

What can be done with this knowledge? What I do, in this small way here, is retell it. The poet Mourid Barghouti writes in *I Saw Ramallah*, 'But I do know that the stranger can never go back to what he was. Even if he returns. It is over. A person gets displacement ... and there is no cure.' The book is his memoir of returning to Ramallah thirty years after leaving as a young man in 1966 to study in Cairo. He'd left his home expecting to return, but was not allowed to after the 1967 war.

I didn't yet know this history as I wandered around Bella's Tel Aviv home. I was focused on establishing my own faint connection to her past. Leaving, I walked up along the narrow footpath to the corner, where I hailed a taxi. As usual, the driver asked what had brought me to Israel, and as usual I told him that my grandmother had lived in Tel Aviv for many years. He swept his hand before us, telling me, 'When your grandmother lived here, all this was sand, only a few roads.' I tried to imagine my father as a boy, if he were to have lived in that Tel Aviv, walking over the sands to a Hebrew language school. I thought about how he'd said he'd have preferred that to living far from his family in England. The driver probably didn't know that when Bella lived in Syrken Street, the nearby Palestinian village of Al Mas'udiyya (Summayl) had shared the same sands. Quite possibly the local children, Jewish and Palestinian, had played together (or perhaps that's me having a moment of magical thinking). The village was home to over 800 residents, much larger than the few dozen who were recorded living there in the mid-1800s. Their houses were stone-built, and there was an Ottoman secondary school, workshops, gardens and stores. The residents of this village fled on 25 December 1947, under threats from the Haganah, one of the paramilitary Zionist organisations responsible for dozens of massacres and the destruction of 500 villages during the Nakba. Today just one house still stands in the Al Mas'udiyya (Summayl) village, the former home of a man called Muhammad Baydas and his family.

Many Israelis do not know these local Palestinian histories, nor could they point to the many sites that have been razed, rebuilt and renamed. The knowledge is hidden from them, and many don't want to know. It was in the early days of my research that I read *Young Tel Aviv* by historian Anat Helman. It was then I realised just how little Palestinian history was included in Israel's histories – even vivid, well-researched works such as this one. I searched other texts and found the same problem of erasure and absence. In *Young Tel Aviv* there was no mention of these villages, but of Palestinians ('Arabs') living on the vague outskirts, or working as peddlers or sitting outside their 'primitive' stalls, as if they had inhabited only Jaffa to the south.

*

In one of the few letters that Ruth kept, Bella mentions in passing that the 'Arabs are often discriminated against'. During a time when the Palestinians were being increasingly marginalised, Bella had at least noticed. By pointing this out, she was like some other Germans whom she knew, such as Anna Essinger, Bunce Court's founder and director. Anna Essinger wrote to my father, her former pupil, in January 1948 when he was living in postwar Melbourne, just a few months after the bloody British-mandated partition of India and Pakistan in August of 1947. During the days and weeks of Partition, people were forced from their homes of many generations; neighbours became enemies. Millions of Hindus, Muslims and Sikhs were killed, mutilated, wounded, raped, displaced. At the same time, violence, street fights, raids on Palestinian villages and massacres were taking place in Mandate Palestine as the British withdrew and the day of independence drew near. Anna Essinger wrote to my father, 'I wish there was another Gandhi for Palestine. I am so uncertain of the outcome of the partition, and one cannot see the end of it unless some spiritual leader arises.' I've held on to Bella's observation of discrimination against Palestinians, her tiny sliver of a 'Gandhi' moment, for all it's worth since first reading it among my cousin Lisa's mementos.

Arrivals, departures and the Palestinian No

The original plan had been for the whole family to live in Palestine once the children had finished their schooling; that is, if they received the necessary approvals. By the time Willy and Bella got the certificate to immigrate to Palestine, the *al-Thawra al-Kubra*, against the British administration had begun. They went to Palestine alone while Michael and Ruth continued their studies at Bunce Court school: studying in a progressive environment, speaking English, living in country Kent, far from the pogroms in Germany and violence in Palestine. Willy could still afford to pay the annual fee to the school. They wrote to the children regularly (sadly, only one or two of these letters were kept).

But much went wrong for them in Palestine. Their marriage was struggling, and Willy couldn't get a business going. Neither of them was the kibbutzim type; many kibbutz residents had trained in agricultural work, were mostly young, frequently socialist, and were mostly Eastern European Jews. Willy and Bella were like most German Jews in British Mandate Palestine: professionals, struggling with the Hebrew language, older.

*

With persecutions and pogroms increasing in Germany following the extreme violence of *Kristallnacht* in November 1938, which caught the attention of world media and progressive politicians and humanitarian organisations, the first Kindertransport children began to arrive in England in December 1938. Some of these children were sent to live and study at Bunce Court school, substantially increasing the numbers of children enrolled there. The Kindertransport evacuation was the initiative of a broad delegation working on behalf of refugees, comprising Jewish groups, as well as Quakers and others. Anna Essinger was tasked by the government with setting up the reception camp for the 10 000 children who arrived over the nine months before the commencement of war. In Germany, delegates prioritised children most in peril, including teenagers who were in concentration camps or in danger of arrest, or were threatened with deportation, children in Jewish orphanages, and children with a parent in a camp. With support from the government and the BBC, the Refugee Children's Movement made public requests for families to take in the children. The British action was soon followed by similar Kindertransports to the Netherlands, and other countries. Australia took 37 German and Polish children and teenagers in 1939. To begin with, many believed that the children would later return to their families and homes.

Ruth finished her schooling in September 1938, earning a School Certificate, and joined her parents in Tel Aviv. Five years younger, Michael was just starting secondary school. Ruth's absence from Bunce Court seems to have made little difference to him. She hadn't been an attentive older sister.

Even so, my father thrived at the school and has many vivid recollections of the friends he made, the lessons, the musical ensembles and choirs the children and teachers performed in, the kindness of his teachers. His first girlfriend was another student, Peppi Ungar, originally from Danzig, and decades later my parents visited Peppi and her husband at their home in Israel on the coast near Haifa.

But all the while, he insists he didn't ever receive any affection or love, that he missed out on the love of a mother. But, I ask him, what of the other children? They too were separated from their parents. He had lived apart from the other young children for the first three years, and it's this experience of the double isolation and abandonment that shaped this feeling of being unloved. When I ask him whether Tante Paula had been affectionate towards him, he dismisses her as just a nurse, not someone who knew how to show affection. I do and don't believe him, though I can see this is his *felt* knowledge: he felt unloved. This is what he was left with.

While I have been finishing this book, thousands have died in Gaza, thousands of children have been orphaned. With every line I write about 'then', of my father's story and his family history, I think sickeningly of 'now' and the suffering that's being endured, and the generations of suffering to come. Dad and I have talked about it, how traumatic it is to understand the suffering of others, to be able to do nothing to stop it, to feel the shame, a new shame that he most certainly never expected to be feeling in his nineties.

*

When Ruth arrived in Tel Aviv, she found her parents both very busy, and 'out quite a lot. Exactly what they did I do not know.' She describes Bella's work as:

> finding accommodation for refugees from Germany who had entered Palestine illegally since the British were restricting Jewish immigration to appease the Arabs. The Jewish refugees who arrived on ships from Cyprus had to run a British blockade and were met by little ships which took them ashore.

These refugees were part of the Aliyah Bet migration, those fleeing Europe without papers and trying to get through the British blockades. Once they reached land, they'd receive assistance from the clandestine local organisations Bella was working with. I've done a few spot checks of Bella's address book to correlate names with those of known activist women and organisers. One page includes details for Zessi Rosenblüth, a significant social work leader in Mandate Palestine, and a member of the Jewish–Palestinian peace association Brit Shalom. Possibly Bella knew other social workers in Tel Aviv and Jerusalem. The refugee organisation she worked with may have been Mossad l'Aliyah Bet, but there is no record of her name in its archives. Many of the women involved went unrecorded unless the individual had significant seniority.

Ruth's recollections of Willy's work are even vaguer: 'I believe my father tried various business enterprises to make some money, but in this he did not succeed.' I've asked my father what he remembers from Willy about his business efforts, but Willy's months in Palestine weren't something that he talked about with his son.

In mid-June 1938 Willy applied for the family to immigrate to Australia after an application to the USA was rejected. A German friend had landed in Melbourne, and had reassured Willy there were business opportunities. According to Ruth, 'despite being an ardent Zionist, he had to look elsewhere to settle'. Details are sketchy, only that he had met 'a Mr Patkin from Melbourne' who suggested he go to Australia and was willing to 'guarantee him and help him to get a Landing Permit'.

My grandfather wasn't the only immigrant to want to leave; there was much movement into and out of the territory as Jews tried to find a country they felt they could survive or, ideally, thrive in. The hardships of living in Palestine were significant. There were food shortages, lack of infrastructure such as roads, hospitals, schools, footpaths and public transport. Social welfare was provided by private organisations in lieu of a state-based system. Wages were low, to say nothing of the ongoing conflict between the British forces and the Palestinian resistance.

Ruth described herself as missing her school friends, of being alone and bored much of the day. She'd long forgotten the Hebrew she'd learned at school in her last two years in Germany, and this limited who she could talk with. Bella enrolled her in a secretarial course, which Ruth hated. She learned to cook the evening meals, with Bella setting out a recipe for Ruth to follow. 'Mutti's method of teaching me how to cook was to give me the recipe and explain what to do then [leave] me to it. At meal time she would give her appraisal of my efforts. We cooked on kerosene stoves, I presume because the block of flats was not connected to gas.' She describes an accidental fire, and Bella's all's-well-that-ends-well amusement:

> One day I must have let too much kerosene on to the stove and it caught alight, I alerted the neighbours who called the fire brigade. There was not much damage apart from a very blackened kitchen and a frightened Ruth. My mother took it rather well, in fact she laughed at the sight of me.

It's one of my treasured images of Bella, of her laughingly shrugging off the filthy kitchen and the worried, grimy daughter, sooty and dishevelled from the fire.

*

In January 1939, four months after Ruth's arrival, Willy left for Australia aboard the *Strathallan*, arriving as a stateless person in February 1939. The revised plan had been for the family to migrate together, and for Michael to go to a local school in Melbourne. The Australian documents arrived, but as Ruth explained, 'for some reason one was issued for my father, mother and brother with a separate one for me. This meant that on arrival in Melbourne Vati had to surrender his permit and apply for another one for Mutti and Micha.'

Dad concedes there was a problem with the landing papers; each member of the family should have had an individual certificate, but didn't. At other times he says that Bella didn't want to leave Palestine. More recently, he's conjectured that Willy didn't want her to follow him. Maybe there's a grain of truth in all these stories.

A strange fact of my father's recollections is that while he has had possession of Ruth's short autobiography for some years, and he'd spoken to Willy during those years, key facts did not 'sink in'. A traumatic experience can resist new information ferociously well. We know that is true of societies, and for individuals. Though my father has softened and shifted in his thinking, the fundamental experience of being suddenly left at Bunce Court and then feeling abandoned for the duration of the war shaped everything he knows and feels about Bella. Even now, he is suspicious of the immigration permit errors that Willy had to deal with. Just the other day, which is to say in the past couple of years (2023 or 2024) he said again that Bella 'wanted to stay in Tel Aviv and live her own life without having to look after me'.

'Late in April 1939,' wrote Ruth, 'Bella said she thought that there might be a war soon.' Bella didn't want Ruth to delay leaving, Ruth wrote, because 'my Landing Permit for Australia would expire on 17 August and my Certificate of Identity on 31 July'. Bella told Ruth 'that it would be wise if [she] went to join Vati now, rather than wait until her and Micha's Landing Permits arrived'. What strikes me about Bella in each of these brief glimpses is how pragmatic and decisive she was.

Mother and daughter drove to the Jerusalem consulate for the visa documents 'in a hired car with other passengers ... very fast to avoid getting shot at by Arabs from the roadside'. Ruth had wanted to see the Old City while they were there, but 'Mutti said it was too dangerous'. The situation in and around Jerusalem *was* more dangerous than in Tel Aviv, for both Palestinians and Jews. Tel Aviv was a site of some violence, but in the main, the British forces were targeting Palestinians in their farms, villages and the towns north and west of Tel Aviv and Jaffa. Palestinian violence towards Jewish migrants more often took place around Jerusalem than Tel Aviv.

They had shared seven months together, then Ruth boarded the train for Port Said and the boat to Australia. She arrived in Australia on the *Maloja* in May 1939.

Looking back, Ruth said that 'Mutti and I had not become very close, the time was too short and she was also preoccupied with other things. Hence I do not remember being upset at leaving her.' Perhaps for both, these separations were now normal; they were just two Jews among hundreds of thousands on the move.

Bella warned Ruth to not go out alone in Port Said 'because there was White Slave traffic and it was a very dangerous place for young girls'. Port Said was known for its friendly guides who'd approach unwary male travellers at the port and lead them down increasingly dark streets to brothels run by madams who were 'bold, betrimmed Jezebels of Austrian, Russian, Greek and French origin'.

How worried was Bella about sending Ruth on this long journey to Australia on her own? Her warning wasn't unfounded, though it's unlikely that she had any specific worry about the Jewish slavers and enslaved women who had been Bertha Pappenheim's focus.

With the opening of the Suez Canal in 1869, Port Said had become an international centre of 'flows of people, goods and ships', which included prostitution and the sex-trafficking of abducted girls and women. Since 1910 there had been international scrutiny and indignation over 'white slavery', so much so that the League of Nations had voted for the International Convention for the Suppression of the White Slave Traffic treaty (1910), and then the more inclusive 1926 Slavery Convention.

Ruth says that she *did* go out that night in Port Said and safely boarded the RMS *Maloja* the next day.

Bella remained in Tel Aviv, waiting for the necessary immigration papers for herself and Michael to arrive. I don't know what she lived on; presumably Willy sent her funds, though possibly not much because she'd complained to Ruth that he was a 'miser'. She was forty-seven years of age, highly trained and experienced, so it's possible she also had some paid employment. Older than most, but still of working age.

*

As the situation in Europe for Jews worsened, more applied to enter Palestine, or made their way over without permits. Hundreds of Aliyah Bet immigrants drowned at sea. Some were returned to the cities they'd fled. Between 1946 and 1949 well over 50 000 Jews were deported from Palestine and held in detention camps in Cyprus, or were intercepted on their way to Palestine. People who reached land but were caught without legal documentation were deported. A few thousand came overland through countries that directly bordered Palestine, such as Syria and Lebanon. There was also extensive undocumented entry by Syrian Arabs and Bedouins from the British Protectorate of the Emirate of Transjordan (established by the League of Nations in 1921; now Jordan). The Bedouins' livelihoods, which included pastoral work, had been disrupted by the British. They needed to work on farms during harvest months. British Mandate officials 'viewed labour migration with suspicion and actively tried to discourage it'. Iranian and Iraqi Jews fleeing persecution by ultra-nationalist groups and the state were also entering overland, but the British, hell-bent on restricting incoming Jews to enforce the quota, were unsympathetic to these Mizrahi Jews' claims of persecution.

Thus, there were tens of thousands of undocumented people entering Palestine, who, along with certified migrants, needed the assistance of residents with humanitarian skills such as Bella's and those of other women who'd trained in progressive education, social work and much-needed humanitarian skills.

World War II

Just as Bella and most of Europe had feared, in September 1939 the war began. Ruth had safely arrived in Australia and Michael was safe at school in the English countryside: though like other schools, the school evacuated from Kent, near the east coast, to the west, at Trench Hall in Shropshire, out of the flight path of the Luftwaffe bombers.

The outbreak of war sealed Michael's fate: there were few berths to be found for Bella to travel from Haifa to England to collect him and then bring him to Palestine or Melbourne, where his father and sister were waiting. As the war continued, there were no safe transits anymore.

In June 1940, Italy joined the Axis war front. Britain and France had a significant presence in the Middle East; Italy wanted dominion as well. Palestine, became a target. Trade was disrupted, the citrus export market was threatened, and unemployment rose. The city of Haifa began preparations to defend itself from military attack, including building bomb shelters. Within weeks, Italian war planes were making raids on Haifa's port, oil terminal and refinery. The Haifa district was populated with over fifty Palestinian villages and Bedouin camps, plus Jewish settlers, a total population of around 200 000 at this time. For two months the city was repeatedly bombed by Italian forces, with many Palestinian, Jewish and British civilians killed.

Bella was, I imagine, calm, maybe resigned, amid these threats.

She'd known war and civil violence through much of her life. She'd worked with child and adult survivors during World War I, had worked and lived in East Prussia after the devastating Russian invasion of 1914. In Berlin she'd witnessed violent street attacks and knew of murders by Nazis.

Then one afternoon in September 1940, Tel Aviv was unexpectedly bombed in an Italian raid. The town hadn't been fearful, the military hadn't regarded it as a potential target and so didn't have any air raid warning systems or bomb shelters prepared. One hundred and thirty-seven people died, including over fifty children and the elderly residents of a nursing home. These first bombs fell in Bograshov and Trumpeldor streets, half a kilometre from Bella's flat.

Reading about the bombings for the first time, I wondered how much Willy and Ruth had known about them. Had they worried that Bella might have been injured or the apartment damaged? The raids were extensively reported in Australian papers, especially the regional papers from the hundreds of small towns that had sent so many of their young men to the distant war in Europe and the Middle East. Willy and Ruth would have known of the bombing from reports in the Melbourne papers and the *Australian Jewish Herald*. Did Bella send a telegram to reassure them she was unhurt?

A few kilometres away, the Palestinian village of Al-Mas'udiyya, home to over 700 residents (now the site of Ramat Aviv), was also hit. Seven people died there, including five children, and one Australian soldier. Tel Aviv didn't have adequate medical facilities, and Australian soldiers, along with residents, drove the dozens of wounded adults and children to Jerusalem. By mid-1941, 500 bomb shelters had been built in Tel Aviv. Haifa was still a target and was bombed many times over the next two years. Tel Aviv, Acre and Jaffa were also bombed again. These air raids made the threat of a ground invasion ever-present.

Egypt and Syria were both sites of intense conflict during

the war. The Italian fascist Radio Bari had been broadcasting propaganda in Arabic through the Middle East and North Africa since 1934. It had distributed radios at reduced prices in Libya and countries under British and French control, including Palestine, Egypt, Tunisia, Algeria, Syria, Lebanon and Morocco. Once war began, Radio Bari's focus was to reignite anti-British sentiment among Palestinians. But Italy's actions were unsubtle, and in Libya large-scale Italian settlements were displacing the Arab population and creating anti-Italian resistance.

Everyone in the coastal Palestinian cities understood a war was underway, and those living nearer to the heavily guarded Syrian and Lebanese borders in the north understood the threat of invasion by Axis forces. But despite the tensions and hostility between many Palestinians and Jews before World War II, and the Italian propaganda efforts, during and after the air raids there was a practical solidarity between the Palestinian, Jewish and Christian communities. It was to last only as long as the war continued.

*

A ground invasion was a very present threat to all the Palestinian communities. When the British war cabinet withdrew its policy of not allowing Palestinians to be armed, the Jewish Council of Women's Organizations successfully lobbied for a Palestinian women's corps, based on Britain's Auxiliary Territorial Service. In January 1942 the *Australian Jewish Herald* headlined its front page with the words 'Dramatic Scenes'. A public Recruiting Week had been launched in Tel Aviv that month, and Bella was among the first sixty-two women enlisted, with the rank of corporal. A small group of sixty women, including Bella, left for Cairo to be trained as officers and NCOs for the ATS. In February the *Australian Jewish Herald* characterised the Jewish ATS women as both assertive and self-sacrificing:

> In spite of the heavy burden which the Jewish women in Palestine have been carrying since the beginning of the war in their assistance to the war effort ... they are not content only with their work in passive defence but want to be organised for active war service within the army in the fields in which women are able to give expert service.

By the time I read that old newspaper article, I knew enough about Bella's life to think: yes, that's my grandmother through and through.

More than 3600 Jewish women from Palestine volunteered to serve in the British armed forces in the Middle East during the war. Many others were not willing or able to leave employment, families and their children for the army. A few in the ATS were Christian and Palestinian, but organisers viewed the ATS as a Jewish nation-building effort and resisted it becoming a bipartisan defence force.

To begin with, seventy-five recruits, including Bella, were based 'at the front' in Egypt, driving military vehicles, working as technicians, in military hospitals, offices and military storerooms. I have a bundle of photographs from Bella's ATS years in Egypt. What I notice in the images, most of them tiny two-by-three-inch snapshots, black and white but quite crisp in their tones, is how confident and purposeful she and her colleagues are. They smile despite the seriousness of their work, and look proud. From the English-language records of the Palestinian ATS, which talk in very general ways about the work the women undertook, it's clear Bella must have been one of the oldest, well over the official age of recruitment when she enlisted. In some photos, she appears to be the oldest by two decades. Her seniority, then, was perhaps based on her age and work history, her language skills in Hebrew, English and German. Possibly she also had some Arabic, as she used a few words in a letter to Ruth.

Corporal Bella Messer (*second from right*) with friends in Tel-Aviv, during leave, 1942; and 'in the trenches', lying alongside a trench she and other ATS women have dug, Egypt.

The ATS women's days were arduous. But they were comrades and shared a purpose of protecting Palestine and supporting the troops. In an English-language oral history, one of the younger women, Hannah Tilayeff Roberts, said:

> We had to discover how to drive in the dark, over desert, through quicksand and sandstorms. We had to learn how to maintain and repair the vehicles ... Life in the desert was hard. Mornings and nights were bitterly cold, while the days were very hot. Often we had sandstorms, when the sand penetrated everything, even our food. But we were young, full of energy and working for a cause that made it all worthwhile.

In a letter to Ruth dated 17 December 1943, Bella talks about how far she is from Ruth who by now must be a mother. The letter is written in German and was sent from Egypt to Ruth in Melbourne. In 2007 I sat down with my father and he began translating the letter at the dining table. I turned on my phone's voice recorder, as I have done so many times. (Listening to the recording in 2024, I can hear my mother walk past at one point. Later, she asks us if we'd like a cup of tea. It's a beautiful moment for me, hearing her voice again, so confident and relaxed, just words in passing.) This recording of my father talking about Bella is one of the earliest that I have. He read the letter in a voice much younger than his voice is now, which has the slower raspiness of very old age:

'*Corporal B Messer, 195172, 503 Company ATS. No 1. Convalescent Depot ME*. Hm, I don't know what ME stands for.

'*My dear good Ruchen* [little Ruth], *yesterday I wrote you an airletter but today I wanted to write again properly, and to answer your long letter from the 5th of October. The knowledge that this letter will arrive at a time when the baby* [Dad's nephew, Leigh, born in 1943] *is already probably born, makes me so impatient and longing.*

You will understand, Häse –' meaning little hare, he tells me, '*the fact that I am at this time not with you, is something I will never get over and I'm very unsure whether the sacrifice that I'm making* –' Here Dad paused, trying out a couple of translations, '*that I'm bringing to the efforts*, or *my efforts – and the result – whether it corresponds with the result*.'

He stopped and said, 'It's a very difficult sentence. I don't understand what she's saying, actually.'

'Isn't she talking about her work in the army?' I said.

'This is what I don't know. And then she says, *I'm trying to comfort myself with the thought that since the outbreak of the war, I could not in any case have travelled to Australia. But, will you actually need me when I'm there? You will not need me with Frank and baby* – This was before,' said Dad, 'that she [Bella] knew that [Ruth had] separated from Frank – *and your home and your circle of friends and acquaintances. I'm very conscious of my uselessness, or better un-usefulness* – these are words I really should look up in the dictionary – *and incompetence, I'm very conscious of. And also, Michael will not need me. He, perhaps even less than you. It is more difficult with boys. What do you want actually? A girl or boy? I imagine you will be happy with whatever fate sends you, so long as the child is healthy. And what kind of name have you chosen? I'm quite excited when I think about all of this*.' Dad pauses, again trying out a series of translations. '*I'm certain*, or *I think* or *I expect that Vati will be more concerned about you and try harder than he ever did with me. And that is how it should be*. – Oh, and here – *I sit here in the Convalescent Depot and I'm convalescing*. I really should translate the rest.' (He didn't, because we were distracted by other things, or perhaps it was time for me to go to work, or home to my children, who were youngsters then.)

'Why is she in the Convalescent Depot?' I asked, wondering what she'd been ill with.

'She's sick.'

'What, the flu, or …?'

He read on. '*Two summers in Egypt cannot be done away with magic, and one and three-quarter years of heavy work and living in such a large group of people, which I'm not used to. I was very down and nervous. The doctor after the second sick break …*'

It didn't occur to me at the time to wonder about Ruth not having said anything to her mother about her marriage problems with Frank, whom Willy had not liked – for good reason, as it turned out.

In her autobiography, Ruth mentioned that Bella had been good friends with the younger women she served with. She was a mother figure to some. Boyfriends, parents, politics, work, I imagine they'd have talked about it all, along with news of the war, their futures, music, film, and the rest.

The ATS recruits were paid, but only 75 per cent of what their male counterparts earned. Even at the lesser female rate, as a corporal Bella's economic independence was assured while she was in the ATS. This would have lessened her financial dependence on Willy, something she deeply resented, according to Ruth. She'd been earning an income for years until she married, and in her final letter to Ruth protested Willy's grudging financial control. But like so many women across Europe, Australia and the USA, once the war and their service roles came to an end, economic insecurity and dependence returned.

The *Australian Jewish Herald* published an article in 1942 titled 'Palestine's Women Soldiers'. The journalist, Miriam Shir, reported on a trip she'd made to an ATS training camp, location undisclosed, other than that it was situated alongside a male soldiers' camp. The visit gave Shir an 'odd, proud feeling to see soldiers – English and Australian and Free French and whoever might be passing by – salute our Palestinian girls in their trim officers' uniforms.' Shir also happens to admiringly describe a 'middle-aged' sergeant, who is like Bella in age and background (but not her), a soldier 'who had been prominent in social service and in women's organisation work for many years'.

Postwar, what work was available to Bella, or whether in her mid-fifties she had employment at all in a predominantly young society, is unclear. She continued to live in Tel Aviv until getting a berth on the *Partizanka*, boarding at Haifa with a couple of hundred others leaving Palestine. More passengers were taken on at Port Said and Malta, before the *Partizanka* arrived in Fremantle on 8 January 1948.

The fortunes of war

As late as April 1943, *The Australian Jewish News* was reassuring its readers that inmates of the Theresienstadt camp 'now receive mail' and relatives and friends could send messages through the Red Cross. Theresienstadt was very effectively being used as propaganda, presented by the Nazis as a resettlement camp and even as a 'spa town'. In fact, it was a transit camp to extermination and forced labour camps. For an inspection in 1944 by the Danish and International Committee of Red Cross, it was transformed through an intensive 'embellishment' into a tidy town. To prepare for the inspection, over 7000 prisoners were moved to Auschwitz. Food supplies were increased, prisoners were trained how to behave, children were even provided with toys.

In January 1943 eyewitness accounts had begun to emerge of the use of gas chambers in the camps. It certainly was not yet known that there were dedicated extermination camps: Auschwitz-Birkenau, Treblinka, Chelmno, Bełżec, Sobibór and Majdanek. Witnesses in Europe were attempting to get news of the atrocities out.

The *Australian Jewish Forum* republished a terrifying account from a witness to the killings in the Warsaw Ghetto. The Polish resistance fighter had escaped to Britain, and made this report in December 1942, reprinted, in part, in Australian papers in May 1943:

> Tell them 'there [outside the Nazi-invaded countries] that there are moments when we hate them all; we hate them because they are safe there and do not rescue us. Because they don't do enough. We are only too well aware that in the free and civilised world outside, it is not possible to believe all that is happening to us ... We are all dying here. Let them not retreat until the civilised world will believe us – until it will undertake some action to rescue those of our people who will remain alive.'

That same month, other Australian newspapers republished a British news report on what was taking place in Holland. From the *Daily Mercury* in Queensland came a graphic account titled 'Nazi atrocities':

> A secret paper from Holland which reached London a few days ago gives a hair-raising description ... The prisoners arrive packed in cattle trucks where they are met by well-fed, smartly uniformed German brutes who drive them into the camps ... the bayoneting en route to make them run often turns out to be fatal ...

The vast extent of the many thousands of concentration camps, forced labour camps, transit and prisoner-of-war camps in German-occupied Europe was not known by the public outside of Europe, though there were persistent rumours, and the issue was not prioritised by the Allied governments who did have knowledge. The BBC's war news services were listened to across Europe and Commonwealth countries, but reports on the murder of Jews were patchy. There was the problem of having no visual evidence; the infamous photographs of starved inmates and piles of bodies at Buchenwald and Bergen-Belsen that first hit the newspaper headlines in 1945 hadn't been possible until journalists and army photographers accompanied Allied soldiers into the liberated camps.

*

Dad told me that when he visited the USA in the 1980s, his cousin Alice Fink said she felt that Willy and Bella could have done more to help her parents and brother get out of Germany. Perhaps more effort and money could have gone to others in the extended family; but there were so many who needed help. Could Willy have demonstrated to the Jewish Agency that issued the certificates for immigration to Palestine that he could support his own mother, Emma, or Bella's widowed sister, Hedwig? Which of them would have gone? I wonder how much time Bella and Willy thought they had to settle in, to establish themselves and what they might have aimed to do to help others of their family and friends.

Bella's oldest sister, Hedwig, had long been a Berlin widow by the 1930s. Perhaps they tried to get Hedwig out, but she was in her early-fifties and few women without financial means obtained visas to any country. Of her own immediate family, Hedwig was the only one Bella was leaving behind – with what feelings of fear or dread, guilt or heartache?

Willy's brother, Arnold, was long divorced and perennially insolvent – and still estranged from Willy, having almost bankrupted their business and abandoned his wife (Helga's mother) years earlier. Their mother, Emma, was an elderly woman and not eligible for a visa. Willy's sister and brother-in-law, Ella and Georg Redlich, also remained; they had none of the necessary skills, no savings or international sponsors. Of the seven members of the Redlich family who'd lived at Starnberger Strasse 3, only Alice survived because she was already in England in 1939. The others were all deported.

Most of the German Jews transported to Theresienstadt and Auschwitz were Berliners. Hedwig was transported to Theresienstadt in June 1942; Emma in August.

Ruth wrote about not knowing the seriousness of the situation in Germany when she was a teenager in England and Palestine, and then a young woman in Australia; of not knowing of the plight of Jews in the ghettos and concentration camps. It seems that Willy and she didn't discuss the war and the fate of Jews. She hadn't been told about her grandmother Doris's suicide. In her autobiography, she admitted to being focused on herself, and being busy with employment, motherhood, relationships, her membership of the Communist Party, and not giving a thought to family who had remained in Germany.

> While all this was happening I was completely absorbed in my own life [in Melbourne] knowing nothing of all this, even having a holiday in Lorne [a seaside town a couple of hours south of Melbourne] in the summer of 1942. When I ponder over it I feel very bad and sad. But we didn't know. My father never talked of what might have happened to his family.

She was like many others, Jewish and non-Jewish, who said, 'the world didn't know'. And they were right. Outside the countries where the atrocities were taking place, most people did not know until the end of the war. Only then did international news reports begin to emerge.

Ruth's Jewish identity was a part of her, but not her focus. She was looking towards a brighter future for the world: she saw herself as a class warrior, a communist woman who was taking action to make a better society. It was something she was living every day as a young, smart but uneducated migrant, barely out of her teens, moving from boarding house to boarding house, working

Communist Party of Australia march in support of Soviet Jews, May Day, Melbourne.

in factories and as a domestic servant, then marrying, becoming a mother, then a single mother. Communism spoke to her – and perhaps, too, was a way to avoid the past and the present horrors of the war and the yet-to-be-named Holocaust.

Perhaps my family's response to this catastrophe was like that of many others traumatised by events that were shockingly inhumane. Ruth turned to politics, working hard on issues of workers' rights, support services for migrant women, nuclear disarmament and local politics. My father turned to science, coming to specialise in Australia's unique marsupials and its monotremes, the platypus and the echidna: those strange creatures that both lay soft eggs and suckle their young (not through teats but through many pores in their bellies). Willy continued in business, and through his business grew many connections with Melbourne's Jewish community.

Family and friends who had died or disappeared, such as Minnie and Julius, the details of what had happened in the camps, the complete horror of those years, was not spoken about. The trauma was there within them, nevertheless. They knew, as the world came to know, but it wasn't something they talked about.

Bella was not spoken about. Like many survivors of terror and atrocities, her survivors needed to turn their attention to creating a new life for themselves. Such is the way of our human world it seems, atrocity and recovery and a new life if the conditions are kind enough. My father says he truly did feel grateful to be alive in Australia.

Now: Jerusalem and the archives

I made three trips to Israel between 2015 and 2019. The first was just a few days taken with Katharina, my younger second cousin (Rolf's daughter), travelling from Berlin and staying with Katharina's aunt Hanna (Rolf's sister) at Hanna's house in Tel Aviv. This first visit was to see family; to spend time with Katharina and Hanna, and meet Hanna's teenage children, look around Tel Aviv and do a couple of day trips to the coast.

The second visit was undertaken for this book. I wanted to get a sense of Bella's daily life in Palestine, a feel for the physical place, the kinds of people she'd have known. It's one thing to read about a time and a place, but to look at the same skies, to walk the same sands and dip into the ocean she may have swum in, to have seen her house: that's the physical connection that the children of migrants, exiles and refugees seek time and again, going back to the place their parents and grandparents came from. Did I succeed, did I feel satisfied? Momentarily. Yes. A little.

There were also specific matters that needed settling, for my father's sake and my own. I wanted to return to Sydney with three questions answered: Was it true, as he believed, that Bella had immigrated to Palestine with her lover Walter Strauss and not Willy? Had she spent her time there partying with friends and lovers instead of bringing Dad back from Bunce Court? And who was this Walter Strauss who had caused the deep rift between her and Willy?

On my second trip in 2018, I engaged a young academic to help me. The research assignment was imprecise; I had so few details to start with. My man in Jerusalem was Yonatan Harel, a PhD candidate in Philosophy at the Hebrew University of Jerusalem, where all those decades ago Walter Strauss had become head of the Department of Hygiene (aka Public Health). Before leaving for Israel, I'd shared photos with Harel of Bella in Palestine, along with my father's document, 'A History of My Family', so that he understood the facts that we had to hand. I'd told him Bella had taken her own life, that she then disappeared from the family record, and that I wanted to know more about her in every way, and I needed help from him to learn something of her life in Palestine and whatever else he could help me with about her years in Germany. I had her ATS photographs, some names from her address book, a few letters, her Syrken Street address, the name Walter Strauss, and Ruth's remarks about her Aliyah Bet activism.

Coming out of the bus terminal into downtown Jerusalem for the first time was a shock. In my previous visit, I hadn't visited Jerusalem because Hanna said the place made her nervous; it was too dangerous. I hadn't been scared going there, but made the mistake of standing still just outside the exit gates to use my phone map to orient myself, unsure which way was north, and was brusquely told to move away by the armed guard. Looking around me, I was startled by the distinctive black clothing of the Hasidic men in their long coats and stiff hats. Women were dressed in below-the-knee skirts and snoods; others were going about their day in the Western dress of jeans and jackets, or some other combination familiar to me. Jerusalem was nothing like the more liberal and secular Tel Aviv. I could have been in a different country. There was an intensity on the streets near the terminus that I found unnerving. It was the religiosity, though it should have been the young IDF soldiers who frightened me, with their assault rifles and packs slung on their backs as they made their way to or from leave. But I was already used to IDF soldiers, most of them young conscripts undertaking the required military service. They were always out on leave, or returning to base with their large kit bags, frequently carrying arms. I knew that as a non-Palestinian they were unlikely to be a threat to me.

I slid into a taxi, putting my jacket back on in the chilly mountain weather. As we drove, I caught glimpses of the staggered hillside of the Mount of Olives cemetery across the valley, the dark smudges of the cypresses growing tall among the chalky white limestone of the pathways and ancient Jewish graves. I saw glimpses of East Jerusalem, where the Palestinian Israelis live – not that the term is used in Israel; they're Arab Israelis there. Their schools are underfunded, and checkpoints, road barriers, Jewish settlements and soldiers are everywhere.

I arrived at the university early and strolled across the landscaped courtyards. The day was sunny, the grounds beautifully kept, with views across the valleys and the city. Many of the limestone buildings were prominently named after their American benefactors. In a spacious courtyard near the shade of the stone pavilion I spoke briefly with a small group of cheerful men and women who were studying for their diplomas as tourist guides.

The student cafeteria was quiet and mostly empty of people during the mid-semester break. Harel appeared, smiling and tentative like me, a slim man with dark hair and friendly eyes. He was in his early thirties. He'd been recommended to me because of his languages, and his knowledge of twentieth-century German Jewish culture. He was fluent in Hebrew and German and his English was good, too. That is, he was perfect. We talked about his children and I was a little taken aback that he'd achieved so much in so few years: marriage, two children, military service, teaching and postgraduate study. We didn't discuss politics or religion. I had a feeling we both knew that we'd have different politics, and because this was his home, his culture, because he possibly carried wounds from his military service or had lost friends, or perhaps even felt a complex guilt for having harmed or killed a Palestinian, I didn't speak. I did notice a mark that might once have been a wound from his service in the IDF.

He told me he'd not been able to find a written record of Bella anywhere in the various national archives in Jerusalem. She hadn't joined any major political parties, nor could he find her name amid the records of the organisations she'd very likely been associated with, based on what Ruth had recorded of her mother's activities, and Bella's rank of corporal at the start of her work in the ATS. She wasn't in the records of the Aliyah Bet resistance movement. That she was missing wasn't significant, though it was disappointing. She was like many women community workers and volunteers who went unrecorded and are now mostly invisible to history. But she was also different, because since she was a teenager she'd striven to work and to participate; this was something that struck Harel forcefully. In his more formal, Germanic-philosophic-English phrasing, he said he believed that for Bella the 'general cause' of working for the social good and her sense of freedom and independence had been stronger for her than the caveats and impositions of the 'social codes' for women, and for Jewish women.

Harel and I made our way from the university café out into the bright sun of the day and then to the archive office in another building. He had arranged for an archivist to locate and retrieve Walter Strauss's file. The old manila folder was thick with papers and photographs, certificates and clippings; thick in part because in those years, the university records were documented thrice: in Hebrew, German and English. We were allowed to take the file into a small room with a desk and chairs.

Now for the first time I was seeing an image of Strauss. He was handsome, straight-backed, broad-shouldered, with a good head of hair even in middle age, and a Roman nose. He didn't have the gentle demeanour of my grandfather, nothing of the sweetness I'd often seen in Willy's expression. He looked indefectible, and as if he knew it.

When and with whom had he sailed into Haifa? Dad's cousin Susanne Arendt, Hedwig's daughter, was living in Fort Worth, Texas, when Dad met her in the 1980s and she told him that Bella had arrived in Haifa with Strauss. He'd believed her. What a rumourmonger she was, a *Klatschbase*! The university employment records included his immigration records, proof that he had immigrated with his wife and son from Berlin to Palestine, on a different ship from Willy and Bella, in 1937. But the damage was long done; Dad and Susanne had met in the early 1980s, and it had taken me thirty years to get to the university and read the document that disproved what she'd told him. Why had she said it? Was it an honest mistake? Or had she become a bit mean-spirited with age?

Strauss had been ambitious: the evidence was there in letters, minutes of department meetings, appeals regarding his appointment as head of the Division of Hygiene – a post which comprised the departments of Social Medicine, Preventative Medicine and Malaria – and in his international standing as an epidemiologist. We also found evidence of his arrogance and calculation towards academic competitors. 'Please excuse me,' wrote Judah Magnes, the well-known New York reform rabbi and advocate of a 'bi-national' Arab and Jewish state, objecting to Strauss's appointment, 'excuse me for bringing up this matter in this personal way. This is not, as you know, entirely to my taste ... Prof. Strauss did everything he could to blacken the name of Prof. Kligler before the Committee of Inquiry.' (Jacob Kligler was the founder of the university's departments of Hygiene and Bacteriology.) In minutes from 1950, one of Strauss's supporters said that 'Prof. Strauss's personal difficulties with co-workers were due [to] the fact he was a perfectionist who rejected incomplete and incompetent work by others.' Harel and I were intrigued by the allegations and counter-allegations that swirled around Strauss and left the room feeling we'd feasted on a delicious ancient controversy.

We debriefed about the day and next steps, then Harel left to take his children for a horse-riding lesson. I hailed a taxi back to the bus terminal. The driver asked me where I was from. I told him Australia, and said I was here researching the life of my grandmother who had lived in Palestine during the war. 'There is no Palestine!' the driver said to me angrily, giving me a fright. 'There has never been a Palestine!' An old Palestinian penny, a remnant of Bella's life, came to mind. I think I'd found it in one of her boxes. Fearful of more anger, I said not a word in response.

His words were a fierce echo – shared widely by other Israelis, though not all – of former prime minister Golda Meir's statement that 'there was no such thing as Palestinians' in an interview with the *Sunday Times* on 15 June 1969, the second anniversary of the Six-Day War:

> It is not as though there were a Palestinian people in Palestine considering itself as a Palestinian people and we came and threw them out and took their country away from them. They did not exist.

The Irish writer and critic Philip Ó Ceallaigh has spent most of his adult life in Eastern Europe, and is interested in writers who critique rather than expound nationalism. He's the translator of *For Two Thousand Years*, a short semi-autobiographical novel by Jewish Romanian writer Mihail Sebastian (1907–1945). The novel's title references the 2000-year history of antisemitism, though it is set in Romania in the interwar years. Ó Ceallaigh quotes from a scene in *For Two Thousand Years* in which:

> One man argues that the rise of fascism makes Zionism

> about Jewish survival. To which another retorts that [Jabotinsky] is himself a fascist: 'And no less of a fascist because he's a Jew ... Land makes its own terrible demands ... What will you do with the indigenous Arabs, who also have the right to a natural death, rather than abruptly by Zionist extermination?'

Ó Ceallaigh writes that the novel is a prescient account 'of life lived among the intellectuals who accepted – some of them slowly – the rationales of fascism and racism'. It is a reminder and a warning that any person can become complicit in (or worse, a participant in) the extermination of others, and to not do so demands thought and active resistance.

My Jaffa apartment

On my last trip to Israel in 2019, I'd decided to live amid, or at least near, a Palestinian community by living in Jaffa. Today, the Palestinian population is a minority of only around 15 000. Up until the Nakba, Jaffa had been very cosmopolitan, with a population of over 80 000 and a prosperous international trade port. The famous, beautifully juicy and bright 'Jaffa orange' variety had been developed by the local Palestinian farmers in the mid-nineteenth century and became the principal export product.

I was renting a roomy bedsit with lots of art on the walls, a desk, and sunlight, in the second-storey apartment of the artists Galit and Jan Rauchwerger. After leaving Russia in 1973, Jan had moved to Jaffa at a time when hardly any Israelis lived there, and it was a much smaller community. My guess is that this building was among the many that Palestinians had lived in until 1948; it was well over a hundred years old, judging by its design and the thickness of its walls. Now, some streets are being gentrified, with new apartments with sea views going up.

Galit and Jan had raised their four children here. Galit's photographs and lithographs and Jan's oils, many of them portraits of Galit, her curly triangular bob of hair distinctive in each, hung on the walls in my two rooms. The windows looked out on palm trees, and balconies overflowing with ivy and crimson bougainvillea, cacti, nasturtiums and geraniums.

To reach the apartment from Yefet Street, I would walk up a narrow laneway off the street, the flanking walls trellised with vines and ferns, past a wandering flock of peacocks, and the occasional house cat. The curlicued front gates opened onto a stone-paved garden courtyard that various of the residents tended. To get to my flat I'd then walk up two flights of wide and solid internal stairs. This stairwell was the building's bomb shelter.

Sitting at the kitchen table one day, my worktable, Galit and I drank tea and chatted. I showed her photos of Bella, and the photographs she and Willy had taken on their 1934 tour of Palestine. We were each interested in the other's projects. I asked her about the next exhibition she was working towards, and her work at a refugee project helping Somali women settle in Israel.

After I cleared away my breakfast things, I spread my books and notes across the kitchen table. I worked with the curtains open and with views of the tall date palms and crimson bougainvillea flowering from neighbouring gardens. From the Catholic school and church down the road I heard the morning bells. From the mosque, the calls to prayer. From the courtyard and the lane, the screech of the birds. Sometimes, voices speaking Hebrew or Arabic would waft up from below. One time, a peacock flew up onto the balcony's railing. Some days I was writing furiously with these sounds accompanying me; more often, writing tentatively.

Wanting to know something can be dangerous when knowing will lead to a new burden: the decision to act or not, to acknowledge what you know and then do something, or not to act if there are good reasons for your inaction. We all of us choose what we speak out about. I thought of Mohsin Hamid's novel *Exit West*, in which the 'natives' (citizens) are intractably pitted against the 'migrants':

> And then the natives and their forces stepped back from the brink ... Perhaps they had grasped that the doors could not be closed, and new doors would continue to open ... too

> many native parents would not have been able to look their children in the eye, to speak with head held high of what their generation had done.

That could be me; it is certainly true of many of 'us', in our WEIRD (Western, Educated, Industrialised, Rich and Democratic) nations.

*

One morning during this November visit, my landlady Galit woke me. She was, unaccountably, standing beside my bed, very early, telling me to get up, whispering perhaps, but speaking urgently. And then I heard the missile warning siren winding up, wailing louder and louder, a sound I knew from news and entertainment, never before from real life.

She hurried me down into the stairwell with the others in the building, all of us in PJs and track pants, one of the children with just a blanket draped around them. There was the wailing siren, then a silence, then a vast and muffled thud, which I felt bodily, through my skin into my chest; a deep bass boom. The Iron Dome interceptor missile had detonated one of the rockets in the skies above southern Tel Aviv. We waited some more in the stairwell, to see what the next siren would say, the others checking the government's missile-alert app on their phones. Nothing more, so we returned to our apartments. Later I read that it was not Hamas, but a rogue cell that had fired the rockets from Gaza.

Galit and I talked about the rockets. She said that she and other Israelis lived with the complexity of the fear, the shame and the anger with their government daily. I wished I knew more Israelis like Galit, who believed that some kind of reconciliation and future peace could be possible. Even if it wasn't going to be possible, they would not stop their peace work.

Only the day before the missile attack, I'd been on a tour of the Gaza border and nearby towns, yeshivas, and villages which had once been home to Palestinian farmers and families. The tour has changed, but is still offered; it had been jointly managed by Jewish and Palestinian peace activists. Today 'Gaza' tours focus on the resilience of the Israelis living in the moshavs and towns that survived the Hamas terrorist attack of 7 October 2023. It's a tragedy that so many of the men and women killed and taken hostages were themselves peace activists.

On the tour I took in 2019, led by Eliyahu McLean, we stood at lookouts along the Gaza border, some with public telescopes, and looked across the kilometre of no-man's-land, past the electric fences, seeing only the taller buildings of the city that reached above a seven-metre wall with its sensors and remote-control machine guns.

At the northern Eretz Gaza border, I talked to Abbas, a Palestinian taxi driver. Middle-aged and of generous spirit, he knew our guide, Eliyahu McLean, well. They'd been encountering each other for many years at this border. Abass's taxi service involved driving Palestinian workers with permits into and out of Gaza.

We were hours on the road, passing remnant Palestinian villages and visiting Sderot and Ashkelon, towns that have suffered numerous rocket strikes because of their proximity to Gaza (and which were hit again on 7 October). We were shown piles of black rocket cases, heard about the local children's PTSD, viewed a children's playground with its concrete huts and tunnels painted to look like play areas, but there in case of attacks. The walls in these towns near Gaza, but outside the militarised zone, were pitted and chipped by the blasts.

Going on this tour was an action in itself; in a small way, the tour group's presence affirmed that not everyone's back was turned upon the Palestinians and those Israelis who want coexistence and recognition of Palestinians' right of return to their former homes. A day later, one of the towns we'd been in was hit by Hamas rockets;

such events were 'normal'. As we travelled the area, McLean and the local participants we met talked to us about their lives, history, and the importance of dialogue. McLean has been an interfaith peace activist of many years, an Orthodox Jew who has forged relationships across a broad spectrum of Muslims, Jews, Christians and Druze. In the immediate aftermath of 7 October and the years since, he has continued his peace work and inspired others to do so too.

After that sudden early rising on the morning of the missiles, I had spent the rest of the day discombobulated, unable to focus on anything much, disoriented when I walked out into the empty streets. The streets were quiet; there were almost no cars on the roads. My local, the Café Yafa, was closed. I kept walking and found a café that was open. Entering it, I asked what they would do if there was another attack during the day. The young woman said they had a stairwell to go to. She spoke in a desultory way. Life would go back to its strange-to-me 'normal' the following day. The rockets had been intercepted. It was a day that was quickly merging into many other days.

I rang my cousin Hanna, who lived in central Tel Aviv about a twenty-minute drive away if the traffic was bad (which it often was). She was despondent and on edge about the coming days. Her daughter was in her first year of her military service. She wasn't stationed in the south, near Gaza, she was in the north near the Syrian border, but a welcome event for the families of new recruits had been cancelled. Hanna had received permission for me to come along, and I'd been eager to go.

I hadn't told Hanna about my tour to the towns and the Gaza border the day before, or the trip I was leaving on early the next day. From Sydney I'd contacted the Road to Recovery, an Israeli association of volunteers who drive Palestinian patients from checkpoints at the West Bank and Gaza to Israeli hospitals for critical treatment. I was put in touch with Avigdor Cahaner, a retired professor of agriculture and a volunteer driver. That year drivers had already made over 10 000 trips, assisting 20 000 Palestinian patients, many of them children, to get critical care.

We were to leave his home at around 5 a.m., so the day before I took the bus to his moshav, Rishpon, a cooperative farming and artisans' workshop near the coast north of Tel Aviv. The moshav was founded in 1936 amid a cluster of small Palestinian villages, on land historically cultivated by residents of the village of Al-Haram. Avigdor's parents had settled there decades ago, and he'd raised his family there and was well aware of the moshav's history. The afternoon I arrived we walked around the quiet moshav, talking for hours, eating dinner at a local restaurant.

We set off early the next morning, when it was still dark, arriving at the West Bank border at Qalqilya at around 6 a.m. Avigdor parked the car in among dozens or perhaps even hundreds of cars, mini-vans and buses collecting Palestinian workers, mostly men, for work in Israel. Under the yellow and white floodlights, road dust rose and swirled all around, making it hard to discern faces. The noise was tremendous, with men shouting greetings and directions, others just silently walking towards their transport. Looking towards a yellow gate barely discernible through the crowd, Avigdor lifted the Road to Recovery flag up high on its pole, so the patient and his carer would see it and find us. They were somewhere amid the thousands of workers coming through the fortified gateways. Like the men, they'd queued for hours to pass through the long, caged walkways on the far side of the walls. Nearly 10 000 workers from the West Bank towns of Nablus, Jenin, Tubas, Jericho and Qalqilya walked through this crossing daily.

Then out of the mass of people, Avigdor saw the young woman and her elderly father, walking with a stick. Avigdor had not met them before; most trips it was someone new. He greeted them and Mohammed, the patient, took the front seat, while I sat in the back with his daughter, Amina (I've changed her name here), who spoke English. We didn't speak much to begin with, but we made conversation bit by bit. I didn't want to intrude, she'd been up already for hours, didn't know me. It was another hour or more driving along the freeway beside the rising and falling horizon of the West Bank wall. Then, as the sun rose and the day became warmer, we reached the entrance to Sheba Hospital. Avigdor stopped the car, and Amina got out to pass through the double-glazed checkpoint for Palestinians entering the hospital. As she showed her papers, passport and had her bag checked I wandered around, free to walk in and out of the hospital grounds. I didn't need to get out of the car, and perhaps my free movement was salt in Mohammed's wound, but I wanted to see what was possible for me to freely do. Amina returned to the car, and we drove through to the building where Mohammed was receiving his treatment. Another driver would pick them up that afternoon and return them to the West Bank.

'A Palestinian Day Out'

Before this 2019 visit to Israel, I had contacted the writer and academic Yonatan Mendel and asked if we could meet. Mendel's essay 'A Palestinian Day Out', had been published in the *London Review of Books* a few months earlier. The essay's setting is the long stretch of beaches between Tel Aviv and Jaffa. I knew these beaches reasonably well from my walks and historical researches. The coastline is bracketed by the old Tel Aviv port and the Hilton Hotel at the city end, and the ancient port of Jaffa to the south. The distance between these two points is seven and a half kilometres, but politically and culturally, the distance is vast. In his essay, Mendel focuses on a particular day he spent at one of the beaches, one of the two days each year when Palestinians from the West Bank are allowed to travel outside the walls, other than for work.

During Eid al-Fitr at the end of Ramadan, and two months later during Eid al-Adha, the beach, writes Mendel, 'between Tel Aviv and Jaffa fills with Palestinians from the West Bank. For many children this is the only time they get to visit the seaside, even though their homes in the Occupied Territories may be no more than twenty or thirty kilometres away.' In Tel Aviv it is very possible to ignore the over five million Palestinians living an hour or two away. For Israelis, the majority of Palestinians live unseen behind the walls in the designated areas. They are out of sight. On these two days per year, Palestinian families and the Israelis can be physically close, spread out upon the grassy slopes and the sands.

Though never intermingling, Mendel observes, except in the water.

The Mediterranean's coastlines have seen trade and piracy, and been the source of myths and legends, of freedom for migrants and seekers of asylum, and of enslavement and imprisonment. Sixty-five kilometres south of Jaffa lies Gaza, where over two million Palestinians were imprisoned between the sea, which is barred to them – the Israeli navy patrols the waters – and the towering walls and kilometre-wide no-man's land.

One afternoon, I re-read Mendel's essay and then walked down from my lodgings in Jaffa to the beach. It was a warm day. I waded in, and took a few dives into the mild swell. It's called Alma Beach now. Pre-Israel, it was known as al-Manshiyah. Floating on my back, I looked up towards the town, to the Mahmoudiya Mosque's minaret. People were walking along the sand, paddling, lying on towels. They were locals and tourists such as me, from Japan, Nigeria, Canada, South Korea, the USA. A young woman with long wavy hair curling down her back sunned herself near where I'd laid my towel. She said she was from Italy, and that she had a cousin who lived in Sydney. She was so relaxed, the sun was warm but not too warm, her skin was golden brown from her days here. But it wasn't who was there that day which interested me the most, it was who was not there.

I'd contacted Mendel from Sydney. He is a lecturer in the Department of Middle East Studies at Ben-Gurion University of the Negev, trained in sociology and linguistics. What I knew of him was that he aimed to bring about more understanding of the Palestinian experience.

We arranged to meet at his local, Café Carger, on Mesilat Yesharim Street. I arrived a half-hour early. I was hot, and in the bathroom ran water over my wrists and wiped the damp from my face. It was November and the city should have had some winter rain by now, but it was still close to thirty degrees that morning. It had been a long walk from where the 54 bus had dropped me off, down dusty Shalma Road, past the rubble of building sites where just one or two men could be seen chipping away; past half-made windows gaping onto dark interiors, wiring loose; past motorcycle repair stores, a strip of stores selling old and new shop mannequins and other stores selling metal shelving, and then one that sold both shelving and store mannequins. Another cluster of shops only sold linoleum.

I'd seen Mendel's picture on his university page, but once at the café – imagine fresh green frappes and crunchy salads – I knew I'd never pick him. All the men looked the same here; in their thirties, dark haired, with short beards, brown eyes, casually dressed, half of them with laptops out, all of them handsome. I took a selfie and WhatsApp'd him, and sure enough he was already there. I'd walked past him, the bearded guy with a book. He gave me a wave from a table in the back corner.

We chatted about his essay, Mendel telling me how he'd gone down to the sea intentionally to experience the special day. Much of his work has been about resisting the disappearances of Palestinian history and culture. I explained that I needed help interpreting photographs from my grandparents' trip to Palestine in 1934, and wanted to learn more about the politics of dispossession. This was the trip that Bella and Willy had taken in preparation for what they hoped would be their emigration, their escape from Nazi Germany. Hitler had been Chancellor for a year by this time, and the laws persecuting Jews were well in place. Some of their friends had already settled in Palestine, others in far-off America.

Before leaving Sydney, I had scanned a few of Bella's photographs from the albums and boxes she'd carried with her to Australia. Three photos of Bella with some young girls were particularly intriguing. Who were they, where were they and why was she with them? They were not Western European girls, they were wearing what I'd describe as 'peasant' dress. I thought perhaps they were Palestinian children.

The photographs were different from others of public street scenes and tourist sites such as Mount Carmel, or of Bella riding a camel, smiling broadly. Willy and she took lots of photos, or Willy did mostly, as she's in the shots, not him, along with other people they encountered. Usually they're men out on the streets; some wearing British military hats, others a Turkish fez, others European-style workers' caps. There were Palestinian men in loose trousers and kaftans. Men in transit, and at work. Cars, bicycles, camels, open trucks are shown carrying people or produce. There are no photos of Jewish men in yarmulkes.

At the table with Mendel, I opened my computer and enlarged a photograph of Bella sitting on the stony ground with a girl, the same one I'd shown to a few other people with no success. She had a few dozen photographs from the 1934 trip, almost all of them carefully placed into four small photo albums, each image described in the white ink of her fountain pen on the dark pages of the album, in her best handwriting. This was the one that particularly interested me. I had found it not in the album, but loose in an envelope with a few other left-over photos from the trip.

Bella sits on the ground near a shopfront, close to what I guessed was an Arab Palestinian girl, with her mother and maybe a sister nearby. Bella is wearing a pretty summer dress with petal sleeves, stockings and dress shoes. The girl might be about six. She sits close beside her on the ground, in a simple dress, a loose scarf around her head, her thick dark hair falling free of it. Bella is looking at the girl and the girl is looking towards the camera – Willy must have taken the shot. They're outside a small store, in front of it a woman stands watching. She might be looking at Willy. Bella and the girl seem to be having a conversation, though in what language? In one of her letters to Ruth, Bella used the Arab expression *'malesh'* (in Arabic, *'Ma'alesh'*, in German, *'malisch'*) explaining that it expressed 'simply everything'; 'no matter, don't worry'. So she knew a little, or possibly more than a little, Arabic. I wanted something, even a lot, from

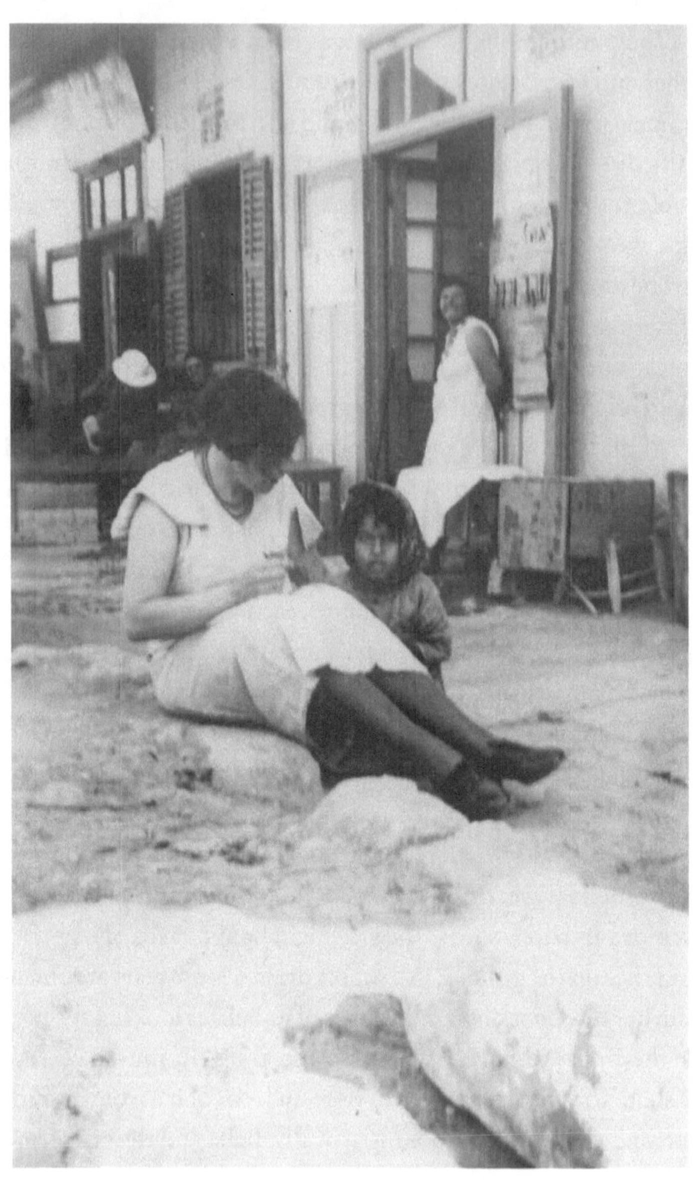

Bella in Zikhron Yaakov with Yemenite Jewish girl.

this photograph. I wanted it to prove she had a redemptive sense of what was going on here, in Palestine.

The first time I came across the photograph I was struck by the fact of Bella sitting on the ground with the girl. She doesn't stand beside her, or lean down towards her. Or even crouch. Her relaxed posture reminds me of so many other photographs of her in which she lounges or hugs my father or Ruth – loosely, warmly. It reminds me of the earliest photograph of her with children in her care, when she was nineteen and in her early twenties, during World War I, working with the orphaned children in Rauschen. This photograph connects me to Bella's history of mothering Ruth and Michael, and her professional care work. And now a new element entered, that she had an interest in what this girl had to say, for why else would she sit with the child other than to talk? If all she wanted was a tourist picture, they'd have posed together as woman and child, or with the girl's mother and sister as a family group for Willy to snap.

Mendel understood perfectly the importance of these visual documentations to reading Israel's pre-Nakba past. I was glad I'd scanned the images and not brought the originals with me, which were only four by four inches in size. On my laptop screen we could enlarge them. He examined the store sign and even though the words were grainy, he deciphered two things: that there was a poster advertising a Jewish socialist play, presented by a touring theatre that supported the kibbutz and labour movement, and that the shop was a Jewish grocery store. The shop sign and the theatre poster were written in Hebrew, faint, but, when enlarged, discernible. The town was Zikhron Yaakov, one of the oldest Jewish towns in Israel, founded in 1882 by Romanian Jews, then later becoming the first settlement for Yemenite Jews fleeing persecution in Muslim Yemen. The girls with their mother were not Arabs, as I'd first thought, but Yemenite Jews, farming people, Mendel thought. He speculated that the group might have come into town to sell produce, perhaps to the grocery store they were photographed outside, or at a street market just out of frame.

Outside Café Carger, the day remained hot, but inside with the doors wide open and the fans turning it was cool enough. I changed to mint tea. At the other tables, people came and went. Mendel had been very generous with his time, and now our meeting was over. I made my way back to Jaffa, elated to have learned so much.

When I had mentioned that Bella had lived in Syrken Street, near Bugrashov Beach, Mendel had told me that there had been Palestinian villages nearby. There hadn't been a trace of them in the propaganda film *The Land of Promise*. The erasure of Palestinian culture was already well underway by the time of the film's 1935 release. It was after Mendel told me about the village near Bella's apartment that I decided to learn more, and found the villages at the *Palestine Remembered* website. Satellite pictures and demographic maps showed three or four villages within a few kilometres of Bella's home: Jarisha, al-Mas'udiyya, al-Jammasin al-Gharbi, Ijlil al-Qibliyya and Ijlil al-Shamaliyya. Villages unknown to most residents of Tel Aviv.

What is lost was needed

A few days after our meeting, Mendel invited me to attend a book launch the next week at Dar Al-Tifel Al-Arabi (Arab Children's House), an education centre in Sheikh Jarrah, East Jerusalem. As the contributors' discussions commenced, I realised with some shock that there were both Jewish Israelis and Palestinian academics seated together on the panel; indeed these people had contributed to the same publication. There was tension and elation in the room, a sense of urgency that I wasn't used to from the many book launches I've attended in my years as a writer and teacher. Holding the launch of *From the River to the Sea: Palestine and Israel in the shadow of 'peace'* at this historic Palestinian institution in East Jerusalem was decisive. The building had been a palatial Palestinian home, and then an orphanage and school for children, founded in 1948 by the late Hind al-Husseini. She had been a social worker and teacher, the daughter of a wealthy family.

In the days after the infamous massacre of Deir Yassin villagers carried out by Zionist Irgun paramilitaries in April 1948, al-Husseini came across a group of girls from the village wandering through Jerusalem. The horrific murders, rapes and destruction of their homes had occurred a few weeks before Israel was proclaimed, and was followed by the destruction of other nearby villages. The Deir Yassin massacre was one of the signal events of the Nakba, prompting hundreds of thousands of Palestinians to flee their homeland.

Al-Husseini converted her grandfather's mansion in Sheikh Jarrah into a shelter and nursery for over fifty of the orphaned Palestinian children. This was the origin of the Dar Al-Tifel Al-Arabi education centre and bookstore of today.

The audience sat in tense, keen silence, many of us taking notes. When the panel had finished, and we began to gather informally for drinks and conversation, I approached one of the German academics in the audience, Dr Anja Zorob. She was teaching in the democracy and human rights school at Birzeit University in the West Bank. 'Are any of your students here tonight?' I asked, still unaccustomed to the restrictions on movement, the myriad rules, zones and crossing points.

'They'd love to have come,' she replied, 'but they can't get permits to leave Ramallah.' What an innocent she must have thought me!

There is much at stake for Israeli academics and public intellectuals within Israel; and the awareness that others in the international community condemn Israel's policies of settlements, economic deprivation, imprisonment and policing, the accusations of genocide and apartheid. The criticisms are sometimes rejected on the basis that only if you're an Israeli Jew can you understand Israel's actions. Except at events such as the book launch, or when I went the following week to see the 2019 documentary *Gaza* at a half-filled cinema in Tel Aviv, my own position was ambiguous to others until I stated it outright. I felt myself the guest, the inexpert, a silent defender (a contradiction of course) of Palestinians' right to return and to nationhood.

I couldn't tell beforehand what my tentative conversations would lead to. Each day I felt that I too, like all the Israelis around me, left too much unasked and unsaid. This seemed to be how most people functioned in Israel in order to manage the emotional, moral and practical schisms with which they live: disillusionment with their government and its powerful international allies; or anger at those like me, who don't live there but have opinions and criticise Israel; or resentment of the Orthodox sons and daughters exempted from military service and the men in the yeshivas who receive government pensions and aren't required to do paid work; or fear that enemies surround the country and could at any moment attack. This fear is both ancient – from centuries of pogroms, massacres and displacement, culminating in the Holocaust – and recent, due to Israel's regional geopolitical tensions.

Some Israelis feel hatred and racism towards Palestinians, the Arabs they accuse of being terrorists who couldn't and wouldn't negotiate; others such as Galit, Yonatan Mendel and Avigdor believe that injustices have been done to Palestinians, that the land needs to be shared, that weapons must be laid down, that dialogue is a first step to peace. Many Israeli Palestinians find the idea 'absurd' that Jewish Israelis 'might be persuaded through dialogue to see Palestinians as human ... given that Israelis live in a militarised state in which dissent is punished', as Isabella Hammad in her 2023 Edward W Said Lecture titled 'Recognising the Stranger', presented just days before the 7 October attack.

Palestinians make up 20 per cent of Israel's population, though not all identify as Palestinian. Many run shops, including those that are open for business on Shabbat, drive taxis and buses, work as doctors, surgeons, lawyers and teachers. The vast majority have lower education outcomes and lower incomes than the Jewish population. Palestinians live as a diaspora even within Israel's borders: people from Gaza cannot leave, except a minority who work in Israel on construction sites (though since 7 October, they are stateless and cannot leave at all and have been replaced by Thai and other Asian-nation workers). Palestinians from East Jerusalem are residents, not citizens, and those living in the West Bank similarly cannot leave without a work permit.

*

On 7 October 2023, six of the Road to Recovery volunteers were murdered by Hamas. Other peace activists were taken hostage and died in captivity. Oded Lifshitz, aged 84 years, and his wife Yocheved Lifshitz, aged 85 years, both Road to Recovery volunteers, were taken hostage. Yocheved was released in October 2023, making headlines when she took the hand of one of her captors and wished him peace ('Shalom'). Her husband Oded died in captivity in 2025.

Yael Noy, the organisation's CEO, says there are fewer volunteers now, but those who remain are determined to continue, and are driving around 140 Palestinians daily to and from Israeli hospitals and the West Bank. The time spent in the private car is a meeting place between Palestinians and Israelis, Noy said in May 2025, 'not possible anywhere else ... one hour of peace together is a hope for better days'.

*

The Yafa café and bookstore, which had stayed shut on the morning of the missiles, is at the corner of Yehuda Margoza and Yefet streets, a few blocks from Galit and Jan's flat. Café Yafa is Jaffa's first bookstore for Arabic language books after the war of 1948 closed the others. Established in 2003 during the Second Intifada, its founders – Michel Elraheb, a Christian Arab, and Dina Lee, who is Jewish – wanted to create a space for dialogue. It was soon after my meeting with Mendel that I met a Palestinian man, Abu-George, at the Café Yafa, an older gentleman who'd been a child in 1948. His words changed me.

At the front of the café, awnings with broad yellow and white stripes sheltered the small tables and chairs scattered outside. It was cheerful and looked much loved. The food gave me a feeling of being home, of familiarity – stuffed peppers, maqluba, the Middle Eastern salad of chopped cucumber, tomato, red onion and so forth, a salad of many names. The café's walls were lined with bookshelves, stocked mostly with Arabic language books, and others in Hebrew and English, political analyses and histories, some poetry and fiction. The music was local, Egyptian and Moroccan. There were a few paintings for sale, and framed posters, plants creeping their green way from shelf to shelf, and small photographs of influential Arab men. Edward Said was the only one I recognised.

I'd sit at one of the smaller tables working on my laptop and, most of the time, not breathe a word of who I was or why I was there, or what I wanted to know. Small tour groups of six or eight people, usually Jewish, would come in for lunch and an educative chat with Michel El Raheb. I'd discreetly observe.

Café Yafa also hosted film and music nights. Following the Nakba, Jaffa lost 95 per cent of its Palestinian population, and now, after seventy years of Israeli 'modernisation' and gentrification, there isn't a movie theatre left. The new cinemas are all in Tel Aviv. Mendel had written how there'd been more than six movie theatres in Jaffa, including the Apollo, the Farouq, Nabil, Orient, Rashid and the magnificent Alhambra. When the Alhambra opened in 1937 it quickly became central to Palestinian cultural life in Jaffa. Designed by Lebanese architect Elias Al-Mor, the art deco building had been luxurious and expansive, very modern, with seating for over a thousand patrons.

After the 1948 war, the Alhambra was seized by the state of Israel, resold, left empty, and decades later purchased by the Church of Scientology. Restored and renovated, it opened in 2012 as the 'Ideal Center of Scientology for the Middle East'. The mayor of Tel Aviv claimed that its reopening testified to Israel's spirit of religious tolerance: 'Within just a few blocks of the center, you'll find numerous synagogues, several mosques and churches, 4000 years of Abrahamic monotheistic religions expressing themselves,' he said. 'The Scientology center is simply showing that Tel Aviv is one of the most pluralistic cities in the Middle East.' It seems incredible that

Scientology could want to insinuate itself into Israel, let alone Jaffa, in a building that had once been an icon of modern Palestinian culture and community.

One Wednesday night I returned after dark to the improvised cinema inside Café Yafa. I was probably the only foreigner amid the two dozen film-goers chatting convivially on the scattered café seating. I was endlessly nervous about asking local Palestinians for their time, asking them to speak from the heart about their politics or their lives, or the past. I had often seen Abu-George at one of the outdoor tables with a few other men. Many people said hello to him; dapper, lean-faced, proud, charming. Somehow, I learned that he was raised in Al-Mas'udiyya, one of the villages near Syrken Street, where Bella had lived. Here was someone who'd lived within a mile of my grandmother. Before the film began, I asked Jiries Copti for an introduction. He was a film producer who was often working at the café, and he curated its mid-week evening film screenings. Jiries was in his thirties or early forties, self-possessed but also warm. We went over to Abu-George, Jiries explained in Arabic what I wanted to do, and we made a time to meet the next day.

Because I was undertaking research that related to my work at the university where I taught, I was to use a university-approved Participant Consent form, the text of which had gone through a university ethics approval process. The researcher gives the participant the form to read, make alterations if need be, and sign before the interview. So, the next thing that I did was give Jiries my form, which set out the aims of the project of writing this book, and how I was going to use the material. The page had my university letterhead and named the Hebrew University of Jerusalem (HUJ), which was hosting me in Israel.

We were standing in the doorway between the café seating and the kitchen with its platters of salads and cakes ready to go out. He read it carefully, then said, 'You know HUJ is the most racist university in the country?'

Every encounter was an education in a new, often discomforting truth. 'No, I didn't know,' I think I said. Did I say that or did my surprised expression say as much? He wasn't baiting me; he was asking and informing me. I remember the adjustment I made; transfiguring all the people I already knew at HUJ, along with those from my own university, to the people I'd met working at HUJ in sociology, history, Middle East studies; wondering what they'd think of this statement. Thinking through the history, what little I knew of it from Walter Strauss's HUJ days. I was shocked. I didn't exactly know what he meant as to why it was more racist than other universities, and I wasn't quick enough to ask.

Was it to do with the university's international status and the American philanthropic backing? Did it employ fewer Palestinians? Offer Palestinians fewer scholarships? Were its units of study promoting a particular view of the conflict and its history? I read reports, for instance, of the university allowing Special Patrol Units and Border Police to operate from the campus that year for incursions into the East Jerusalem neighbourhood of Issawiya (which is part of the Occupied Territories, along with the West Bank and Gaza). Over sixty HUJ academics and hundreds more from Academia for Equality (Israel) protested to the university.

Issawiya is a volatile, crowded, poor, proud and struggling community. Its land had already been annexed by Israel in 1968 and given to the university; other areas had been annexed for Jewish settlers and industry. With the university requesting the closing of the gate to the neighbourhood's southern entrance in 2007, the 20 000 people living in the area have had only one entrance to their neighbourhood. So little wonder that Jiries said what he'd said about HUJ.

One of HUJ's professors, Nurit Peled-Elhanan, won the 2001 Sakharov Prize for Freedom of Thought, the European Union's highest award for human rights work, for her advocacy for peace in the Occupied Territories. A professor of language and education, her book *Palestine in Israeli School Books: Ideology and propaganda in education* demonstrates that racism towards Palestinians is endemic in Israeli school books. Contemporary violence and historical massacres such as at the village of Deir Yassin are presented as unfortunate but necessary. Peled-Elhanan's research shows that Israeli children 'grow up internalizing the message that Palestinians are people whose life is dispensable with impunity ... and whose number has to be diminished'.

Israeli Jews such as Peled-Elhanan and her husband, Rami Elhanan, who advocate for peace despite their own personal losses, are surely key to any future peace. Their daughter Smadar died in the 1997 Ben Yehuda Street suicide attack in which three Hamas suicide bombers blew themselves up in a Jerusalem pedestrian mall, killing five Israelis including Smadar, aged thirteen. For every death there is another death. Bassam Aramin's daughter Abir, aged ten, was killed at close range by an Israeli soldier in 2007. Bassam grew up in Hebron, a city in the West Bank. At age seventeen he was jailed for seven years for throwing stones at Israeli soldiers. In jail he saw the film *Schindler's List*, adapted from the Australian writer Thomas Keneally's novel *Schindler's Ark*. Seeing that film, he told listeners at the Australian National University in May 2023, changed his life. The two fathers are friends and peace activists. (Their friendship is the focus of Irish writer Colm McCann's 2020 novel *Apeirogon*.)

Here I was at Café Yafa, having flown in over international borders, bussed across disputed terrains, passed through walls and armed gateways. I felt humbled, ashamed of my physical and intellectual freedoms, which had come out of my family's own history of persecution and my father's good fortune to end up in Australia. I felt humbled by my great distance from the Holocaust and that my family now lived safely on the other side of the world.

The next day Abu-George and I sat down at one of the Café Yafa tables I was now so familiar with. Usually, he'd be out the front smoking, but for me we sat inside so that the traffic noise wouldn't interfere with my audio recording.

'Could you tell me about what you remember of your village?' I asked after we'd made some conversation, much of it provocations from him to see, perhaps, how I'd react, or to vent: that Jews are natural migrants, it's in their history so why don't they just go, again; and that it was Jews who committed the murders in the Nazi camps. He spoke gently, with Jiries translating. These were antisemitic tropes I was familiar with: that it was Jews who'd manned the gas chambers and dug the pits, and they were complicit in the atrocities, which then somehow negated the role of the Nazis. I wasn't used to hearing this said to my face, I'd only ever read these words before. I had a strong sense he was testing me. Was I going to listen, or yell at him, walk off, break down?

In many circumstances when I've asked people about their lives, for this book and other projects, people want to talk. They want to share their recollections of past places and ways of life. They want their 'small' histories to become known. They are glad to have found an interested, curious listener. Abu-George was not like that.

'Could you tell me about what you remember of being in your village?' I asked.

His response was emphatic. 'I won't share my memories of the village I was forced from with my family, to help you remember your grandmother. It's not "interesting" to me, as it is for you. I'm a refugee in my own country. That's what I know. That's what you need to know.'

In my eagerness to find traces of her life and to find how she'd fitted in to the seismic shift that was taking place in Mandate Palestine, in the creation of this narrative, in the shoring up of my father's relationship to his own past, in all of that effort and focus, and even while I was always thinking of what had been a consequence of her migration ... I'd been callous to the reality of living in exile. Abu-George was only a few kilometres from where he had lived as a boy but was irrevocably separated from that place. He *was* a refugee in his own country. I had known that, but not fiercely enough, not enough that it hurt me too. From a man who'd lost his home as a boy, I learned so much through these words. And I am reminded now of the novelist Goce Smilevski's words, when he says, 'What is lost at a certain moment can never again be compensated, because what is lost was needed at the moment it disappeared.'

Walter Strauss

At some point in the 1930s Bella fell in love with Walter Strauss. When exactly, I don't know. Then Willy discovered a letter from Walter to Bella and their marriage was never the same again. How I wish that wasn't true, that she'd met Strauss much later in Palestine, so that my idea of my grandparents' marriage, evidenced by the photographs of Willy and Bella in the mid-1930s that show them so carefree and happy together, could be 99 per cent true. In these images my grandparents are touching, laughing, horsing around together. Surely that's love. Or is it some kind of emotional pragmatism amid the Nazi violence, persecutions, and then flight?

It's 2022 and my mother has been living in a dementia unit for two years. The brain injury from an infection she suffered in 2020 worsened the dementia and left her too confused to return home. She is walking, enjoys going outside into the gardens, can hold conversations, but needs twenty-four-hour care. She's leaving us very slowly, leading us down the long lane to the end of her life, which will come the following year. She knows me till the end, and I know her. Sometimes we just look into each other's eyes.

My father has continued alone at the Balmain house, and one day during that year I realise that he's brooding too much on his past. His focus on the early traumatic years is beginning to worry me and my brothers. Without our mother around to talk to – they were great conversationalists together – and occupy his attention, he spends more and more time thinking back on his youth. We

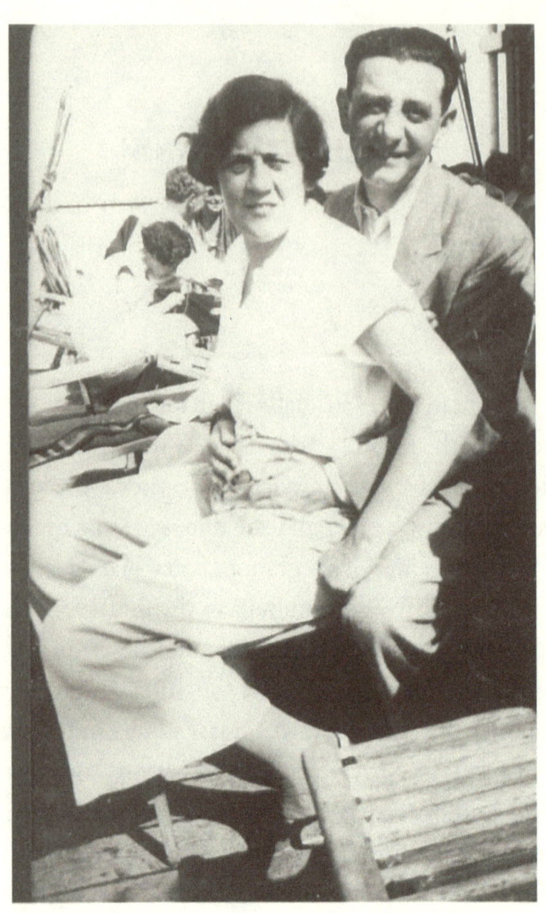

Bella and Willy on *Vulcania*, November 1933.

phone, drop round, try to get him out more, all the things you do when you're worried about someone you love being lonely.

It's a strange kind of conversation we've been having all these years of me working on this book; Dad, an elderly man, getting frailer each year but tenaciously holding on to what he recalls of past events and his experience of them. Why does he spend so much time on those memories, most of them anguished? Is it because I'm writing this book? But I am writing this book in part because he talked about his past for years when I was growing up. Is that what trauma does to a person? Holds you down, sits on your chest, won't let you forget. I so want him to believe he was once loved – yes, imperfectly – but loved nevertheless by Bella.

On the day in 2022 that I'm thinking of, we strayed back to Walter Strauss and my father mentioned that Bella and Walter first met in Berlin. I asked him how he knew this. He couldn't recall. Then I remembered that Ruth had written something about Walter in her autobiography. 'Let's see what Ruth says,' I said, opening the laptop I'd brought with me and pulling up the document. We sat at the table, reading. His relationship with his sister hadn't been warm, though my mother had been very fond of her. But then, she preferred to be fond of everyone in the family.

I suspected he'd not read Ruth's twenty-five pages before. I noticed lines I'd previously highlighted in yellow. What was not highlighted now glared at me. In the chapter titled '1938–39 Palestine and Coming to Australia', she'd written this about being in Tel Aviv in 1939 after Willy had left for Australia:

> Mutti and I were now left alone together and got to know each other a bit after the 3 year separation. During these 3 or 4 months I got to know a little bit about her past ... what I remember most was that she complained about Vati. How mean he was with money, how he slept while she was in difficult labour during my birth and wouldn't have anything to do with me for the first few months after I was born.

Dad didn't comment on Ruth's account of Willy's response to her birth; it was remarkably similar to my mother's story about my birth. In 1960, husbands sat outside the maternity wards in the waiting rooms. Dad found the wait too stressful, went home, took a sleeping pill and didn't return to the hospital for so long the midwives suspected he'd bolted.

At the next lines he muttered 'Aha!' Tapping the screen, he said, 'You should have read this passage more carefully, Jane, seeing as *you're* the one writing the book about my mother.'

Yes, indeed. Ruth had written:

> ... Dr. Walter Strauss, a relationship that went back to when they lived in Berlin. His wife was always ailing and would not divorce him, and he had a sick son who caused him much worry and who he would not leave.

So, Bella and Walter had definitely known each other in Berlin. What came next was shocking, and I couldn't understand how I had overlooked it. Ruth wrote:

> Vati later told me that while he was willing to divorce my mother – though he loved her very much, Dr. Strauss would not leave his wife and son, and that Mutti attempted suicide as a result. This all happened back in Berlin, but when exactly I don't know.

She'd tried to end her life long before her death in Melbourne. I was stunned.

'Did you know this, Dad?'

He paused. 'I don't think so.'

This distraught woman was his mother and my grandmother, and her griefs were coursing through our veins, part of the pulse of our lives. An individual's drive to take their life, those final moments in which the decision is made and acted upon, are unfathomable for those who are left, and perhaps too for the person who ends their life.

By the time of this conversation, I'd made three trips to Israel, the last in 2019. I knew vastly more about Walter Strauss than I, or indeed anyone in the family, had known about him previously.

I'd found photographs of him during my month of research in Tel Aviv and Jerusalem in 2018. He was handsome, chisel-faced, tanned, and much taller than my grandfather Willy. He'd become a professor of public health at the Hebrew University of Jerusalem, and the letters and department records of meetings showed he was ambitious. He knew people in the USA, Germany, Britain. Postwar, he'd been invited back to Germany to give a speech at the Wilhelm University of Berlin, the same university from which the Nazis had evicted him in 1933. The speech that he gave contained nothing resentful or accusatory and referred only obliquely to what had taken place in Germany during the Third Reich. He'd lived a long and prosperous life in Jerusalem, owned a large house in one of the best neighbourhoods, and in the 1960s was honoured by Israel's Prime Minister Ben-Gurion for his contributions to public health planning in Tel Aviv. He died aged in his nineties, on the Hebrew date of 3rd of Tammuz, 5750 in 1990, survived by his wife and son.

There was, too, Willy's testimony to Ruth that he'd always loved Bella. But some love is useless, isn't it, if it's not the love you want. What did Willy love about her? Perhaps he generously loved all that took her away from him: her intelligence and curiosity, her independence. Or perhaps it was the ways she brought out the boisterous and carefree in him. Perhaps he loved her for their shared capacity for change and adventure, or for bringing their children into the world. He'd photographed her sitting up high on a camel in Palestine. He'd photographed her crouching on the road to Haifa talking with children. In another, a picnic scene with friends, she's crawling through his wide-spread legs in a field with the forest behind them. There are photos of them laughing and hugging each other on a sailing boat with friends. She's there with her leg slung over his; in another they clownishly pretend to fall off a seat together. When Willy's arms encircle her waist, and he catches her gaze in a way that seems to encapsulate the secret chemistry between this married couple – had this been nothing more than a scene performed for a camera, again and again? Marriages are complex beasts with their own currents, digestive systems, bitter excrements.

Walter Strauss was still in Berlin with his wife and young son between 1935 and 1937, when Bella and Willy were also in Berlin and Ruth and Michael were at Bunce Court school. Perhaps it was Dad's vague memory of Strauss being in Berlin when his parents still lived there that underpinned his belief that Bella had sent him away so that she could have affairs and go to parties?

How had I managed to forget this vital paragraph of Ruth's about Bella's first attempt at ending her life in Berlin? Surely the content of that paragraph should have impressed itself upon me emphatically. It had not.

The fact is, I didn't want it to be true. I had been willing my grandmother to be a less flawed woman than perhaps she had been. Less suicidal, less hysterical, less of a nympho, less unloving. Willing her to be more forgiving and self-effacing than was visible in Ruth's account. But in writing these words down, I see myself marking her with the same stamp of censure that my father and his father had struck against her. I realised that I was guilty of what Linda Kinstler has said about her investigation into her Nazi grandfather's past: 'To probe the past is to submit the memory of one's ancestors to a certain kind of trial.' Mine was not a trial of Bella; my grandparents were not perpetrators of atrocities. But they were under investigation.

I might guess at but finally know nothing absolute about what was in Bella's heart or loins, or how she experienced her marriage to Willy, or who she loved the most as a mother, or if mothering was even important to her. There is so much that is forbidden to women, so much more is unforgivable in a woman, than in a man. I cannot believe my grandfather's or father's accounts unquestioningly. Which is not to say they're untrue, but they're only very partially true.

Soon after re-reading Ruth's account I needed to share my shock. I read some of it aloud to my writer friend Michelle Hamadache. She stopped me at Ruth's account that Willy had stayed away from Bella and baby Ruth: 'Well, *that* would kill a marriage, wouldn't it,' she said matter-of-factly. 'Right from the very start.'

Yes, the harm may well have been done within their very first year of marriage, in the hurt of being left alone during a long labour, seven months after they'd married, and then Willy showing an aversion to his baby exactly when the mother needs to see the father's love. Childbirth was frightening, many women and their newborns died. And Bella had been working until she married, for many years earning an income, but was now financially dependent on Willy. Ruth's scant words contained all the themes of the women's liberation movements to come.

Ruth's account continued but was frustratingly opaque as to how she felt about any of it. In Ruth's pages there's little self-questioning, just as she was in daily life. Her focus is on what took place and when. As an ardent communist, she's always illuminating the social and economic situation that the working class and migrants like herself were experiencing. She would have liked to go to university as her brother did, but the only university graduates and professionals she'd known in her twenties were the men she'd worked for as domestic help with her baby, Leigh, in tow. Not fair, not fair at all!

Grave relations

There are a couple of last things I need to say about Ruth. She'd also held things close for a long time. Dad describes her as 'secretive', but that's a strong word – he and my mother have both described me as secretive when I just wanted to be private about some of my shit. I think that Ruth was fearful of looking too closely, and packed away everything that had been traumatic, and there'd been lots of that. I visited her when she was valiantly and painfully dying of mesothelioma in Bellingen Hospital, a small hospital in the beautiful river town of Bellingen in the hinterland of the New South Wales mid-north coast. I was there in part because Dad wasn't. He and Judy were both putting it off, delaying and obfuscating down in Sydney. Ruth was seventy-nine years of age, Dad was seventy-four, it was 2001.

After lurking in her lungs for more than fifty years, Ruth's mesothelioma was terminal (it always is). All the way back in the 1960s, her then husband Clem Berman had worked as an engineer at the Victorian State Electricity Commission. He'd come home from work, pull off his clothes, drop them in the laundry sink. She'd wash them, inhaling the minute asbestos fibres as she sorted his shirts, trousers and socks then placed them in the copper. It can take decades for mesothelioma to become active. Clem had been a staunch 1950s Communist Party member, a heavy smoker and drinker, and hadn't lived long enough to die of it. He'd died decades earlier from a heart attack.

In the Bellingen hospital, Ruth's oncologist stopped by to see her, standing in the doorway to her room. Ruth's long-time partner (her third 'husband') Jack was on a chair next to her bed, his beard grey, his blue eyes steady on her. I loved Jack. My cousin Lisa did too, we all did because he was so friendly, warm-hearted and normal. He was Paul Newman–handsome with that same gleam and warmth to his blue eyes. In the immediate aftermath of the war, Jack had been a young Australian soldier posted to Japan to work on the post-bomb remediation. He'd fallen in love with a Japanese woman he met in Nagasaki. He wasn't allowed to marry and return with her, and they'd parted in despair. Twenty-five years passed before he met Ruth on a Contiki tour in Europe and he fell in love a second time. That had all happened a long time ago.

Ruth's oncologist was in his thirties. His red hair was already thinning, and he had a pale complexion that coloured easily. He asked her how she was, and when she answered, he flushed.

'I'm going home,' she said decisively.

A heartbeat later he had tears in his eyes. It took me a moment to understand. He said a brief, heartfelt goodbye.

There was Ruth at one end of the bed, her stomach swollen with pleural fluids, and me standing near the bed. With my arrival, Jack had left to run errands in town and have some lunch. Ruth handed me her typed memoir. It wasn't long, maybe twenty or so A4 ring-bound pages. 'Will you read it?' she asked. 'You're the writer, tell me what you think of it.' We talked about her experience of writing it, that she'd started it during a course run by the University of the Third Age. I put it into my bag.

Sitting up, thin except for the mound of her stomach, her hair grey, Ruth hesitated.

'I felt guilty about Mummy, all these years. I should have done more for her.'

'What would you have done?'

'Spent more time with her.'

When Mutti died, Ruth said she was immersed in CPA politics and campaigning; the party was putting numerous candidates forward in elections throughout Melbourne. She had Leigh, who was six, she was madly in love with Clem, and she worked.

'I wasn't paying attention to how lonely she must have been.'

'Was she lonely?' In 2001 I still knew very little about Bella. I didn't even know what name to use for my grandmother for this conversation.

'Vati wouldn't take her out, she said, and as a married woman she couldn't socialise on her own without him. And Micha was busy with his friends and university studies.'

If I said, 'Grandmother' or 'Grandma', well, that sounded very odd for a person I'd never met. I called her 'Bella' and 'your mother' and 'my grandmother'. The most I knew then was that Bella hadn't loved my father, that she was a bad mother as far as he was concerned, that she'd taken her own life, and there was bitterness from my father towards Ruth about this – for being the most loved, the confidante, the child who received the letter.

Ruth said she'd never visited Bella's grave. 'I felt too responsible, too guilty.'

'Where is she buried?' I asked. Ruth said that Bella's plot was at Springvale Botanical Cemetery in Melbourne. She couldn't tell me much about it, as she'd never been there. I made a calculation. Fifty years had passed. A friend of Ruth's dropped by, and I left in search of a cup of tea. There was much to think about while I was sipping on the too hot, too weak hospital tea. Tea that made you spoon in sugar just to give it the flavour of something. Fifty years in a cemetery with your daughter living a few suburbs away. It was strange that Ruth hadn't gone even once, taking young Leigh with her, and some flowers.

When I got back to her room, she asked, 'Will you go and visit the grave? Would you mind doing that the next time you go to Melbourne?'

Bella with her grandson Leigh. Ruth's shadow is cast upon the wall. This is the last photo taken of Bella.

I said I would go. Ruth was grateful; always calculating the cost of things, she knew it was going to take a plane fare for me to go. She was relieved. She couldn't have asked her son. Almost sixty, Leigh lived nearby in a yurt he'd built at Thora, a village outside Bellingen. Her brother; well she could hardly ask Dad to go in her stead given she'd lived in Melbourne all those decades.

Dad kept putting off visiting Ruth in those last months. He'd say, 'I'll go, just not right now.' The two of them, Ruth and Dad, were not so dissimilar in some ways, both avoiding confrontations with the past.

'Go now, go soon,' I said when I got back to Sydney on the Monday. 'She doesn't have long to live. It's terminal and fast.'

'It's not as if we were close,' he said. 'Ruth stayed a member of the CPA for too long, not just on the books, but as an *active* member, way after Khrushchev's speech,' he said, scoffing and dismissive. In 1956 Stalin's cult of personality and the utopia of Soviet communism had been exposed as a lie. In his speech, Nikita Khrushchev revealed Stalin's extreme abuses of power and his orchestrated murder of millions: political opponents and dissidents, peasants, army officers; the displacement and starvation of the general population. Dad said something disparaging about the CPA's aims. Ruth had not resigned her membership. As if this had anything to do with his sister's dying.

'You'd been a member until then,' I reminded him.

'I only joined for the social life. I wasn't active.'

I'd heard this claim before. He liked this version of himself.

'Not because of the politics. I never believed in communism,' he said.

*

I went to the cemetery in the winter of the next year, driven by my oldest Melbourne friend, the composer Jane Hammond, daughter of the artist Mary Hammond, the child of peasant Yugoslavs who'd made good from almost nothing. It was raining heavily, freezing cold. We both wore long overcoats, giggling at the weather's augury as we walked the paths with the map we'd been given at the Information Desk. But when we found her plot, our laughter went. The rose bushes that edged Bella's row were bare bald stumps pruned to the quick for the coming spring. She was represented by a small memorial plaque on a small square block that sat a few inches above the soil. She was now only as large as a stone you might stumble over on a hike. I felt the loneliness of the pruned rose bush, its short branches jutting out in the rain.

When I returned to Sydney and showed Dad the photograph I'd taken, he pointed out that the date of her death on the plaque was incorrect by one day. An administrative error.

Return from Israel

Years passed, the visit to Bella's grave had taken place long ago, and now I was showing my parents something they'd never in their wildest dreams imagined seeing. Photographs of Walter Strauss, Bella's lover. I was sitting with Mum and Dad in the garden of their Balmain home, it was sunny but not too hot and I'd recently returned from the trip to Israel where I worked with Yonatan Harel and we'd been shown Walter Strauss's file at the Hebrew University of Jerusalem.

In the decade before this, my parents had been to Israel, Egypt and Jordan. I'd paid little attention to their trips, as at that stage I was raising children, working hard and travelling very little. If we got ourselves to Forster up the coast of New South Wales for a holiday, that was an achievement.

My trips to Israel were nothing like those my parents had made, when they spent time with Dad's friends from Bunce Court days and toured the key historic sites. My father had always supported Israel on the basis that Jews needed a safe homeland.

But by now Dad's attitude to Israel's policies and actions towards the Palestinians had changed considerably. 'I don't know the solution,' he said one day after we'd listened to a speech by Netanyahu on the news, 'but what's happening is wrong.' Bibi Netanyahu had been prime minister for years, in fact he had been prime minister twice: from 1996 to 1999 and then again from 2009. His politics were belligerent: 'The key power that must, must not be in their [Palestinians'] hands is the question of security,' he said. 'I don't want them either as citizens of Israel or subjects of Israel.'

My parents had always been interested in international politics, so they knew about these developments, but on this day we weren't talking Israeli/Palestinian politics. I was back, full of excitement about what I'd learned, and proud too. I'd journeyed a long way with much uncertainty and found out some things I found quietly incredible. I brought out my laptop and cleared the courtyard table where we'd been eating lunch together. I wanted to share with my father the incontrovertible proof that Bella and Walter Strauss had not arrived in Palestine together. I'd seen his immigration record for myself in the HUJ archive, I said. I opened my laptop, and showed them the scan of the document in Hebrew, which Harel had translated for me. It stated that he'd arrived by ship, with his wife and son. Dad was pleased by this, interested, as was my mother. Both always preferred the less salacious versions of life.

'Really?' my father said in some excitement, impressed by the factuality of the image in front of him, even though none of us could read it.

'So Dad, don't you think that perhaps Susanne [his aunt Hedwig's daughter in the US] was perhaps spreading a rumour when she told you that Bella had immigrated with Walter?'

'But why would she do that?' he asked.

This was exactly where our discussions tended to fall apart, because here I would be speculating about why others in the family were so antagonistic towards Bella. Yet Bella and Susanne had also been friendly and shared letters. Hedwig had been a much-loved older sister and, as Ruth remembered it, their favourite aunt.

I remember that afternoon so well. It was such a beautiful day, and my mother still lived in her home and could keep abreast of our conversation, though no longer lead it as she'd done before. Writing this, I miss her, and miss seeing where she belongs, in her home.

I clicked on the links that the HUJ administrator had sent me for the photographs of Walter Strauss. I showed them the images of the man whose name my father had known for all these decades but had never seen nor really known anything about. As we looked at him – olive-skinned, handsome, oozing confidence and clearly capable of great charisma – I told them about his career, his beginnings as a lecturer in epidemiology and the science of public health, then a professor, then head of the institute. His confidence was abundantly clear; he couldn't have been more different from my grandfather. Dad was well used to university politics so was interested to hear about the wrangling and bitter accusations back and forth in the lead-up to Strauss's appointment as head of department. He'd loathed his own head of the Biochemistry Department at Sydney University for his bullying and favouritism.

'He and Bella had a lot in common professionally,' I pointed out, as they'd both worked in areas of public health and welfare. My mother agreed, as to her it was vital that a love partnership involved compatible minds.

'In those days,' she said, 'really until the 1970s, women had to *attach* themselves to educated men when they couldn't get the education themselves.' It had happened to her: Dad had the PhD before they married; she didn't begin her first university degree until she was in her forties.

And then in a daring move, I said, 'In a way you are more like Walter than you are like your father. You became a scientist like him. She'd have wanted to talk to you about your work. She'd have been so proud of your research, of who you became.'

He thought about this, and seemed to like this possibility. Mum agreed, saying something quite gentle about Bella, and the two of them seemed momentarily wistful, both having been motherless for so many decades.

I put forward my thesis, that Bella and Walter were indeed in love, but that it wasn't just an affair, wasn't just sex. That they shared real interests and purpose, and that Willy, no matter how much she'd loved him, simply wasn't that kind of man. He'd not been to university, he wasn't working in the public sector; he was well-read and thought about politics and culture, but he was also a businessman through and through. It's how everyone in their families had made their livings for generations, as manufacturers of men's and women's apparel. In Walter, Bella had stepped into the world of men (and some women) who had a direct impact on society.

The found letter

It's December 2022, and I'm trying to finish this book. I wake with it, walk through my day with it, sleep with it. Everything unfinished about it has taken over my life. I'm drawing down on my savings to tide me over, and that can't go on for much longer (though it does, for another few years). Then Dad rings me in some excitement. Fuyu has found a box of letters. Himari and Fuyu are agricultural science graduates on a gap year in Sydney. They're staying with Dad in Balmain in exchange for keeping an eye on him and cooking a few meals each week. He'd asked Fuyu to get on the stepladder and bring down a box from the top of the linen cupboard. From the stepladder he'd asked Michael, 'Would you also like me to get down this box?'

It was just a small box such as you buy from an Australia Post shop to send a small pair of shoes, or a few paperbacks or some such. Dad rings me up, tells me what's inside, I drive over. The box is filled to the brim with letters. Handwritten and typed, stamped, dated. Pages are browning, white, blue. Notepad paper and airmail paper. There's a history of papers of the twentieth century in this box! He's placed the box on the couch near where Indie the cat often sleeps. The living room, indeed every room, is now littered with his things. 'You were never this untidy when Mum was around,' I tell him.

There is a 1972 letter to Dad from his father, Willy (five years before he died), explaining some things about Bella. That she'd had affairs, but that Willy had always loved her. Letters Michael sent to Peppi, his first girlfriend from Bunce Court after she'd migrated to

Israel and he to Australia in the late 1940s, and which she gave back to him on a visit he and Judy made sometime in the 1980s.

There's a letter to Peppi from 1950 in which he writes about Bella's death the year before.

There's a letter from Anna Essinger in answer to one he sent her late in 1948 asking does she know why he's so 'anti-social', is it because he didn't have a mother?

There's a letter from Bella. The letter I hoped for, the missing letter is here. It is one of two letters Bella wrote to him in the two weeks before she died. One short, one long. Both letters have been read. The envelopes have been opened. Dad says he has no memory of receiving the letters or reading them, but agrees he must have read them.

'*Dear Muppelschen,*' he reads out to me, from Bella's letter dated ten days before her suicide. Holding the letter in his hands, which shake slightly with his great age, he reads it to me. Bella had written to him where he was staying in Launceston. At the end of the university year, he'd got himself a summer job down there at the post office, and then after Christmas the plan was to hitch around Tasmania, camping and hiking.

'Why does she write that?' he asks himself, pondering why she'd use the word *Muppelschen*. 'This is something you'd write to a child, but I was a young man.' He's genuinely perplexed. The grief is welling in me. In English, the word can be translated as puppy. The suffix '-chen' makes the noun an endearment.

'It's an endearment for one's child, Dad. Like in English it might be "sweetie" or "my little possum" or something like that.'

'But I was twenty-two!'

'Yes, but you're her child, and you always will be her boy even when you're a man, so she's being motherly.' Even now, my father's capacity to not understand these nuances surprises me. 'It's a mother's endearment to her child, whatever his age is.'

'She's saying goodbye', he says sadly.

The letter continues, written front and back across two pages, asking about the family he's staying with and hoping that they're welcoming, congratulating him on doing so well in his studies that year. She's seen his results and is going to phone Willy at work to let him know. She wants to know if his socks are warm enough, and are his hosts feeding him enough. She's happy about the pay he's getting at the post office job. She mentions that Ruth will be going away on 23 December with Clem and Leigh. It's such a lovely, chatty, warm letter.

Friday 23 December was the same day that she took the pills, after leaving the final letter for Ruth to say she had waited till she had gone on her holiday.

'She was saying goodbye to you, Dad.'

He knows. I feel overwhelmed by how sad this is. Her loving letter that he didn't understand. It's another lovely, bright-lit day in Sydney when we're talking but it feels that the world has shrunk to me and the perimeter of my skin and this thread of talk with him.

'All these years, *seventy* years and you didn't remember this letter. If you'd remembered, and read it again, your whole life could have been different.'

'I don't know why.'

More than seven decades had passed with him believing Bella never said goodbye. And in that absence, Willy stepped in with his stories about Bella, and Ruth never reassured her younger brother, 'Mutti loved you, never forget it. I know she did.'

Handwritten letters are so beautiful. The soft paper: its fold marks, the paper folded in half and then in half again before it's slipped into the envelope. Its December date stamp. The fountain pen ink and the cursive loops, its valleys and curls. The rest at the full stop.

And then she comes to the end of the fourth page, there's no space left, and she writes, 'love to you for this coming new year, and for next year and all the years that follow'.

And now

I once again accompany my father to see his oncologist at the Kinghorn Centre in Victoria Street, Darlinghurst. This is something we do regularly, with my brother Jacob taking it on more lately. While we're waiting for Dr Joshua, Dad asks what I've been up to and I say, 'Not much, just trying to finish the last twenty or thirty pages of the book, I'm so close I can see the end now.'

'Really?' he says with some excitement that this book, which has gone on and on for years, might manifest itself as a real thing. Got to see it to believe it!

After the consultation, I leave Dad in the foyer and go off to get the car. He walks very slowly, shuffles along these days, and it's hilly around here. I've parked a few streets away, near the National Art School where Louis did his art studies, alongside its tall sandstone walls built by convicts more than 200 years ago. I like this walk to and from the car, past the terraces and the cafés, the corner plant store, the old wares store that's been on the other corner for decades, the much older pub, the streets mainly walked by locals. I've known these streets since the 1980s when I spent so much time here. The squats and cheap rents are long gone.

I pull up outside the Kinghorn Centre, get out of the car and Dad totters out with his walking stick, his legs skinny in his loose jeans. I help him get seated and buckled in. We're silent for a few minutes as I drive off, then he asks me, 'What are you calling the book again?'

'*Raven Mother*,' I say.

'Will it have pictures in it?'

'If you feel okay about having family photos in it, yes, definitely. If that's alright with you.'

'Yeah,' he says in a tone of 'of course'.

I wonder if he's recalling words from *Alice in Wonderland*, which he used to read to me, where Alice thinks to herself, 'What is the use of a book without pictures or conversations?'

The traffic is slow along this section of the single lane of Victoria Street. We inch past the public St Vincent's Hospital and then the private clinic. To the right of us is Green Park and the famous wall, the old beat, and the beautiful octagonal bandstand beneath the trees, built in the 1920s. Whenever I walked down along this section of Victoria Street at night, past the park, I was never worried about the men. There's also a Gay and Lesbian memorial and a memorial for the murdered heart surgeon Victor Chang.

'Shouldn't it be *Raven Mother?* with a question mark?' Dad asks.

We've talked about this before. He doesn't like the title, thinks it's misleading for it seems like a statement.

'A question mark would be terrible. What book do you know of that has a question mark in its title, other than self-help?'

'I suppose so,' he says.

'The reader will realise why it's called that once they read the book, and that Bella didn't abandon you, that she's not a bad mother, a *Rabenmutter*.'

'But she *didn't* abandon me, in fact she made sure I was safe,' he says.

'Dad, it was you who used the word about her, that's how you felt about what had happened. You said many times, "She abandoned me". That's one of the reasons I've been doing this book.' What a confusing turnabout this is from him!

'But over time,' I continue in the same unhurried pace as the slow traffic, 'we've talked about what I've discovered, so your ideas about her have changed. For both of us, we've changed through the process of me doing the book.' I've not put this into words with him quite like this before, or even to myself. We've both changed.

'Yes, I suppose that's true. I do think differently about her now.' He seems a little surprised by this, maybe. It's hard to tell when I'm watching the road. By now we're heading down Oxford Street in a gnarl of cars and vans. The sun is shining, there's a breeze. Even though his years of feeling abandoned and unloved will always be there, the constant grey backdrop to his long, long life, today he's with one of his loving children, on a perfect spring day in Sydney.

'Did you know,' I say, 'ornithologically speaking, ravens don't abandon their chicks. The expression is completely misleading. Unfair, really.'

'I wonder why that is. The raven is a threatening-looking creature though, isn't it.' He pauses for a bit, thinking. 'Will the book have photos?' he asks again. 'I've been reading someone's memoir,' he says, trying to remember whose book it is. 'The pictures really help.'

'Yes, it will have pictures.'

Afterword

This book was born from, and carried by, difficult conversations about family and the impacts of war and migration. These are conversations we need to have.

As the daughter of a Jewish refugee who arrived in Australia as a stateless person, I hope that *Raven Mother* shares not only my family's history and the tragedy and resilience of Jewish experience, but also honours the histories, resilience and terrible losses of Palestinians. I have tried to place these histories in conversation with one another. What's here is a gesture in the right direction, I hope. Let us hold these complex stories together and share them openly, in dialogue with others.

I live and write on Gadigal land in Sydney, Eora Nation country. I am grateful that this precious land is shared, while acknowledging that it was never ceded. First Nations Australians whose ancestors arrived over 60 000 years ago live here, along with people from many other nations whose families arrived as convicts, settlers, refugees fleeing war and persecution, and migrants searching for a better life.

Mohsin Hamid writes, 'We are all migrants through time.' We are also, always, migrants across this earth.

*

With regards to names: recognising the precariousness of identity, I refer to the Sinti people indigenous to Germany as Sinti rather than as Romani or Roma. While the term 'Arab' was freely used for Palestinians for much of the last century and persists today to deny Palestinians distinct national identity, I've avoided using the term except when referring to specific older texts.

References

AAP, 'Scientology May Be Demonized Around the World, but in Israel It Barely Makes Waves', *Haaretz*, 8 November 2012, <www.haaretz.com/2012-11-08/ty-article/scientology-no-demon-in-israel/0000017f-e8d3-dc91-a17f-fcdff0920000>.

Ahmed, Aijaz, 'Tanzimat: A brief outlook of secular reforms in the Ottoman Empire', *VFAST Transactions on Islamic Research*, vol. 9.2, 2021.

Al-Salim, Farid, 'Introduction' in *Palestine and the Decline of the Ottoman Empire*, I. B. Tauris & Company, London, 2015.

Aljazeera, 'Who are Israeli settlers, and why do they live on Palestinian lands?', *Aljazeera*, 6 November 2023, <www.aljazeera.com/news/2023/11/6/who-are-israeli-settlers-and-why-do-they-live-on-palestinian-lands>.

Allen, Ann Taylor, 'Pestalozzi, Fröbel, and the Origins of the Kindergarten', in *The Transatlantic Kindergarten: Education and Women's Movements in Germany and the United States*, Oxford Scholarship Online, January 2017.

Alroey, Gur, 'Journey to Early-Twentieth Century Palestine as a Jewish Immigrant Experience', *Jewish Social Studies*, vol. 9.2, 2003.

Amara, Ahmad, 'Beyond Stereotypes of Bedouins as "Nomads" and "Savages": Rethinking the Bedouin in Ottoman Southern Palestine, 1875–1900', *Journal of Holy Land and Palestine Studies*, vol. 15.1, 2016.

Anderson, Charles W, 'The Suppression of the Great Revolt and the Destruction of Everyday Life in Palestine', *Jerusalem Quarterly*, Institute for Palestine Studies, vol. 79, Autumn 2019.

Arielli, Nir, '"Haifa Is Still Burning": Italian, German and French air raids on Palestine during the Second World War', *Middle Eastern Studies*, vol. 46.3, 2010, p. 33.

Australian Jewish Forum, 'The Ghetto Speaks', *Australian Jewish Forum*, 1 May 1943, p. 12.

Australian Jewish Herald, 'A.T.S. Now Totals 1800 Women', *Australian Jewish Herald*, 11 February 1943, p. 7.

Australian Jewish Herald, 'Dramatic Scenes', *Australian Jewish Herald*, 15 January 1942, p. 1.

Australian Jewish Herald, 'Women's Auxiliary Service for Palestine', *Australian Jewish Herald*, 13 February 1942, p. 8.

Australian Jewish News, 'Theresienstadt Concentration camp', *Australian Jewish News*, 20 October 1943, p. 4.
Australian National University, 'We Need to Talk: Peacebuilders Rami and Bassam in conversation at ANU', Australian National University News, 10 October 2025, <history.cass.anu.edu.au/events/we-need-talk-peacebuilders-rami-and-bassam-conversation-anu>.
Aytekin, Ayse Betul, 'How peace flourished in Ottoman Palestine: A story of coexistence', *TRT World*, <www.trtworld.com/turkiye/how-peace-flourished-in-ottoman-palestine-a-story-of-coexistence-15612345>.
Azem, Ibtisam, *The Book of Disappearance*, translated by Sinan Antoon, Syracuse University Press, New York, 2019, p. 84.
Baer, Elizabeth R and Myrna Goldenberg, *Experience and Expression: Women and the Holocaust*, Wayne State University Press, Detroit, 2003.
Banko, Lauren, 'Refugees, Displaced Migrants, and Territorialization in Interwar Palestine', *Mashriq & Mahjar: Journal of Middle East and North African Migration Studies*, vol. 5.2, 2018, pp. 38, 41, <muse.jhu.edu/article/778327/pdf>.
Barclay, Katie and Nina Javette Koefoed, 'Family, Memory and Identity: An introduction', *Journal of Family History*, vol. 46.1, 2020.
Barghouti, Mourid, *I Saw Ramallah*, translated by Ahdaf Soueif, Bloomsbury, London, 2004, p. 4.
Bashīr, Bashir, Goldberg, Amos (eds) and Khūrī, I and Rose, J, *The Holocaust and the Nakba: a new grammar of trauma and history*, Columbia University Press, 2018.
Baum, Vicki, *Grand Hotel*, translated by Basil Creighton, Whitefriars Press, London, 1930, <archive.org/details/in.ernet.dli.2015.174657/page/n1/mode/2up>.
BBC, 'WW2 People's War: An archive of World War II memories – written by the public, gathered by the BBC', 15 October 2014, <www.bbc.co.uk/history/ww2peopleswar/>.
Beiner, Ronald, 'Walter Benjamin's Philosophy of History', *Political Theory*, vol. 12.3, 1984.
Ben-Gurion, David, 'Diary: 21 April 1949', Ben-Gurion Archives, cited in Hanna Yablonka, *Survivors of the Holocaust: Israel after the war*, New York University Press, New York, 1999, pp. 18, 19.
Benjamin, Walter, *Berlin Childhood around 1900*, translated by Howard Eiland, Belknap Press of Harvard University Press, Cambridge, Massachusetts, 2006.
— 'Hear Walter Benjamin's Radio Broadcasts for Children', Poetry News, Poetry Foundation, 20 June 2012, <www.poetryfoundation.org/harriet-books/2012/06/hear-walter-benjamins-radio-broadcasts-for-children>.
— 'Thesis XVII' in *Illuminations: Essays and reflections*, Hannah Arendt (ed.), translated by Harry Zohn, Mariner Books Thesis, 2019, p. 207.
— *Radio Benjamin: Walter Benjamin* (ed.), Lecia Rosenthal, translated by Jonathan Lutes, Diana Reese, Lisa Harries Schumann, Verso Books, London, 2022.

Berg, Nicolas, 'Why Was Goethe the "Patron Saint of German Jews"? Reconsidering a central topic of George L. Mosse's oeuvre 30 years Later', *Journal of Contemporary History*, vol. 56.4, 2021.

Berkowitz, Michael, 'Stefan Lux (1888–1936): A calculated suicide before the Second World War', *Journal of Modern Jewish Studies*, vol. 18.1, 2019.

Berman, Ruth, *Autobiography of the years 1922–1956*. Copy held by Jane Messer.

Bernstein, Deborah and Shlomo Swirski, 'The Rapid Economic Development of Israel and the Emergence of the Ethnic Division of Labour', *British Journal of Sociology*, vol. 33.1, March 1982, p. 67.

Black, Ian, *Enemies and Neighbours: Arabs and Jews in Palestine and Israel, 1917–2017*, Penguin, London, 2017, pp. 48, 49, 53, 64, 68, 90.

Bonifas, Aimé, 'A "Paradisical" Ghetto of Theresienstadt: The impossible mission of the international committee of the Red Cross', *Journal of Church and State*, vol. 34.4, 1992.

Bristow, Edward J, *Prostitution and Prejudice: The Jewish fight against white slavery 1870–1939*, Schocken Books, New York, 1983, pp. 11–47.

Brody, David, 'American Jewry, the Refugees and Immigration Restriction (1932–1942)', *Publications of the American Jewish Historical Society*, vol. 4, June 1956.

Cadbury, Deborah, *The School That Escaped the Nazis: The true story of the schoolteacher who defied Hitler*, Public Affairs, New York, 2022.

Carr, Godfrey, '"The Golden Age of Nothingness": Some German intellectuals and the idea of suicide', in *The Weimar Dilemma: Intellectuals in the Weimar Republic*, Anthony Phelan (ed.), Manchester University Press, Manchester, 1985, pp. 92–109.

Chen, Joanna, 'A volunteer wonders if her dream of coexistence has been destroyed forever', *Forward*, 14 October 2023, <forward.com/culture/564982/road-to-recovery-israel-palestine-coexistence-ngo-volunteer/>.

Cohn, Carol (ed.), 'Women and Wars: Toward a conceptual framework', in *Women and Wars*, Polity Press, Cambridge, UK, 2013, pp. 1–35.

Courbage, Youssef, 'Demography and the Palestine Question (I) 1850s–1948'. Figure: Jewish Migration Waves to Palestine 1882–1948', in *Interactive Encyclopedia of the Palestine Question*, <https://www.palquest.org/en/highlight/294/demography-and-palestine-question-i>.

Cox, Mary, Hunger in *War and Peace: Women and children in Germany, 1914–1924*, Oxford University Press, 2019, p. 266.

Crew, David F, *Germans on Welfare: From Weimar to Hitler*, Oxford Scholarship Online, 2011.

Daily Mercury, 'Nazi Atrocities', *Daily Mercury*, Mackay, Queensland, 29 May 1943, p. 3.

Davison, Roderic H, *Reform in the Ottoman Empire, 1856–1876*, Princeton University Press, New Jersey, 2015.

Denisova-Schmidt, Elena and Lena Nicolas-Kryzhko, 'Rabenmutter

(West Germany, Austria, German-speaking Switzerland)', Global Informality Project, October 2020, <www.in-formality.com/wiki/index.php?title=Rabenmutter_(West_Germany,_Austria,_German-speaking_Switzerland)>.

Döblin, Alfred, *Berlin Alexanderplatz* [1929], translated by Michael Hofmann, Penguin Books, London, 2018.

Doumani, Beshara B, 'Rediscovering Ottoman Palestine: Writing Palestinians into History', *Journal of Palestine Studies*, vol. 21.2, 1992.

Durbach, Andrea, 'Forms of Censorship', The Cross Art Projects, Sydney, 11 May–15 June 2024, <www.crossart.com.au/wp-content/uploads/2024/06/Forms-of-Censorship_Andrea-Durbach.pdf>.

Dwork, Deborah and Robert Jan Van Pelt, *Flight from the Reich: Refugee Jews, 1933–1946*, W.W. Norton & Company, New York, 2009.

Elyada, Ouzi, 'A Female Journalist Reporter in 1930s Palestine: Dorothy Kahn Bar-Adon and the *Palestine Post*', *Media History*, vol. 30.3, 2024.

Englert, S, 'Hebrew Labor without Hebrew Workers: The Histadrut, Palestinian workers, and the Israeli construction industry', *Journal of Palestine Studies*, vol. 52.3, 2023, p. 26.

Erpenbeck, Jenny, *The End of Days*, translated by Susan Bernofsky, New Directions Books, New York, 2014.

Esbrook, Leslie, 'The Greatest Show on Earth: A study of the Red Cross' front row seat at the Stage of Theresienstadt', *Vanderbilt Undergraduate Research Journal*, vol. 3.1, Spring 2007.

Evans, Richard J, 'Coercion and Consent in Nazi Germany', *Proceedings of the British Academy*, 2006, <www.thebritishacademy.ac.uk/documents/2036/pba151p053.pdf>.

Executive Council of Australian Jewry, <www.ecaj.org.au>.

Feidel-Mertz, Hildegard and Andrea Hammel, 'Integration and Formation of Identity: Exile Schools in Great Britain', *Shofar: Interdisciplinary Journal of Jewish Studies*, 23.1, 2004.

Fink, John, 'Report by John Fink (Fly. Hans, September 10, 1991)'. Account of his life 1920–1945 up to liberation from camp. Report requested by the Holocaust Memorial Foundation of Illinois, 8 pp. Copy held by Jane Messer.

Finke, Ursula, 'Ursula Finke, underground life in Berlin', The Wiener Library for the Study of the Holocaust and Genocide, Eyewitness Testimony Collection (coll. 1656), 458. Original in German. Weiner Holocaust Library, <early-testimony.ehri-project.eu/document/EHRI-ET-WL16560458>.

Fischer, Wolfram, Klaus Hierholzer, Michael Holbenstorf, Peter Th. Walther and Rolf Winau (eds), *Exodus von Wissenschaften aus Berlin: Fragestellungen, Ergebnisse, Desiderate: Entwicklungen vor und nach 1933*, Walter De Gruyter [German], 1994.

Föllmer, Moritz, 'Suicide and Crisis in Weimar Berlin', Conference Group for Central European History of the American Historical Association, *Central European History*, vol. 42, 2009.

Fontane, Theodor, *Entanglements – An Everyday Berlin Story* [1887], translated by Derek Bowman, Three River Press, New York, 1986.

Franck, Julia, *The Blind Side of the Heart*, Vintage, New York, 2010.

Geheran, Michael, *Comrades Betrayed*, Cornell University Press, Ithaca, New York, 2020.

Gellately, Robert, *Backing Hitler: Consent and coercion in Nazi Germany*, Oxford University Press, New York, 2001, pp. 130–31.

Gessler, Philipp, 'Central Council representative criticizes Israel', TAZ Publishing, 8 August 2006 [German], <taz.de/Vertreter-des-Zentralrats-kritisiert-Israel/!393917/>.

Giles, Frank, 'Golda Meir: "Who can blame Israel"', *Sunday Times*, 15 June 1969, p. 12.

Gill, Natasha, 'The Original "No": Why the Arabs Rejected Zionism, and Why It Matters', *Middle East Policy Council*, n.d., <mepc.org/commentaries/original-no-why-arabs-rejected-zionism-and-why-it-matters/>.

Goeschel, Christian, *Suicide in Nazi Germany*, Oxford University Press, Oxford, 2009.

Goldberg, SA, 'Blood Ties / Social Ties. Matrilineality, converts and apostates from late antiquity to the middle ages', translated by E Rundell, *Women, Gender, History*, vol. 44.2, 2016.

Goossens, Reuben, 'Remembering those Wonderful days when Passenger Liners were Real Ships', ssMaritime, n.d., <ssmaritime.com/Johan-de-Witt.htm>.

Gopin, Marc, 'Eliyahu McLean' in *Bridges Across an Impossible Divide*, Oxford University Press, Oxford, 2012.

Grady, Tim, *A Deadly Legacy: German Jews and the Great War*, Yale University Press, New Haven, Connecticut, 2017.

Grady, Tim, *German-Jewish Soldiers of the First World War in History and Memory*, Liverpool University Press, 2012.

Granit-Hacohen, Anat, *Hebrew Women Join the Forces: Jewish women from Palestine in the British forces during the Second World War*, translated by Ora Cummings, Vallentine Mitchell, Elstree, Hertfordshire, UK, 2017, p. 46.

Green, David B, '1940: Italy Bombs Tel Aviv During WWII', 9 September 2013, *Haaretz*, <www.haaretz.com/jewish/2013-09-09/ty-article/1940-italy-bombs-Tel Aviv-in-wwii/0000017f-f473-d044-adff-f7fb19a10000>.

Grodzinsky, Yosef, *In the Shadow of the Holocaust: The struggle between Jews and Zionists in the aftermath of World War II*, Common Courage Press, Monroe, Maine, 2004, pp. 167–94.

Groneman, Carol, 'Nymphomania: The historical construction of female sexuality', *Signs: Journal of Women in Culture and Society*, vol. 19.2, 1994.

Halaby, Mona Hajjar, *In My Mother's Footsteps: A Palestinian refugee returns home*, Thread Books, London, 2021, pp. 47, 50.

Halamish, Aviva, 'Palestine as a Destination for Jewish Immigrants', in Caestecker, Frank and Bob Moore (eds), *Refugees from Nazi Germany and the Liberal European States*, Berghahn Books, New York, 2010.

Halpern, Ayana 'Between Universal and National "Social Therapy"? Professional interventions by Jewish social workers in British mandatory Palestine', *European Journal of Social Work*, vol. 22.6, 2019.

Halpern, Ayana and Stefan Kongeter, 'Jewish social work between Germany and mandate Palestine: The story of Dr Mirjam Hoffert', *Medaon*, vol. 11.21, 2017.

Halpern, Ayana and Dayana Lau, 'Social Work Between Germany and Mandatory Palestine: Pre- and post-immigration biographies of female Jewish practitioners as a case study of professional reconstruction', *Naharaim*, vol. 13.1, 2019, p. 8.

Hamid, Mohsin, *Exit West*, Penguin, London, 2017, p. 164.

Hammad, Isabella, *Recognising the Stranger: On Palestine and narrative*, Fern Press/Vintage, London, 2024, p. 28.

Hansen-Glucklich, Jennifer, 'Father, Goethe, Kant, and Rilke: The Ideal of Bildung, the Fifth Aliyah, and German-Jewish Integration into the Yishuv', *Shofar: Interdisciplinary Journal of Jewish Studies*, vol. 35.2, 2017.

Helman, Anat, *Young Tel Aviv: A tale of two cities*, translated by Haim Watzman, Brandeis University Press, Waltham, Massachusetts, 2010.

Herlitz, Esther, 'ATS and WAAF in World War II', *Shalvi/Hyman Encyclopedia of Jewish Women*, Jewish Women's Archive, n.d., <jwa.org/encyclopedia/article/ats-and-waaf-in-world-war-ii>.

Hessel, Franz, *Walking in Berlin: A flaneur in the capital*, translated by Amanda DeMarco, Scribe Publications, Melbourne, 2016.

High Commissioner to Colonial Secretary, 9 September 1938, #557, TNA CO 733/366/4. Exemption from the permit system was made for the Jewish areas of Tel Aviv and its adjacent citrus plain (the Sharon): 'Report on Military Control in Palestine', 34, TNA WO 191/89, <www.palestine-studies.org/en/node/164303>.

Hirsch, Dafna, '"We Are Here to Bring the West, Not Only to Ourselves"': Zionist occidentalism and the discourse of hygiene in mandate Palestine', *International Journal of Middle East Studies*, vol. 4.4, 2009.

Hirsch, Marianne, *Family Frames: Photography, narrative, and postmemory*, Harvard University Press, Cambridge, Massachusetts, 1997.

— *The Generation of Postmemory: Writing and visual culture after the Holocaust*, Columbia University Press, New York, 2012.

Hoffmeister, Donna, 'Growing up Female in the Weimar Republic: Young Women in Seven Stories by Marieluise Fleißer', *German Quarterly*, vol. 56.3, 1983.

Huber, Valeska, 'Connecting colonial seas: The "international colonisation" of Port Said and the Suez Canal during and after the First World War', *European Review of History: Revue Européenne d'histoire*, vol. 19.1, 2012, pp. 141–61, 142, 147.

Hughes, Matthew, *Britain's Pacification of Palestine: The British Army, the colonial state, and the Arab Revolt, 1936–1939*, Cambridge University Press, Cambridge, 2019.
Hugues, Pascale, *Hannah's Dress: Berlin 1904–2014*, translated by C Jon Delogu and Nick Somers, Polity Press, Cambridge, UK, 2017.
Imperial War Museums, <www.iwm.org.uk/history/what-happened-to-people-displaced-by-the-second-world-war>.
Independent Jewish Voices: For human rights and a just and peaceful solution, <ijv.org.uk>.
Isherwood, Christopher, *The Berlin Stories*, New Directions Publishing, New York, 2008.
Jaber, Bay, 'Responding to Cries of Genocide: The Yemenite Children Affair', *PKI Global Justice Journal*, Queens University, 23 September 2019, <globaljustice.queenslaw.ca/news/responding-to-cries-of-genocide-the-yemenite-children-affair>.
Jewish Council of Australia, <www.jewishcouncil.com.au>.
Kahlenberg, Caroline, 'New Arab Maids: Female domestic work, "New Arab Women," and national memory in British mandate Palestine', *International Journal of Middle East Studies*, vol. 52.3, August 2020, pp. 449–50.
Kaplan, Marion A, *Between Dignity and Despair*, Oxford University Press, New York, 1988, p. 184.
— *The Making of the Jewish Middle Class: Women, family and identity in Imperial Germany*, Oxford University Press, New York, 1991, pp. 8, 69.
Kaplow, Larry and Greg Myre, 'Understanding the Map of Jerusalem, Or Trying To', NPR (National Public Radio), 13 May 2013, <www.npr.org/sections/parallels/2018/05/13/610519266/understanding-the-map-of-jerusalem-or-trying-to>.
Keane, Garry and Andrew McConnell (dir.) *Gaza* [Film], Produktion Fine Point Films and Beetz Brothers Film, 2019.
Kershaw, Ian, *Hitler, the Germans, and the Final Solution*, Yale University Press, 2008.
Khalidi, Rashid, *Palestinian Identity: The construction of modern national consciousness*, Columbia University Press, 1997.
Khalidi, Walid, 'Why Did the Palestinians Leave, Revisited', *Journal of Palestine Studies*, vol. 34.2, 2005.
Khoury, DR and L Brand, 'Oppression of Issawiya Neighborhood', *Jerusalem Quarterly*, vol. 81, Spring 2020.
Kinstler, Linda, *Come to This Court and Cry: How the Holocaust ends*, Bloomsbury Publishing Plc, London, 2022, p. xx.
Klorman, Bat-Zion Eraqi, *Traditional Society in Transition: The Yemeni Jewish experience*, Brill, Leiden, 2014, pp. 87–143.
Knudsen, Are and Sari Hanafi (eds), *Palestinian Refugees: Identity, space and place in the Levant*, Routledge, Oxford, 2011.
Kohlstruck, Michael and Simone Scheffler, 'Das Heckerlied und seine antisemitische Variante Zu Geschichte und Bedeutungswandel eines

Liedes', *Ausschluss und Feindschaft, Studien zu Antisemitismus und Rechtsextremismus*, 2011, p. 132, <https://www.static.tu.berlin/fileadmin/www/10002032/Mitarbeiterbilder/Publikationen_Dokumente/Kohlstruck_PDFs/Kohlstruck_Scheffler_2011_Heckerlied.pdf>.

Koren, Shira, 'The Story of Marian Greenberg: The forgotten Hadassah activist', *Women in Judaism*, vol. 7.1, 2010.

Kozminsky, Ohad, '"The Oldest Disease": The charge of antisemitism as a weapon', *Overland*, 17 June 2024.

Kra Krass, Andreas, 'Magnus Hirschfeld in Palestine: The journey of a German Jewish sexologist (February 14–March 13, 1932)', *Queer Jewish Lives Between Central Europe and Mandatory Palestine: Biographies and geographies*, (eds) Andreas Kraß, Moshe Sluhovsky and Yuval Yonay, Bielefeld: transcript Verlag, 2022, pp. 183–220.

Kreutzmuller, Christoph, *Final Sale in Berlin: The destruction of Jewish commercial activity, 1930–1945*, Berghahn Books, New York, 2015.

Lamberti, Marjorie, 'Radical Schoolteachers and the Origins of the Progressive Education Movement in Germany, 1900–1914', *History of Education Quarterly*, vol. 40.1, 2000.

Lau, Dayana and Ayana Halpern, 'Jewish Social Work Biographies Between Germany and Mandatory Palestine', *Soziale Arbeit*, vol. 72.1, 2023.

Leiserowitz, Ruth, 'Population displacement in East Prussia during the First World War', in *Europe on the move: Refugees in the era of the Great War*, Peter Gatrell and Liubov Zhvanko (eds), Manchester University Press, 2017, pp. 23–44.

Leman, Juda (dir.), *The Land of Promise* (November 1935 version), Urim Palestine Film Company, Israel Film Archive, Jerusalem Cinematheque, <jfc.org.il/en/movie/54747-2/>.

LeVine, Mark, 'Conquest Through Town Planning: the Case of Tel Aviv, 1921–48' *Journal of Palestine Studies*, vol. 27.4, 1998.

Liât, Kozma, 'Sexology in the Yishuv: the Rise and Decline of Sexual Consultation in Tel Aviv, 1930–39', *International Journal of Middle East Studies*, vol. 42, 2010.

Lipner, Sandra '*Effingers*: A portrait of German-Jewish life, 1878–1948', book review, The Weiner Holocaust Library, 6 February 2020, <wienerholocaustlibrary.org/2020/02/06/428/>.

Loentz, Elizabeth, 'Jewish Women and Intersectional Feminism: The case of Bertha Pappenheim', *Feminist German Studies*, vol. 39.1, 2023.

Lohr, Eric, 'The Russian Army and the Jews: Mass deportation, hostages, and violence during World War I', *The Russian Review*, vol. 60.3, July 2001, pp. 404–19.

Löhr, Isabella, 'Emergency Committee in Aid of Displaced Foreign Scholars: Building transatlantic networks in science and learning', *Transastlantic Perspectives*, <www.transatlanticperspectives.org/entries/emergency-committee-in-aid-of-displaced-foreign-scholars/>.

MacDonald, Callum A, 'Radio Bari: Italian wireless propaganda in the Middle East and British countermeasures 1934–38', *Middle Eastern Studies*, vol. 13.2, May 1977, p. 205.

MacLean, Rory, *Berlin: Imagine a city*, Weidenfeld & Nicolson, London, 2014.

McMahon, Serena, 'Netanyahu's Not-Quite-2-State Solution', 30 September 2018, 4.43 PM ET, Heard on *Morning Edition*, NPR, <www.npr.org/2018/09/30/653094273/netanyahu-at-odds-with-trump-over-two-state-solution>.

Makamson, Collin, 'Kinderdorf Pestalozzi: "Building a world in which children can live"', National World War II Museum, New Orleans, 27 April 2021, <www.nationalww2museum.org/war/articles/kinderdorf-pestalozzi-refugee-children>.

Markus, Andrew, 'Jewish Migration to Australia 1938–49', *Journal of Australian Studies*, vol. 7.13, 2009.

Masalha, Nur, 'Settler-Colonialism and Disinheriting the Palestinians: The appropriation of Palestinian place names by the Israeli state' in *Palestine*, Bloomsbury Academic & Professional, London, 2018.

Masalha, Nur, Mahmoud Hawari and Ghada Karmi, 'Palestine chronology', The Palestinian History Tapestry, <www.palestinianhistorytapestry.org/history-references-for-embroidery-panels/>.

Matthäus, Jürgen and Emil Kerenji, *Jewish Responses to Persecution, 1933–1946: A source reader*, Rowman & Littlefield in association with the United States Holocaust Memorial Museum, 2017.

Mausolf (nee Hirschfeld), Bella, 'God in Heaven Help Us', account of escape from Nazi labour camp with Helga Verleger and two other young Jewish women during a forced march, 1945, 123 pp. Copy held by Jane Messer.

Mellen, Emily, 'Across the Waves: Radio Bari, the fascist radio heard across the Mediterranean', Centre for Global Inquiry and Innovation, University of Virginia, 2021, <cgii.virginia.edu/projects/across-waves-radio-bari-fascist-radio-heard-across-mediterranean>.

Mendel, Yonatan, 'Fantasising Israel: Tel Aviv's centenary', *London Review of Books*, vol. 31.12, 25 June 2009, <https://www.lrb.co.uk/the-paper/v31/n12/yonatan-mendel/fantasising-israel>.

— 'A Palestinian Day Out', *London Review of Books*, vol. 41.16, 15 August 2019, <www.lrb.co.uk/the-paper/v41/n16/yonatan-mendel/diary>.

Mendelsohn, Daniel, *The Lost: A search for six of six million*, 4th Estate, London, 2007.

Messer, Jane, 'A Bit of a Jew', *Westerly*, vol. 29.4, 1984, p. 59.

— 'Suicide in Nazi Germany: Transformative family history', *Life Writing*, 18 September 2022.

Messer, Michael, 'My Family History', 10 pp. Copy held by Jane Messer.

— 'My Reminiscing' as told to Zoe Thurner, volunteer, Friends of Montefiore, October 2024, 47 pp. Copy held by Jane Messer.

MHM Admin, 'Who Were Truus' Children?', Melbourne Holocaust Museum, 25 February 2022, < https://mhm.org.au/2022/02/25/truus/>.

Miron, Guy, 'From Bourgeois Germany to Palestine: Memoirs of German Jewish women in Israel', *Nashim: Journal of Jewish Women's Studies & Gender Issues*, vol. 17.1, 2009.

Mishra, Pankaj, 'The Shoah after Gaza', *London Review of Books*, vol. 46.5, 7 March 2024, <www.lrb.co.uk/the-paper/v46/n06/pankaj-mishra/the-shoah-after-gaza>.

Morris, Benny, *Righteous Victims: A history of the Zionist-Arab conflict, 1881–1999*, Knopf, New York, 1999, pp. 123, 147.

Moule, Doreen, *Friend or Foe?: The fascinating story of women's internment during WWII in Port Erin & Port St Mary, Isle of Man*, Rushen Heritage Trust, 2018.

Mouton, Michelle, 'Missing, Lost, and Displaced Children in Postwar Germany: The great struggle to provide for the war's youngest victims', *Central European History*, vol. 48, 2015.

Muslih, Muhammad, 'Arab Politics and the Rise of Palestinian Nationalism', *Journal of Palestine Studies*, vol. 16.4, 1987, pp. 88, 91.

Near, Henry, 'Experiment and Survival: The beginnings of the kibbutz', *Journal of Contemporary History*, vol. 20.1, 1985.

Norrell, Tracey Hayes, *For the Honor of Our Fatherland: German Jews on the Eastern Front during the Great War*, Lexington Books, Lanham, Maryland, 2017.

Norris, Jacob, 'Transforming the Holy Land: The ideology of development and the British mandate in Palestine', *Humanity*, vol. 8.2, Summer 2017, p. 269.

Ó Ceallaigh, Philip, 'When is a people not a people?: Academic and diplomat Rashid Khalidi brilliantly interweaves his history of Israel,' *Irish Times*, 15 February 2020.

O'Donahue, Saskia,'Meet the Israeli charity supporting Palestinians amid the Gaza war', *Euronews*, 2024, <www.euronews.com/2024/01/13/meet-the-israeli-charity-supporting-palestinians-amid-the-gaza-war>.

Oz, Amos, *A Tale of Love and Darkness*, translated by Nicholas de Lange, Houghton Mifflin Harcourt, Boston, 2004.

Ozacky-Lazar, Sarah and Yoav Stem, *Locals: Conversations with Arab citizens in Israel*, The Tami Steinmetz Center for Peace Research, Tel Aviv University, 2019.

Palestine Remembered, 'Village Statistics of 1945: A classification of land and area ownership in Palestine', <www.palestineremembered.com/index.html>.

— 'Welcome To al-Mas'udiyya', <www.palestineremembered.com/Jaffa/al-Mas%27udiyya/index.html>.

Partners for Progressive Israel, 'Kolot-Voices of Hope, Post-October 7 Series, The Road to Recovery', Partners for Progressive Israel, <www.progressiveisrael.org/kolot-voices-of-hope-the-road-to-recovery/>.

Patek, Artur, 'Sketches from the History of Aliyah Bet – Clandestine Jewish immigration', Jan Jacek Bruski (ed.), *Jews On Route To Palestine, 1934–1944*, Jagiellonian University Press, Krakow, 2012, p. 155.

Penslar, Derek J, 'Herzl and the Palestinian Arabs: Myth and counter-myth', *Journal of Israeli History*, vol. 24.1, 2005.

Peri, Oded, 'The Muslim Waqf and the Collection of Jizya in Late Eighteenth-Century Jerusalem', *Ottoman Palestine 1800–1914: Studies in Economic and Social History*, 2023.

Potten, Dorle (Dorothea), 'Des Kindes Chronik, A Chronicle of Childhood', account of the life of Potten's German Jewish parents and aunts Anna, Paula and Bertl Essinger, including images and archival documents, 400 pp. Gift from Dorle to her friend Ruth Berman. Copy held by Jane Messer.

Potts, Charlotte and Kate Brady, 'Descendants of Nazi victims fight for German citizenship', DW (Deutsche Welle), 2 December 2020, <www.dw.com/en/descendants-of-nazi-victims-continue-fight-for-german-citizenship/a-52295031>.

Rabbani, Mouin, 'Palestinians and Their Discontents', *Critical Sociology*, vol. 49.6, 2023, pp. 935–37.

Raichel, Nirit and Tali Tadmor-Shimony, 'Jewish Philanthropy, Zionist Culture, and the Civilizing Mission of Hebrew Education', *Modern Judaism*, vol. 34.1, 2014.

Ritschl, Albrecht, 'Fiscal Destruction: Confiscatory taxation of Jewish property and income in Nazi Germany', VOXEU Column, Centre for Economic Policy Research, 30 May 2019, <cepr.org/voxeu/columns/fiscal-destruction-confiscatory-taxation-jewish-property-and-income-nazi-germany>.

Rittner, Carol and John K Roth (eds), *Different Voices: Women and the Holocaust*, Paragon House, Minneapolis, Minnesota, 1993.

Riverine Grazier, 'Savage Air Raid on Tel Aviv', *Riverine Grazier* (NSW), 13 September 1940, p. 2, <trove.nla.gov.au/newspaper article/139820223?searchTerm=Tel Aviv%20raid>.

Rose, Jacqueline, *The Question of Zion*, Melbourne University Publishing, Melbourne, 2005.

Rosenberg-Friedman, Lilach, *Birthrate Politics in Zion: Judaism, nationalism, and modernity under the British mandate,* translated by Haim Watzman, Indiana University Press, Bloomington, Indiana, 2017.

Rozin, Orit, *The Rise of the Individual in 1950s Israel: A challenge to collectivism*, Brandeis University Press, Waltham, Massachusetts, 2011, pp. 162–79.

Saß, Anne-Christin, 'Reconstructing Jewishness, Deconstructing the Past: Reading Berlin's Scheunenviertel over the Course of the Twentieth Century' in Simone Lässig and Miriam Rürup (eds), *Space and Spatiality in Modern German-Jewish History*, Berghahn Books, New York, 2017.

Sabbagh-Khoury, A, 'Colonialism by Purchase: Coercion and replacement in rural Palestine', *Politics & Society*, 1 September 2025.

Sahhar, Micaela, *Find Me at the Jaffa Gate: An encyclopaedia of a Palestinian family*, NewSouth, Sydney, 2025.
Sai, Englert, 'Hebrew Labor without Hebrew Workers: The histadrut, Palestinian workers, and the Israeli construction industry', *Journal of Palestine Studies*, vol. 52.3, 2023.
Said, Edward W, *The Question of Palestine*, Vintage Books, New York, 1979, pp. 8, 12.
Saleh, Zainab, 'The Denationalization of Iraqi Jews: The Legal and rhetorical production of otherness', *Palestine/Israel Review*, vol. 1.2, 2024, pp. 392–94.
Sanagan, Mark, *Lightning through the Clouds: 'Izz al-Din al-Qassam and the making of the modern Middle East*, University of Texas Press, Austin, Texas, 2020, pp. 112–13.
Scheer, Tamara, 'One Empire or Two States? Dualism and States of Emergency in Austria-Hungary Before and During the First World War', *First World War Studies*, vol 14. 1, 2023, pp. 115–35.
Scheer, Tamara, 'Only a Myth? The Solely English-speaking Habsburg army conscripts from the United States, 1868–1918', BIAAS Blog, Botstiber Institute for Austrian-American Studies, 11 May 2020, <botstiberbiaas.org/only-a-myth/>.
Schulte, Regina, 'The Sick Warrior's Sister. Nursing During the First World War', in Abrams, Lynn and Harvey, Elizabeth (eds), *Gender Relations in German History: Power, agency and experience from the sixteenth to the twentieth century*, Routledge, 1996, p. 123.
Sela, Rona, 'Presence and Absence in "Abandoned" Palestinian Villages', *History of Photography*, vol. 33.1, 2009.
Sela-Sheffy, Rakefet, 'Integration through Distinction: German-Jewish immigrants, the legal profession and patterns of bourgeois culture in British-ruled Jewish Palestine,' *Journal of Historical Sociology*, vol. 19.1, 2006.
Shafir, Gershon, *Land, labor, and the origins of the Israeli–Palestinian Conflict, 1882–1914*, Cambridge University Press, Cambridge, 1989, pp. 81–82.
Shehadeh, Raja, *A Rift in Time: Travels with my Ottoman uncle*, Profile Books, London, 2010, pp. 7, 26.
— *We Could Have Been Friends, My Father and I: A Palestinian memoir*, Profile Books, London, 2022.
Sherwood, Harriet, 'Academic claims Israeli school textbooks contain bias', *The Guardian*, 7 August 2011, <www.theguardian.com/world/2011/aug/07/israeli-school-racism-claim>.
Shir, Miriam, 'Palestine's Women Soldiers', *Australian Jewish Herald*, 18 December 1942, p. 5.
Smith, Charles D, *Palestine and the Arab–Israeli Conflict*, 9th ed., Bedford/St. Martin's Press, Boston, 2007, p. 118.
Sochen, June, 'Both the Dove and the Serpent: Hadassah's work in 1920s Palestine', *Judaism*, vol. 52, 2003.

Stanislawski, Michael, *Autobiographical Jews: Essays in Jewish self-fashioning*, University of Washington Press, Washington, 2012.

Stegemann, von Wolf, 'The song as an incitement to hatred of Jews – The "Heckerlied" and its anti-Semitic variant in the Weimar Republic and under National Socialism', *Doresten unter Hakenkreuz: Die juidische Gemeinde 1933–1945,* 1983, <www.dorsten-unterm-hakenkreuz.de/2012/05/28/das-lied-als-anstiftung-zum-judenhass-das-heckerlied-und-seine-antisemitische-variante-in-der-weimarer-republik-und-im-nationalsozialismus/>.

Steir-Livny, Liat, 'Shattered Encounters: From my father's house (1947) to my father's house (2008)', *Pivot: A Journal of Interdisciplinary Studies and Thought*, vol. 6.1, 2017, pp. 29–30.

Sydney Jewish Museum, 'Post War 1945–1950. Government Policy – Discrimination', The Australian Perspective, Sydney Jewish Museum, n.d., <holocaust.com.au/the-australian-perspective/post-war-1945-1950/>.

Talk Matters – Jews and Arabs Together, 'May 2025 – Yael Noy, Director of Road to Recovery (1284)', Talk Matters – Jews and Arabs Together, YouTube, <www.youtube.com/watch?v=wWG0G31bwuY>.

Tamari, Salim, *Mountain Against the Sea: Essays on Palestinian society and culture*, University of California Press, Los Angeles, 2008, pp. 150–66.

Taylor, Melissa Jane, 'Family Matters: The emigration of elderly Jews from Vienna to the United States, 1938–1941', *Journal of Social History*, vol. 45.1, 2011.

Tergit, Gabriele, *Käsebier Takes Berlin* [1931], translated by Sophie Duvernoy, New York Review Books, 2019.

— *The Effingers: A Berlin saga* [1951], translated by Sophie Duvernoy, Pushkin Press, London, 2025.

Terrestrial Jerusalem, 'The Baffling Siege of Issawiya', *Terrestrial Jerusalem*, 4 December 2019, <t-j.org.il/2019/12/04/the-baffling-siege-of-issawiya/>.

Tessler, Mark A, *A History of the Israeli–Palestinian Conflict*, Indiana University Press, Bloomington, Indiana, 1994, p. 177.

The Road to Recovery, 'Road To Recovery – The Year 2019 in Review', <www.roadtorecovery.org.il/Site/uploads/Annals/The-Road-To-Recovery-Annual-Summary-English_2019.pdf>.

Thoenig, Mathias and Thierry Mayer, Seyhun Orcan Sakalli, Johannes Buggle, 'How asylum policies deterred Jewish migration out of Nazi Germany: A quantitative assessment', Centre for Economic Policy Research, 25 January 2021, <cepr.org/voxeu/columns/how-asylum-policies-deterred-jewish-migration-out-nazi-germany-quantitative>.

Timberg, Scott, 'Observing Terror: A conversation with Philip Ó Ceallaigh, translator of "For Two Thousand Years"', 15 June 2018, *Los Angeles Review of Books*, <lareviewofbooks.org/article/observing-terror-a-conversation-with-philip-o-ceallaigh-translator-of-for-two-thousand-years/>.

Toller, Ernst, *I was a German: The autobiography of Ernst Toller,* Read & Co. Books, Bristol, UK, 2013, pp. 9–10.

Tryster, Hillel, '"*The Land of Promise*" (1935): A case study in Zionist film propaganda', *Historical Journal of Film, Radio and Television*, vol. 15.2, 1995.

Turner, Mandy (ed.), *From the River to the Sea: Palestine and Israel in the shadow of 'peace'*, Lexington Books, Lanham, Maryland, 2019.

United Nations General Assembly, '1951 Convention Relating to the Status of Refugees', United Nations, Treaty Series, vol. 189, 28 July 1951, p. 137, <www.unhcr.org/1951-refugee-convention.html>.

United Nations High Commissioner for Refugees [UNHCR], '"The Long Journey": Digitizing the Palestine refugee experience', United Nations, 28 November 2013, <www.unrwa.org/newsroom/press-releases/%E2%80%98-long-journey%E2%80%99-digitizing-palestine-refugee-experience>.

United States Holocaust Memorial Museum, 'Aryanization', Holocaust Encyclopedia, <encyclopedia.ushmm.org/content/en/article/aryanization>.

— 'Nazi Camps', Holocaust Encyclopedia, <encyclopedia.ushmm.org/content/en/article/nazi-camps>.

— 'Theresienstadt: Red Cross visit', Holocaust Encyclopedia, <encyclopedia.ushmm.org/content/en/article/theresienstadt-red-cross-visit>.

Velde, Theodoor H van de, *Ideal Marriage: Its physiology and technique*, translated by Margaret Smyth, London, 1951.

Verhey, Jeffrey. *The Spirit of 1914: Militarism, Myth and Mobilization in Germany*, Cambridge University Press, 2000. pp. 68, 112, 201.

Verleger, Helga, 'Account of the Transport to the East which left Berlin on 26 September 1942, written by me after the liberation, by Witness Helga Verleger', circa 1945–1946, 7 pp. Copies of handwritten and typed narrative held by Jane Messer.

— 'They lived in Wedding: Personal histories of Jewish citizens', translated by Michael Messer from the German publication *Am Wedding Haben Sie Gelebt: Lebenswege Jüdischer Bürgerinnen Und Bürger* [They Lived in Wedding: Life Stories of Jewish Citizens] Berliner Geschichtswerkstatt [Berlin History Workshop], Walter Frey / Metropol Verlag, 1998. Copy of translation held by Jane Messer.

— USC Shoah Foundation, creator, & S Lessig, S Helga Verleger oral history (interview code: 31984), 27 May 1997 (S Lessig) [Video recording], USC Shoah Foundation, 1997.

Verleger, Rolf, 'Anti-Israel protests. "Who got us into this mess?"', Interview with Rolf Verleger and Tobias Armbrüster, Deutschlandradio, 22 July 2014. [German], <www-deutschlandfunk-de.translate.goog/anti-israelische-proteste-wer-hat-uns-das-denn-eingebrockt-100.html?_x_tr_sl=de&_x_tr_tl=en&_x_tr_hl=en&_x_tr_pto=sc>.

— *Israels Irrweg: Eine Jüdische sicht* [Israel's misguided path: a Jewish perspective] vol. 131, *PapyRossa*, 2008 [German].

— 'Israels Unrecht auf geraubtem Land' ['Israel's injustice on stolen land'], *Frankfurther Rundschaur*, 15 January 2019 [German], <www.fr.de/meinung/israels-unrecht-geraubtem-land-11237654.html>.

Von zur Mühlen, Patrick, 'The 1930s: The end of the Latin American open-door policy', in Frank Caestecker and Bob Moore (eds), *Refugees from Nazi Germany and the Liberal European States*, Berghahn Books, New York, 2010.

Wagener, Volker, 'German "Wolf Children": The forgotten orphans of WWII', DW News (Deutsche Welle), 11 February 2017, <www.dw.com/en/german-wolf-children-the-forgotten-orphans-of-wwii/a-41214994>.

Watson, Andrew, 'Unheard-of Brutality': Russian atrocities against civilians in East Prussia, 1914–1915', *The Journal of Modern History*, vol. 86.4, 2014, pp. 795, 818, 824.

Weinthal, Ben, 'German Jews Feud Over Criticizing Israel', *Forward*, 9 March 2007, <forward.com/news/10301/german-jews-feud-over-criticizing-israel/>.

Weitz, Eric D, *Weimar Germany: Promise and tragedy*, Princeton University Press, 2007.

Wiles, Rich, 'The Deir Yassin Massacre: Why it still matters 75 years later,' *Al Jazeera*, 9 April 2023, <www.aljazeera.com/news/2023/4/9/the-deir-yassin-massacre-why-it-still-matters-75-years-later>.

Yablonka, Hanna, *Survivors of the Holocaust: Israel after the war*, Palgrave Macmillan, London, 2016.

Yuval, Ben-Bassat, 'Reactions to Zionist Activity in Palestine before and after the Young Turk Revolution of 1908 as Reflected in Petitions to Istanbul,' *Middle Eastern Studies*, vol. 49.3, May 2013, pp. 355–56.

Zadoff, Noam, 'A Political Circle: Brit Shalom', in *Gershom Scholem: From Berlin to Jerusalem and back*, Brandeis University Press, Waltham, Massachusetts, 2017, Project MUSE, <muse.jhu.edu/book/66698>.

Zochrot, 'From Nakba to Return: al-Mas'udiyya (Summayl)', n.d., <www.zochrot.org/villages/village_details/49275/en?alMasudiyya__Summayl>.

Zweig, Arnold, *De Vriendt Goes Home*, translated by Eric Sutton, William Heinemann, London, 1934.

Acknowledgements

I've been assisted by many. Thank you to my father, Michael, for the hundreds of conversations we've had over so many years. To my dear friends and writers, Michelle Hamadache and Mary-Ellen Mullane, for the sustained encouragement, our conversations and your insightful comments on many draft pages. Also, to Malcolm Knox, Philippa Donovan and the excellent Kim Swivel for the editorial insights and many questions.

It's been a pleasure to work with NewSouth Publishing from the very start, and my sincere thanks go especially to Paul O'Beirne, Elspeth Menzies, Katherine Rajwar and Linda Funnell. The book has found such a good home. Hats off to the Australian Society of Authors' Virtual Literary Speed Dating program, through which *Raven Mother* first met NewSouth Publishing.

Thank you, dear Rolf Verleger and Katharina, Anne, Simon, Hanna and Noam for welcoming me to your homes in Germany and Israel. Katharina, you have brought family together. Rolf and Hanna, our conversations in Cyprus about Bella were priceless. Over many years, the friendship of our cousins in the USA, the Fink and Frazer families, has been precious. This book is also for Alice Fink and Helga Verleger. Lisa and Leigh Morgan, I'm grateful that you shared the precious family archives with me, and Lisa, thank you for our years of friendship as cousins. Suzanne and Micha, Jan and Stefan Kossack, thank you for sharing your Berlin with Louis and me. Dearest Elke, we will ride again! Jane Hammond, I'm grateful in so many ways, including for the drive out to Springvale all those years ago. Lee Kofman, your friendship, along with your generous letter of support, came at a critical time.

You're not with us any longer, but dear Ruth Berman, Mary Hammond and Jack Sennett, thank you for sharing your recollections and insights about Bella and family. I love and miss you all.

To my former colleagues at Macquarie University, Marcelle Freiman, Jean-Philippe Deranty, Robert Reynolds, Gil Davis, Tanya Evans and Randa Abdel-Fattah, the enthusiasm, letters of support, introductions and translations were instrumental to getting *Raven Mother* underway. Many thanks.

Critical information about the Riess and Messer family members was provided by the genealogists and historians Claudia Stock (Germany) and Paul Cheifitz (Israel). On the Isle of Man, Petra Randle at GerManx Tours, Sarah Christian and staff at the Manx National Heritage museum, and Robyn Hughes and staff at the Isle of Man Public Record Office: your professionalism and the care you showed during the research into my great-aunt Minnie's experiences on the IoM are much appreciated.

Many people in Israel and the Occupied Palestinian Territories provided generous assistance. Thank you for your trust, the conversations and for sharing your knowledge and experiences: Yonatan Harel, Yonatan Mendel, Galit Rauchwerger, Eliyahu McLean, Avigdor Cahaner, Noa Cahaner McManus, Hela Yaniv and the Road to Recovery, Jiries Copti, Abu-George, Jumal Zuhair Maraga, Mohtaseb Al-Mohtaseb, Ala' Hassan Shihadeh, and the archive unit at the Hebrew University of Jerusalem.

Raven Mother would not have been possible without the financial support of Creative Australia and Create NSW; the grants and the knowledge that I had the support of writing peers have been invaluable.

Two of Australia's national treasures, Trove and the National Archives of Australia, hold the digital archives that were essential to my research.

Parts of this book were written with the generous financial support of DAAD, the German Academic Exchange Service. Other parts of this book were written during residencies at Varuna National Writers' House. In-kind support was generously provided by the Centre for Creative and Cultural Research, University of Canberra and visiting fellowships at the Centre for Transdisciplinary Research, Humboldt University of Berlin, and the University of Potsdam.

And dear Martin, thank you for our many conversations about history and family, for your assistance with military histories, and for never asking, 'When will it be finished?'

www.ingramcontent.com/pod-product-compliance
Lightning Source LLC
LaVergne TN
LVHW091114080826
845145LV00008B/1916
9781761170638